Elizabeth Champney

Entertainments

Comprising directions for holiday merry-makings, new programmes for amateur performances, and many novel Sunday-school exercises

Elizabeth Champney

Entertainments
Comprising directions for holiday merry-makings, new programmes for amateur performances, and many novel Sunday-school exercises

ISBN/EAN: 9783337045425

Printed in Europe, USA, Canada, Australia, Japan

Cover: Foto ©Lupo / pixelio.de

More available books at **www.hansebooks.com**

ENTERTAINMENTS.

COMPRISING

DIRECTIONS FOR HOLIDAY MERRY-MAKINGS,

NEW PROGRAMMES FOR AMATEUR PERFORMANCES,

AND

MANY NOVEL SUNDAY-SCHOOL EXERCISES.

Collected and Edited by
LIZZIE W. CHAMPNEY.

"Experience tells us that it is times of gladness which especially need a sanctifying power, a presence of the Lord."—*Trench.*

BOSTON:
D. LOTHROP AND COMPANY,
FRANKLIN ST., CORNER OF HAWLEY.

DEDICATED

TO

KATE CAMERON.

"Why should we weep that such is her lot,
Beautiful, sainted, and never forgot?"

CONTENTS.

	PAGE.
INTRODUCTION	9
MISSIONARY CONCERT.—Scenes in Mission Fields .	14
THE EVANGEL OF THE MORNING STAR.—An Allegory. *L. S. Stillson*	34
TEMPERANCE CONCERT EXERCISE. *Mrs. C. F. Wilder*	53
EXERCISE FOR CHRISTMAS DAY, OR EVE . .	70
"CHILDREN'S DAY" SERVICE.—Lily Sunday . .	82
SUNDAY EVENING EXERCISE.—Death and Resurrection	90
FLOWER CONCERT	94
MAY DAY IN DOORS	99
THE FAIRY QUEEN.—A May-Day Cantata. *W. Eustis Barker*	109

CONTENTS.

	PAGE.
FOUR ODES FOR DECORATION DAY. *Kate Cameron.*	119
MRS. JUNE'S PROSPECTUS.—Recitation for Spring Festival	126
FOURTH OF JULY EXERCISE	128
THANKSGIVING EXERCISE	136
THE PILGRIM'S PROGRESS.	142
A CURE FOR TRAMPS.—Temperance Drama. *Lizzie W. Champney*	155
SUNDAY EVENING EXERCISES. *Fannie M. Steele.*	
I. Courage In Doing Right	169
II. Love to God	185
III. Love to Men	187
IV. Love of God Shown in Nature	188
V. Influence of Little Things	190
VI. Lessons from Flowers	199
VII. Little Deeds of Kindness	200
VIII. The Temple Service	203
IX. Jesus Only	214
X. The Gospel Armor	217
XI. The New Jerusalem	225
XII. The Delectable Mountains	229
XIII. Three-minute Sermons for The Children	237
BEAUTY AND THE BEAST.— A Play in Three Scenes. *Susan Hale.*	267
LIVING PICTURES. — Fifteen Tableaux. *Fannie M. Steele.*	290
A BIRD CONCERT	299

	PAGE.
ANOTHER BIRD CONCERT	311
A PORTRAIT OF A FELLOW-CITIZEN	312
MOTHER GOOSE ENTERTAINMENT	314
SONGS OF SEVEN	335
AN IDYL	337
BABES IN THE WOOD	339
OTHER GOOD THINGS	343
ACCESSORIES AND DECORATIONS	345

INTRODUCTION.

The love for festivals, and especially for religious festivals, is so universal that we must regard it as one of the innate cravings of the human mind.

The element of entertainment must enter even into religion, if it is to be dear to the popular heart. Entertainments at any rate, the multitude will have, it only remains for Christians to decide whether they shall make this mighty power a Christian force, or leave all the merry and bright things of this life in the service of Satan.

Festivals were very dear to the primitive church. An ancient writer calls them:

> " The title pages
> Of all past, present, and succeeding ages;
> The inventories
> Of future blessedness;
> The florilegia of celestial stories;
> Spirits of joys; the relishes and closes
> Of angels music; pearls dissolved; roses
> Perfumed; sugared honey-combs; delights
> Never too highly prized—
> Who loves not you, doth but in vain profess
> That he loves God, or heaven or happiness.'

" The children of this world are wiser in their generation

than the children of light." The great popularity of the Romish Church among the masses is owing in no small degree to its many festivals. Take for instance the holy days sacred to Mary alone.

> "O, in May how we honored Our Lady,
> Her own month of flowers !
> How happy we were with our garlands
> Through all the spring hours;
> All her shrines, in the church or the wayside,
> Were made into bowers.
>
> And in August — her glorious Assumption;
> What feast was so bright!
> What clusters of virginal lilies,
> So pure and so white.
> Why the incense could scarce overpower
> Their perfume that night.
>
> And through her dear feasts of October
> The roses bloomed still;
> Our baskets were laden with flowers,
> Her vases to fill!
> Oleanders, geraniums and myrtles
> We chose at our will.
>
> And we know when the Purification
> Her first feast comes round,
> The early spring flowers to greet it,
> Just opening are found;
> And pure, white and spotless the snow drop
> Will pierce the dark ground.

The Protestant Church is at length recognizing the aid of entertainment in the religious education of children. Sunday-school celebrations and Sunday-school concerts are becoming more common and are conducted in a more artistic manner than formerly.

It is, however, often a most difficult matter for the Sunday-school worker to arrange a programme for an exhibition or concert which shall be neither silly nor tedious; but, while presenting an attractive and effective entertainment, shall at the same time, inculcate some moral lesson. The labor of drilling the performers, of interesting them in their parts, and superintending rehearsals is in itself sufficient; but, added to this, the manager generally has the task of originating the entire plan, and composing the material used.

Sunday-school literature is very defective in this particular. Very few dialogues, etc., are issued by the publishing houses from which Sunday-school libraries are generally supplied. We know of *no* comprehensive collection for the various festivals of the Christian year; and the various good things which are frequently dropping from the press have but an ephemeral existence, and are seen but by comparatively few who might appreciate and use them.

To relieve the already overworked class, the prime movers of entertainments (of which each Sunday-school has one or two,) of the task of originating, as well as executing, is the object of this work. We offer a collection of *new* entertainments, by persons of great experience in amateur theatricals, in musical matters, in Sunday-school entertainments of all description, and in literary work. The members of this committee have been chosen from different denominations of the Christian religion; the Episcopal, the Presbyterian, the Methodist, the Baptist, the Unitarian and the Congregational societies being all represented, while their residences are widely scattered throughout the different cities of the Union. With their original contributions, prepared expressly for this work and not heretofore published, we have combined selections from other authors; referring to them in skeleton programmes when they can easily be found, and quoting them at length where they exist in a form not readily available for practical use. The little dramas by Mrs. Abby Morton Diaz, the poems by Mrs. A. D. T. Whitney, and Mrs. Mary Mapes Dodge, and the ballads by Bishop Coxe, are reprinted with the kind permission of the authors and of their publishers Messrs. Houghton, Osgood & Co., and Mr. A. K. Loring of Boston, and Scribner & Co. of New York.

The exercises here presented are principally such as are suitable for Sabbath evenings. A number of secular entertainments have also been added for the aid of temperance, missionary and other societies, and with a view to the enlivenment of church, fairs and social circles and the assistance of school exhibitions and holiday merry-makings.

Feeling sure that their work will meet a felt want, and seeing in prophetic panorama the long vista of delightful evenings which it may inspire, the committee,

> HARRIETT G. BRITTAN,
> SUSAN HALE,
> FANNY M. STEELE,
> S. K. STILLSON,
> C. FRANCES WILDER,
> LIZZIE W. CHAMPNEY.

extend their various offerings and their unanimous Happy New Year.

ENTERTAINMENTS.

MISSIONARY CONCERT.

PROGRAMME.

SCENES IN MISSION FIELDS.
"The Field is the World."

1. INDIA.—*Scenes for Children.* - - - - - Miss Brittan.
2. GREECE.—*Tableau and Song.* Ode to Apollo. - Milman.
3. CHINA.—*Recitation.* The Little Chinee. - - Geo. Cooper.
4. FRANCE AND ITALY.—*Dialogue;* in costume.
     *The Vaudois Teacher. - - Whittier.
5. AFRICA.—*Recitation.* Song of Slaves in the Desert. Whittier.
6. NORTH AMERICAN INDIANS.—*Tableaux.*
     Scenes from Hiawatha. Longfellow.
7. PERSIA OR TURKEY.—*Tableau.*
     Scene from Arabian Nights.
8. JAPAN.—*Tableau.* A Japanese Feast.
9. THE FREEDMEN.—*Recitations.* At Port Royal. - Whittier.
     How Persimmons took care of
     de baby, or, Daddy Wafless. L. W. Champney.

* All Recitations not given in this volume are to be found in the works of the authors named.

MISSIONARY CONCERT FOR SUNDAY SCHOOL CHILDREN.

SCENES IN MISSION FIELDS.

I--INDIA.

Let the superintendent, or one of the teachers who has a good voice, take the charge of the evening's entertainment, and after all things are arranged for the tableaux, let him step in front of the curtain, and make a short speech to the audience somewhat like this:

Dear young friends: We are going to try this evening to make you understand somewhat of missionary work — that is, what missionaries do. I suppose you all know that the meaning of missionary, is, one sent. If there was a poor little sick girl who lived in the next street to you, and your mother were to send you to that child with a beautiful basket of fruit, and tell you to say to her that your dear mother was coming with a nice easy carriage to take her for a good long ride — you would be a little missionary to that poor child; you would be sent to her with good tidings or news, something that would make her feel happier at once, as well as give her more hopes of happiness to come afterwards. Well, missionaries, as we generally call them, are those who go on messages of love, to those poor people who are terribly sick, with that most dreadful of all diseases, sin; and they carry with them something that will not only make the poor people happier at present, but they also take the Gospel or good news of more and greater happiness to come. They go to the poor heathen people who know nothing of the one great God, our loving Father God, and nothing of the dear Saviour, who loved us so much that He died to save us; but they worship ugly images which their own hands have made, and they believe in the most silly and ridiculous stories, and they think that all these silly stories are as true as we know our Bible words to be. Now, this evening, we are going to let you see some of the foolish things that are believed in heathen countries, so that you may better understand how much need there is for us to send the Bible to them, if we would obey the command of Jesus to "do to others as we would have them do to us."

We will give you a glimpse of Greece, China, France, Italy, Africa, Persia and Japan; and we will also take you among our own North American Indians, and among our freedmen.

But, first, I will tell you something about the

poor people in India, and what they believe. They are all heathen, and as they know nothing of the true God, of course they know nothing of the beautiful heaven that he has prepared for all those who love him. But they believe that when a person dies his or her soul goes directly before the God Yuma, the judge of the dead. He directly opens a book in which is written down all the good and the bad deeds that man has ever done. Well, you know they believe that there are a great many different gods, and each god has a heaven or paradise of his own. So when Yuma examines the books, if he finds that the man has done more good deeds than naughty or bad ones, the man goes directly to the paradise of the god that he has served most, or who loves him best, and he stays there very happy for a great number of years, and then comes back to this earth and is born again as some other little baby, in a better or richer position than he was before, and this he does many thousands of times, till at last when he has been very very good a great many times, he is taken to the highest heaven of all, where the greatest of all the gods lives, and then his soul becomes a little bit of the great god himself, and he never comes back to the world again. But, if when Yuma is judging the man, he finds from the books that the man has done more naughty things than good, then the man's soul is sent to a dreadfully bad place where he is punished very much, and then he comes back to the world again, yet not as a man, but as some animal; well, if he is good whilst he is an animal, when he dies he will come back to this world again as some better animal, or perhaps as a man again, so that he may again try to be better. Thus you see they believe that all animals — birds, beasts, fishes, insects, and reptiles have all at one time been men, women or children, and some day will be such again. Thus they think it is a dreadful sin to kill any animal, even the smallest insect, like an ant or a fly or a mosquito; it is almost as great a sin to kill a fly they think, even by accident, as it would be to kill a man, and if they do kill an animal it is written down in the book against them as a great sin. While they think it is a very good deed to feed a beggar, and as all animals are very glad when anybody gives them food, they say that to feed an animal is as good a deed as to feed a beggar, and so every time they feed an animal it is written down in the book as a good deed for them. Now, I will show you one way that they have of getting, as the children at school would say, a great many good marks.

SCENE 1st. *The curtain should now rise and show two full grown girls in the Hindoo costume in their own country. It consists of nothing but a sauce wound around the body, with bare feet; but as this cannot be done here, we must try to imitate it as nearly as possible. The young ladies should wear no shoes, but flesh-colored stockings, and to prevent taking cold let them have cork soles inside the stockings. Then they should wear all their under clothing,* but loose enough not to impede any graceful action or motion. Over the under clothing should be placed the sauce, put on first round the waist, the width way of the cloth, reaching from the waist to the ankles; this is wound twice round the body and then brought up over the neck, shoulders and head as seen in photographs. The sauce should be from six to seven yards in length, and from a yard to five feet in width, according to the height of the wearer, the width going from the waist to the ankle. The sauce may be composed of any kind of cotton cloth, but white muslin, or Turkey red with a bright colored border all round it, is the prettiest and best; only where several are needed, it is best to have a variety. Each of the young ladies also should wear a quantity of mock jewelry, chains, necklaces, mock pearl beads, bracelets, armlets, etc.; these may be simulated by broad bands of gilt paper round the arms, with silver bangles on the ankles. Before the dialogue begins, the superintendent, or whoever has charge of the exercises, should inform the audience that as they do not understand Bengalee, he has requested these Bengal ladies to speak in English.

As the curtain rises the two women should be discovered with a little girl about five or six years of age, dressed in the same way. One woman should be seen seated cross-legged on the ground with the little girl seated on her lap. The other should be standing up, but stooping over, holding in her left hand a large leaf in which is about a teaspoonful of granulated sugar. With her right hand she takes up a few grains, and going to different portions of the room, she drops them down in the corners on the floor. The woman that is seated then addresses her:

"What are you doing, Benoth?"

Benoth. "Oh! Mohenee, yesterday I met with a terrible misfortune. I was very tired, and I was stretching and yawning, and while my mouth was open a mosquito flew into my mouth. I commenced to cough to get it out but I could not, and I swallowed it and thus of course killed it; and, oh, that great sin will be written down in the book against me!"

Mohenee. "But what are you doing now?"

Benoth. "Well, you know that will be a dreadful big black mark against me, and so I am trying to do something now by which I may get a great many little good marks."

Mohenee. "But what is it you are doing, pray do tell me?"

Benoth. "Why, you know for every beggar we feed we get a good mark, and to feed an animal is the same as to feed a beggar. But I am very poor; and a horse, or a dog, or a cat—it takes a big bit of food to give them a dinner; but one grain of sugar is sufficient to give a dinner to an ant, so that from this one spoonful of sugar I can feed hundreds of ants, and so get hundreds of little good marks to set against that one great big black mark."

Mohenee (jumping up with her little girl). "Oh, Benoth, what a splendid thought! why we can get a lot of good marks very cheaply then. Come, Golap, (*to her little daughter,*) we will go and get some sugar to feed some ants too, for I dare say, by accident we may have killed some insects also. Come along."

(*Moves across the stage with her little daughter. Curtain falls.*)

SCENE 2d. *Represents the heathen mother's hopelessness on the death of her child. The curtain rises, revealing a common wooden box, (for the Zenana ladies have no furniture in their rooms,) a Zenana lady clothed the same as before — as these women marry so young, she might easily be represented by a young girl of fourteen or fifteen — a little girl of six or seven, and a young lady to represent the missionary lady, who should be dressed in white, with a large straw hat. She should hold in her hand the picture of the sacrifice of Cain and Abel which she has just been explaining, showing them how the sacrifice of Abel typified the Lamb of God slain for us. The little girl is kneeling in front of the lady, her arms resting on the lady's lap, her eyes fixed intently on the lady's face, and the lady is teaching her the verse, "But Jesus said, suffer little children, and forbid them not, to come unto me; for of such is the kingdom of heaven." After repeating it two or three times, the little girl addresses the lady:*

"Maam Sahib, I do love that Jesus who you say died that we might go to heaven. What can I do to show him that I love him?"

Lady. "Do you love him, Golap? (*Golap means Rose.*) If you love him you must try and obey him. He says if we love him we must keep his commands."

Golap. "But what does he want me to do? I do not know; tell me, that I may obey him, and show him that I love him."

Lady. "Well, dear, he tells us we must never steal, we must never tell lies, we must be kind and loving to each other, and little children must obey their parents. Then you must believe in Jesus and pray to him to make you good, and you must not worship those ugly idols which are only made of clay, and cannot see you or hear you if you pray, but you must pray to the one great God in heaven to take care of you and make you good for Jesus Christ's sake."

Golap. "Oh, I do not worship those Takors, for they are only made of clay I know, and if I let one fall it will break to pieces directly, and then it can not punish me for doing it, but I will pray to that good Jesus who lives up above those beautiful stars, and then perhaps when I die he will take me to live in that beautiful place in heaven with him."

Lady. "He will dear if you will only love and serve him."

(*Curtain falls.*)

SCENE 3d. *Curtain rises, disclosing the same Zenana lady sitting on the ground, rocking herself backward and forward, and moaning and weeping and wringing her hands in greatest distress. Her sauce or cloth not only drawn up over her head, but falling down so as to cover* her face. *The missionary lady is coming in. She goes up to the woman and putting her hand on her shoulder she says:*

"Why, Bo! Bo! Bo! (*the title by which a young married woman is always addressed,*) what is the matter?"

Bo. "Oh! don't you know, have you not heard that my Golap is gone, lost to me forever!"

Lady. "Gone, why, where has she gone?"

Bo. (*Speaking through her sobs.*) "Oh, that terrible black mother, horrid Kali (*Kali or Kalee as it is pronounced*) the goddess of Begenne, has always hated me, and does hate me, and now she has sent the goddess Dussura (*Cholera personified*) to take away my treasure, my only love, my darling Golap — she is gone, gone from me forever! I shall never, never, see her more; oh, that horrid wicked Kalee."

Lady. "When did Golap die?"

Bo. "Two days ago. Oh that dreadful black mother, to hate me so much as to take my only child from me."

Lady. "It was not Kalee, it was Jesus took your little one; he loved her so much and he wanted her to live with him in heaven, and so he has taken her there where she will have no more pain, or sin, or sorrow, or sickness, or death, and if you will only love Jesus you too can go to live with him in heaven."

Bo. "Oh no! no! I wish I could believe it, but I cannot. It is Kalee hates me."

(Lady starts on seeing a large black spider or cockroach coming towards her on the floor. These poor Hindoos think that because a child has not done either much good or much evil, when it dies, it immediately becomes some insect which lives only a short time; and then when the insect dies it immediately comes to earth again as some other little child, therefore they will never kill an insect, as in doing so, they might be killing a child. A large toy spider or beetle might be obtained, and placed on the ground, where the audience could see it. The lady, knowing that Bo would not kill it, and dreading the insect coming upon her, points to it, and says:

"Won't you put that out of the window?"

Bo. "Put that out of window, send that away? Oh, no! not for the world, that is my only comfort; it came here the day my little girl died, and I gave it some rice and it has remained here ever since, and I know it is my little girl, for it likes to stay near me."

Lady. "Oh, no, dear Bo, your little one is in heaven with the angels round God's throne singing his praises, she will never have any trouble or sorrow again, she will never come to this earth again, but be forever happy with God in heaven."

Bo (moaning and wringing her hands). "Oh, I wish I could believe it; I wish I could believe it; oh, if I could only think I might ever see my little darling once more; but I can't believe it, it is too good to be true; the only comfort I have is in thinking this insect is my darling, and that she likes to be near me."

Curtain falls.

II—GREECE.

TABLEAU.—*Stage arranged to simulate a grove. At the centre and back a large plaster bust, or full-length figure of the Apollo Belvidere, placed upon a wooden pedestal. In front, two young girls dressed in the costume of ancient Greece, as described by the late President Felton of Harvard University. The girls have bare arms, wearing first the chiton or sleeveless vest, which may be made of two pieces of square cloth fastened at the shoulders by brooches, and belted at the waist. Second, a scant skirt made to clear the ground. Third, a sheet may be caught in the belt behind, draped around the limbs, brought again to the back, and over one shoulder, a loaded corner hanging in front. One of the girls, a brunette, should wear a chiton of buff or fawn-colored cashmere, and the sheet should have a broad border of maroon color. The other, a blonde, should wear a light blue chiton, and the sheet which composes the outer garment may be thickly spotted with small stars cut from silver paper. Both wear imitation sandals over their stockings. The hair may be arranged in a loose knot at the back of the head, a la Diana, with a sling-shaped fillet in front, or may be modelled after any classical statue. One holds a laurel wreath, the other a branch of laurel. They sing or repeat alternately the following selection from Millman:*

ODE TO APOLLO.

Lord of the speaking lyre!
That with a touch of fire
Strik'st music which delays the charmed spheres,
And with a soft control
Dost steal away the soul,
And draw from melting eyes delicious tears.

Lord of the unerring bow,
Whose fateful arrows go
Like shafts of lightning from the quivering string,
Pierced through each scaly fold,
Enormous Python rolled,
While thou triumphant to the sky didst spring.

And scorn and beauteous ire
Steep'd with ennobling fire
Thy quivering lip and all thy beardless face,
Loose flew thy clustering hair.
While thou the trackless air
Didst walk in all thine own celestial grace.

Lord of the gorgeous shrine,
Where to thy form divine
The snow-white line of lessening pillars leads
And all the frontispiece
And every sculptured frieze,
Is rich and breathing with thy god-like deeds.

Phœbus Apollo, hear!
Great Lycian king, appear,
Come from the Cynthian steep or Xanthus shore,
Here to thy Grecian home
In visible Godhead come,
And o'er our land thy choicest influence pour.

III—CHINA.

RECITATION.—*By a very small boy. Costume, a long, loose blouse-apron of yellow calico, with baggy, flowing sleeves, over ordinary suit, a hat shaped like an inverted work-basket, braided jute pig-tail fastened within. If a Chinese umbrella can be obtained at a curiosity store, let him hold it behind him, also an armful of cheap Japanese fans and pictures which (having finished his recitation and descended from the platform) he can peddle among the audience, thus adding to the proceeds of the evening. The recitation may be "The Little Chinee," published in the Independent.*

THE LITTLE CHINEE.

Who was it came to town one day,
In such a meek and pensive way,
    But this strange, wee Celestial?
His precious queue hung down behind:
Their Ps and Qs they have to mind
    That side the globe terrestrial.

"How funny!" cried the children there,
"He must have dropped out of the air."
    His almond eyes peeped slyly.
"Me washee, cookee," this he said,
"Me sclubbee flooree, makee bed.
    All samee, A one stylee."

He knocked at doors, his errand told,
Then quietly his hands he'd fold—
    No attitude was finer.
The folks all said: "My! You're too small,"
They knew the dishes he'd let fall,
    He spoke such broken China.

He only smiled and trudged along,
And then he sang this classic song —
    No bird could sing so gayly.
'Twas "Ching chow hi," and "Chop chi bo,
    "Me walkee, pickee my way, oh!
From China-town, by lailee."

He joined the children at their game.
They thought he didn't know the same —
    His smile was tantalizing.
At marbles, tag, and bat, and ball,
That day he took the prize from all
    In manner most surprising.

Now, when the sun was going down,
They followed him beyond the town —
    His pig-tail hung behind him —
And still he wore that pensive smile;
But when he'd gone about a mile
    He vanished. None could find him.

Within a very deep, dark hole,
Beside a giant oak-tree's bole,
    They gazed, with wondering optics;
But he had gone, as each one sees,
Straight down to the Antipodes,
    To ply his little chop-sticks.

Oh! here it was, beyond a doubt,
He'd dug his way right up and out,
    This mild, though artful laddie!
The children call — heard this reply;
"Me top-side up for home. Good-bye!
'The heathen Chinee' — hi! hi! hi!
Me his son! Him my daddy!"

IV — FRANCE AND ITALY.

DIALOGUE.—*In Costume. Characters, Lady, Page and Vandois Colporteur. The time is the second third of the sixteenth century, the reign of Francis I, of France, and the scene is laid in northern Italy or France. The costume of this period offers the richest choice of age for artistic effect. Background a room in the style of the Renaissance. The lady should be dressed in rich brocade, with double sleeves, the inner, tightly fitting with ruffs of deeply pointed lace at the wrists, the outer "angel" or flowing sleeves, open to the shoulder, where there is a small puff. The waist is cut long and pointed; a large ruff completely hides the throat, a gold chain with large pendant, (a small crucifix), hangs over the shoulder. The hair is dressed high, and adorned with an aigrette and strings of pearls. A "rivierre" of jewels runs down the front of the dress. The page wears a velvet doublet slashed in the sleeves to show the linen beneath, and embroidered with dead gold. Long, closely-fitting, purplish gray stockings reaching from hip to heel. Next, the short trunk-hose shall show the foot and knee. A short velvet cape, and a cap adorned with a long white ostrich feather held in the hand. The colporteur should be dressed entirely in black; doublet, trunk-hose, stockings, short cloak thrown over one shoulder, and a small black cap, made by cutting a circle of cloth twenty inches across, gathering the edge and sewing it on a band, say twenty-two inches long, which fits tightly to the head, while the cap itself puffs out loosely above it. The colporteur should kneel, exhibiting his wares, lace and gay silks, in one hand. The poem fits readily into dialogue form. At the proper place he presents the lady with a Testament. The Munchaer Bilder Buchen give sheets of* costumes for the period (second third of sixteenth century), which are very cheap, and will aid those fortunate enough to obtain them, in arranging the dresses for this scene.

V.—AFRICA.

RECITATION.—*Song of Slaves in the Desert.* Whittier.

VI.—NORTH AMERICAN INDIANS.

[Scenes from Hiawatha.—The Arrow Maker's Daughter.]

TABLEAU I. *Background, a wigwam made of blankets wrapped around a frame. In front sits the arrow-maker with his arrows. He is wrapped in a blanket. Hiawatha, in Indian war-dress of buckskin, ornamented with feathers, stands at the left. He leans upon his bow, and gazes with admiration at Minnehaha, who stands just within the wigwam, lifting the curtain. The reader reads from Longfellow's Hiawatha, Part IV, beginning with the lines:*

"Only once his pace he slackened,
Paused to purchase heads of arrows
Of the ancient arrow maker,"

and reading to the end of Part IV.

[Hiawatha and Nokomis.]

TABLEAU II. *Scene, interior of an Indian lodge. Nokomis with gay shawl and handkerchief tied over her head, stands at the door barring Hiawatha's passage out with one arm, the other is lifted warningly. Hiawatha, stands in the centre, with folded arms. See the poem, Part X. If the characters can recite in dialogue from the beginning of the part through the line,*

"Be thou the sunlight of my people,"

the effect will be better than to have it simply read.

TABLEAU III. *Same as tableau I. Hiawatha, lays game at the feet of Minnehaha, and the following selections are recited:*

Arrow Maker. "Hiawatha you are welcome,
Minnehaha. "You are welcome Hiawatha,
Hiawatha. "That our peace may last forever.
And our hands be clasped more closely,
And our hearts be more united,
Give me as my wife this maiden,
Minnehaha, Laughing Water,
Lovliest of Dacotah women!
Arrow Maker. "Yes, if Minnehaha wishes;
Let your heart speak, Minnehaha!'
Minnehaha. "I will follow you, my husband!

(*Hiawatha leads Minnehaha away.*)

Arrow Maker. "Fare thee well, O Minnehaha!
Thus it is our daughters leave us,
Those we love, and those who love us!
Just when they have learned to help us,
When we are old and lean upon them,
Comes a youth with flaunting feathers,
Beckons to the fairest maiden,
And she follows where he leads her,
Leaving all things for the stranger."

TABLEAU IV. (*Not from Hiawatha.*) *Five children dressed in Indian costume, may stand in a row, each number representing a child thus,* 1, 2, 3, 4, 5.

Nos. 1 *and* 2 *recite very distinctly*—"The Choctaw and
the Cherokee,
Nos. 2 *and* 4—"The Kickapoo and Kaw,
No. 3—"Likewise the Pottawattomie.
ALL—"Oh teach us all the law."

VII—PERSIA OR TURKEY.

TABLEAU.—(*From the Arabian Nights.*) *Scheherezade amusing the Sultan and her sister Dinazade with stories and songs. Positions. The Sultan seated cross-legged on a divan smoking a nargile. Scheherezade is seated on the floor at the right; Dinazade, stands at the left, one hand resting on her hip, holding a tambourine, the other arm curved gracefully over her head, as though dancing.* (Costumes, dolls dressed in Turkish costume, after models brought from Turkey by returned missionaries, will be sent by the editor on receipt of two dollars a piece, to any address). *During the exhibition of the tableau, the following poem by Lord Houghton, may be read or recited*:

THE HAREM.
[From Longfellow's Poems of Places—Asia.]

Behind the veil, where depth is traced,
    By many a complicated line, —
Behind the lattice closely laced
With filigree of choice design,
Behind the lofty garden wall,
Where stranger face can ne'er surprise,
That inner world her all-in-all
The Eastern woman lives and dies.

If young and beautiful, she dwells
    An Idol in a secret shrine,
Where one high-priest alone dispels
    The solitude of charms divine;

Within the gay kirk reclined,
    Above the scent of lemon groves,
Where bubbling fountains kiss the wind,
And birds make music to their loves,

> She lives a kind of fairy life,
> In sisterhood of fruits and flowers,
> Unconscious of the outer strife
> That wear the palpitating hours.

VIII. JAPAN. A FEAST.

TABLEAU.—*Suggested by a gentleman for several years a resident of Japan. A large tray is placed upon blocks in the middle of the stage so as to be raised a little distance from the floor. Place on the tray, tiny Japanese tea-cups, and other bits of oriental porcelain. The ladies and gentleman are placed opposite each other sitting on their feet, which are turned under them, as in kneeling, but are not crossed as in Turkish style. The costume is a dressing gown confined at the waist by a girdle. This robe is loose and full for the ladies, rather scant for the gentleman. The numerous fans and pictures to be found at any curiosity shop, will give an idea as to fabric, pattern, and color. Back of the table place a little girl (the waitress,) bending over the company and holding a small tray, on which are tea-cups, a plate of cakes, and a little basket of oranges. As background, use a large Japanese screen. Large decorated vases containing growing plants may be placed on either side of the table.*

IX. THE FREEDMEN.

RECITATIONS.—*At Port Royal. Whittier.*
   How Persimmons took care of de Baby; or, Daddy Wafless. L. W. Champney.

The programme should be varied by interspersing missionary hymns, sung by a choir or congregation. The hall should be decorated with the mottoes, "The field is the world," in illuminated letters over the platform, while on either side, between the windows are the words, Greece, China, India, etc.

The Evangel of the Morning Star.

An Allegory for a Missionary Concert.

BY L. S. STILSON.

CHARACTERS.

ASHTEROTH, *Princess of the Powers of Darkness.*
SUPERSTITION, }
FOLLY, } *Her Attendants.*
SLOTH, }

SPIRIT OF WISDOM,
CHRISTIAN LOVE,
FAITH,
HOPE,
CHARITY, } *Christian Graces.*
TRUTH,
KINDNESS,
ZEAL,

Daughter of the
 " " NORTH,
 " " SOUTH, } *Converts from heathen lands.*
 " " EAST,
 " " WEST,

EVANGELA,
MURIEL,
THERESA, (tall of stature.)
CORINNE,
LOIS, } *Children of the Church.*
UNA, (short of stature),
FRANK, CLAIRE, and other little boys and girls from infant classes.

COSTUMES FOR ACTORS IN ALLEGORY.

ASHTEROTH, *should be represented by a tall, black-eyed and black-haired lady. Her dress, black, with floating gauze draperies of black and red. On the head a black and red (or else steel) crescent, horns curved upward; jet pendants from one side. Hair combed straight back, ornamented with arrows or spears. This is a striking character and costume.*

FOLLY, *has a merry face; wears a dress of many colors, with tiny bells attached.*

SUPERSTITION, *is dressed in black, with peasant kerchief tied around head, and black half-mask down almost over the eyes, to tipify blindness.*

SLOTH, *grey or brown.*

LOVE, *wears white, with gauze draperies edged with rose; flowers at the throat and in the hair. The other Graces, (girls short of stature), wear white dresses, rather short, each relieved with a little color. Each should wear a little shield, bearing her name, suspended over her left shoulder; hair floating in waves.*

WISDOM, *would best be a tall blonde, in contrast to Ashteroth. She is dressed all in white, with white gauze dra-*

peries, dotted with silver stars; a long white veil, and a silver star, or silver arched bandeau above the forehead.

EVANGELA, *is dressed in blue, relieved with white. The other Children of the Church in ordinary dress—greys and browns preferred—to bring the others into relief by contrast.*

The foreign costumes can be best obtained from pictures, and of returned missionaries. Description is inadequate.

PROLOGUE.

An angel from his crown a jewel missed,
Ambition sought it on the heights of fame,
Knowledge from ancient caskets strove to wrest
The treasure all would claim.
Then Christian Love stooped to earth's lowly ways,
To stagnant pools that mortal foot would shun,
Unsoiled her robes, baptized in heaven's white rays
The gem from dust she won.
O children of the light! we'll gain no prize
From wealth of knowledge, or from missal hymn,
But 'mid the lowly, won through sacrifice,
Will gleam the pure soul gem,
Which Christ will set upon His diadem.

SCENE I.

[*Enter* ASHTEROTH *alone.*]

ASH.   Alone! where hide themselves my night-sprung peers,
Terror and Desolation, Ruin, Death?
Once we had force and held the world in thrall,
I touched a victim — Reason left her house.
I spoke — Good vanished from my sight.

I hurled my arrows — Virtue fled away!
Why wanes the strength of evil now? The powers
Of good are gaining on us age by age —
It shall not be! Awake ye Powers of Night!
Rise! Shake the earth with vengeance once again!

[*Enter* SUPERSTITION, FOLLY AND SLOTH.]

Ill met to-day, my laggard followers —
Sloth, Folly, Superstition, ye're remiss
In action, and not valiant as of old.
Hear you: the churches are awakening
To found new missions in the heathen lands;
Where idled ye, not to upset their schemes?

FOLLY. I pray thee, blame not me! I never rest;
I go from church to church beguiling youth,
Tempting them e'er with vanities anew,
Wild revelries, new fashions, proud display —

SUPER. Nor me, great Power, I tell them fortune tales;
With signs and omens, I hinder mission work,
By going to heathen lands and holding men
In heavy chains unable to arise,
And covering with black pall of ignorance,
Which gospel light can never pierce...Behold!

A light screen is suddenly drawn revealing a tableau. Four characters in heathen costume — subsequently presented in Scene II — are seated on the floor, each heavily chained, black tarlatan thrown over all.

ASH. 'Tis well. In heathen lands I ask no more;
What dost thou, Superstition, in churches here?

SUPER. Here too, O Power of Night, I delude men,
By making them worship creeds, regarding more
The letter of the law than spirit, more
The rites of church than helping human souls.

ASH. Good! naught so sure to extinguish Christian zeal —

In this thou rightly judgest.....Sloth hast thou
Been idle like thy name?

SLOTH. [*Rising languidly.*]   Nay, Queen of Darkness,
I've shown the church the bliss of idleness,
Preventing it from doing anything good,
Inventing many excuse to ease the conscience.
When asked for help in foreign mission work,
This frail excuse thou surely will commend—
Oh no, 'tis always best at first to attend
To heathen at home." This artifice never fails;
For such ne'er get beyond *one* heathen at home.
Most men who will not care for souls abroad
Care not for neighbor; so we there are safe.
In other duties, work for Sunday-schools,
Or church, or the poor, I frame excuses fair
For doing nothing, which is doing ill;
Since easy 'tis for Folly then to come
And fill the void with vanities.

ASH.   'Tis true;
But more assiduous be; we Powers of Darkness
Must wiser be than children of the light.
To gain the people 'tis the surest way
To win the infants first.   Lo, here appear
A happy band of Children of the Church.
Be wary now, deride not Christian creeds,
Their Bible-texts and pious hymns; pretend
All to accept, and thus more surely win,
Throwing in at intervals some bone of strife.
Aside! Affrighting them, we thwart our aim.

Enter, talking together, two Children of the Church — THERESA *and* LOIS. *The Powers of Darkness stand aside.*

THER. What if it rain on anniversary?
LOIS. Heaven always smiles upon the children's day.

[*Enter* EVANGELA *at one door.*]

EVAN.   Sisters let us be mindful of the poor,
        To take them fruits and cake on the festal day.

[*Enter* CORINNE, MURIEL *and* UNA *at the other door.*]

THER.   Yes, well you thought of that, Evangela.

        [SUPERSTITION *steps forward.*]

SUPER.   Sweet maiden, may I now your fortune tell?
LOIS.   Oh, thank you, yes, I'd be delighted, quite.

[LOIS *presents her palm to* SUPERSTITION, *who proceeds to examine.*]

SLOTH.   [*Speaks languidly.*]
        Good children do not so distress yourselves:
        The Bible does command, "Eat, drink, be merry,"
        Ye cannot if ye're constantly distressed
        For other's woes. Ye're not your brother's keeper
        If God had meant they should be blest, He would
        Provide a way. Take rest and ease in youth.
SUPER.   [*Still holding* LOIS' *hand.*]
        You have a pleasant fortune, pretty maid,
        You'll marry rich, live long and happy life;
        But now beware—'tis written in this palm,
        And 'tis an ancient omen, if you give
        Fruit to the poor, you'll hungry be yourself.
LOIS.   What! is that true? We must consider then.

[*Another girl holds out palm for her fortune.*]

FOLLY.   Friends, rich attire is needful on that day.
        You should devote your money to fine clothes,
        Not waste it on the poor, yourselves mean clad.
UNA.   Yes, true, my dresses are too old and plain.
CORIN.   And I too need a far more stylish robe.

ASH. [*Aside to attendants.*]
Too well agreed. We must some strife awake.
[*To the girls.*]
You'll pardon me, but my great interest
In your good looking class leads me to ask
Who bears the banner when you march that day?
Which is the honored one of all your class?

THER. [*Rising to full height.*]
Of course the tallest should the banner bear.

UNA. [*Being shortest.*]
No, then the effect were awkward in extreme,
The shortest by all means — 'twere graceful then.

LOIS. What matters height? She who the banner holds
Should be the girl most stylish. I'll — not — say
Who that may be — of course.

MURIEL. Just listen! Style
Our basis of respect!

ASH. If you'll permit
That I decide the question, I will gild
Your banner, handsomest of all the schools.

[*They nod their heads in assent.*]

Let her who is the meekest bear it! [*Pause.*]
[*Aside to her Attendants.*] There!
I've hurled an apple of discord in their midst!

Now follows a grotesque pantomime, two minutes long; all the six moving around with drooping faces, trying to appear " meek ;" EVANGELA *alone natural.*

EVAN. I think that Muriel is the meekest one.
[*All the rest.*] Indeed she's not!

MUR. [*With affectedly "meek" accent.*]
My teacher speaks of one
Who's always meek and gentle. 'Tis not meet
That I should mention who.

CORIN. [*Scornfully.*] Of course 'tis not,
But no one else e'er thought of you as meek.
MUR. [*Indignant.*]
Indeed! my friends have always called me meek,
And if not I, no one of you, that's sure.
UNA. I'm more meek than you, fifty per cent!

Grinning pantomime of satisfaction among the Powers of Darkness. They move around with grotesque gestures of strong delight.

CORIN. Still more am I. If I can't the banner bear,
I leave the class.
MUR. If I cannot, I leave.
EVAN. [*Sadly, pleadingly.*]
O sisters, sisters! this is sad indeed,
When such a peaceful class we've always been.
'Twere better have no banner than such strife.
Come let us leave it to a higher power,
Let us look upward in our time of grief.

[*Steps to front, clasps hands, and looks upward.*]

INVOCATION.

Spirit of Wisdom, O Purest and Best,
Come to earth's children with troubles oppressed.
Torn by dissensions the heart suffers pain,
Bring to us union and comfort again.
Again to the music of peace let us move,
Come, lighten our darkness, O Spirit of Love!

TABLEAU.—EVANGELA *still looking upward in same attitude; other characters facing in various directions. During tableau, distant music — the Angel Song, as given below — growing nearer and nearer, the last two lines sung at door of stage as Graces enter.*

ANGEL SONG.

Come to those we've watched o'er long
Come to the tempest-shaken heart;
Sorrows at our beck depart,
Touched with music anger dies,
Discord melts in symphonies,
When we come — the angel throng —
Singing Love's celestial song.

Enter two by two, six Graces. First FAITH *and* HOPE, *etc., each with her name on small shield, on shoulder and a long green branch in her hand.*

First two GRACES. Where can Christian graces bide?
Second two GRACES. Where no unseen hosts divide?
Third two GRACES. Through sin's mystic mazes wide.
All GRACES. Love alone can be our guide.
EVAN. (*Bowing low.*)
    O welcome, Graces! May you bide with us.
    The spirit wisdom comes she too?
First two GRACES. Not so;
    This message she sends; that your discordant hearts
    Are fitted not to receive her presence pure,
    But Christian Love she sends, the chief of all
    Our band of graces. She will speak to you.

The Graces part a little, cross their wands of boughs above, thus forming double line, and a green arcade under which enters CHRISTIAN LOVE. *She speaks:*

    Through listening ether sped your bitter cry,
    And I am sent on mission of harmony.
    Alas that unto hearts so young should come
    Ambition! It is selfishness supreme
    Which driveth out intent of noble deed.

	I will decide your question of dissent,
	If first a moment I may pause to rest
	From my long journey. (*She seats herself.*)
ASH.	We'll have no influence now ; They'll soon to work.
	With idle hands alone we'll find success.
	But we'll return if but to harrass them.

[*Exeunt Powers of Darkness.*]

LOVE. Care you to listen while I briefly give
        The story of my journeys?
EVAN. *and* MURIEL. Glad we'll hear.
LOVE. I've been to tropic lands where summer reigns,
        The very breeze laden with music sweet —
        The hoopoos' pipings 'mid the banyan groves
        Mirrored upon the Jumna's placid stream ;
        And lulling tinklings of pagoda bells
        Float seaward from the isles of Arracan.
        Alas where nature seems like Paradise
        That man should dwell in darkness ! Girls like you
        Are shut in prison walls, and bound in chains.
CORIN. In chains good Spirit? girls as young as we?
LOVE. Yes, heavier chains than those your eyes e'er saw
        Binds them to earth. They cannot lift their eyes
        To see the light of God, for o'er their heads
        Is spread a heavy pall their eyes ne'er pierce.
        The chains were forged by Superstition's power,
        The name of that thick pall is ignorance.
        Ah, can it be, I said, in Christian homes
        Ten thousand happy children walk in light,
        Rich in possessing churches, schools, and books,
        Yet have no care for those who perish here?
MUR. Poor suffering ones !
UNA. Oh tell us, Spirit pure,
        Who can be sent to free them ?

THER. Is there help
That one of us can give?
LOUIS. 'Twere gladly given.
LOVE. You have not time this year; your great concern
At present is, "Who shall the banner bear?"
Of prime importance that we now decide
"Who shall be chief among us?" The Blessed taught
Who would be greatest, let him minister.
List then whom I appoint; the standard bearer
Shall be that one *Who has done the most for God* ...
...Will she step forward?

[*They drop their heads silently.*]

... What! will no one claim
The honor?... Una thou?...Thou Muriel?
UNA. Not I. [*abashed.*]
MUR. Not I.
THE REST.
And surely 'tis not I.
LOVE. What will you then?
CORIN. We'll strive o'er this no more.
LOUIS. No, rather think of those of whom we've heard.

[EVANGELA *steps forward, and kneels to* LOVE.]

EVAN. Teach us thy holy ministry, O Love,
And our devotion shall our fealty prove.
Show us the way, and we will follow thee,
In this great work appoint to each some part,
And each will yield her offering from her heart,
Pitying the chained,— Oh set the captives free!
LOVE. The inner voice will whisper to the soul,
Each one a little, thus the islands grew,
And if united ye can mountains move.
CORIN. Let us form a mission band in Sabbath-school,

          At evening busy fingers may be plied
          On scarf or picture, glove or broidered robe.
LOUIS. Oh yes, and all we earn shall help to free
          Worse captives far away.

Enter three or four little ones from infant class, FRANK, CLAIR, *etc.*

EVAN. Oh, glorious thought,
          That our young hands can help in God's great work!
THER. I'll net a hammock for the summer woods;
          When told, what good the little sum will do!
LOUIS. And I can knit a shawl for sea-side wear,
CORIN. And I can weave a watch chain from my hair,
CLAIRE. And I will bring this cent that father gave,
          'Twill buy a pen to write the Bible with,
FRANK. And here's my penny "bank" to buy a book,
          To teach some little Hindoo child to read.
LOVE. Happy, thrice happy in your noble work;
          'Tis work for Jesus, Christ the Blessed said,
          " Inasmuch as ye did it to the least of these
          Ye did it unto me." We'll forward then,
          And by and by you'll win your labors' crown.

Exeunt all led by LOVE, *singing the chorus of* " *Marching on, Marching on.*" *Any other Sabbath-school chorus may be substituted.*

SCENE II.

Enter at one door UNA, CORRINNE *and* LOIS, *who carelessly hum the last two lines of a tune. Enter from other door,* MURIEL *and* THERESA.

MUR. O sisters, I've this moment heard good news,
          Four strangers will be here to-day from far,
          And you can ne'er conjecture whence they come.

CORIN. If they were all celestial visitants
        You could not wear a gladder look than now.
MUR.   They're children of our foreign mission schools,
        From east, west, north and south seas unexplored.
CORIN. *and* LOUIS.
        Can this be so?
        Yes we come, the angel throng.
UNA *and* THER.   Oh this is happy news!
        Yes, now they come.

[*Enter* LOVE *with a* HINDOO, *or a Burmah girl.*]

LOVE.   My sisters, happiness!
        Greet you this daughter of far eastern skies,
        A Hindoo maiden.
ALL.   Welcome from our hearts!
THER.   Sit down with us and be our honored guest;
UNA.   And fain we'd hear a story of yourself.
HIND.   My burdened heart o'erflows with thankfulness
        To greet my cherished benefactors here.
        Oh, you can never know how great the work
        Which you have done for me. My mind was blank,
        No knowledge had I of this world of ours,
        I could not trace one word on lettered page;
        Of God or Christ or Heaven I never heard —
        A gloomy state — and yet I knew it not.
        Then Christian Love awoke your sympathies,
        And through your efforts and your offerings
        The light of grace divine pierced e'en my soul.
        Oh wondrous change! If the half your hearts
            could know,
        You'd ne'er regret your toil or sacrifice.
        But thousands of the children of our land
        Are yet untaught, in darkness, as was I.
        O fortunate sisters, you who lifted me,
        Remember them my kindred, raise them too.

[LOVE *leads in an Indian girl.*]

LOVE. You've heard from the Orient, and now the west
        Is asking for your sympathy.
INDIAN GIRL.   Good friends,
        You send away to India, books and men
        With words of peace, good will; have you for us
        But the Gospel of the cannon and the sword?
        Is it a Christian nation that from us
        Takes all we have, and drives us from our homes,
        Till we are left to die upon the plains?
        O Christian children, think of this I pray;
        Appeal you to your fathers; if there be
        Aught beauteous in your Gospel show it us,
        That we may read it in your nation's acts.

Re-enters the Spirits of Evil at the other door. LOVE *leads in a* GREENLANDER *by the hand, who speaks:*

GR.   From ice-bound regions of the pole I come,
        To greet the children of America;
        When ye are caring for more favored climes,
        Forget not us set in by frozen seas.
        There is no zone upon this world of ours
        So cold but warm hearts throb, affections burn.

[LOVE *leads in South American, or* SANDWICH ISLANDER.]

ISL.   "From Greenland's icy mountains," you have heard,
        "From India's coral strand," and where the sun
        The longest lingers on the western hills;
        But there are regions 'neath the Southern Cross
        Where Gospel light and truth have never come.
        O, ye who are thrice blessed in your birth,
        Forget not us in south Pacific seas!

SLOTH. [*To the girls.*]
Oh waste of vital force! They're better off
To rest just where they are. That is best which is.
LOVE. My sisters you have heard the many calls,
North, south, from east, and from the setting sun,
UNA. Alas! I did not think the work so vast;
Whatever we can do will count for naught.
EVAN. But God will take our meaning if we make
Some sacrifice for Him,
[*Steps forward and listens.*] Oh list! far off,
Through throbbing silence I hear a voice
In thrilling murmurs summon me away!
I must obey its call.
LOIS. What can I do
To help this effort on? For many a month
I've saved my silver pieces for a ring.
FOLLY. Yes, and you need the jewel. Bare her hand
Whose fingers are not set with sparkling gems.
LOIS, True, I do not want the ring. [*Meets Love's eye of
tender pleading.*] No, I will give
To God my jewel. It is safe with him.
LOVE. [*Drawing LOIS to her side.*] Heaven will accept
your gift; you've placed it where
Thieves cannot steal it, and no rust corrupt.
SLOTH. Theresa, you will surely take your ease!
Disturb not your young life to overthrow
God's plan; for 'tis a part of Heaven's decree
That some should have the Gospel, some be lost.
FOLLY. Besides you surely can't the money spare;
You've planned a pleasure trip this week, you know,
And recreation is for youth a duty.
LOVE. [*Gently.*] Ah, to temptation will you yield so soon?
THER. No, dearest angel, I will take that price
For the mission work.

LOVE. [*Love embracing her.*] No pleasure is so sweet
         As sacrifice for Jesus, my dear child.
         Do you remember all how once ye strove
         Which one should be the chief on a festal day?
         Ah, nothing so supplants the thought of self
         As some true noble work; and most of all
         Some work for Jesus.
SUPER. [*Clutching the girls' sleeves in desperation.*]
         Let me tell you now
         That money spent on missions is a waste.
         So many sects are working besides yours,
ASH.   [*Aside reproving Super.*] You should say "*ours*,"
             and thus hide the cloven foot;
         We must pretend to be ourselves of the good.
SUPER. [*To girls.*] Our church alone is true, all other creeds
         Are false, their efforts null; so only ours
         Has the right to spread the Gospel.
ASH.   Hence the fact
         That foreign missions are a failure! [*Pause.*]
LOVE.   Hark!
         List to the strains of music far away
         The Spirit Wisdom with her band of Graces.

Distant music growing nearer, and entrance of Graces the same as in scene I. CHILDREN OF CHURCH *speak:*

         Welcome, Christian Graces seven,
         Who reflect the light of Heaven!
GRACES. Hail! the Spirit Wisdom true,
         Blessed children come to you.
CHIL. When Love joins with mortals, then
ALL.   Heaven in peace comes down to men!

[*Branches arched; enter under arch* SPIRIT OF WISDOM.]

SPIRIT OF WISDOM.
         Well done my good and faithful! Ye are blest

　　　　　　　Since each is happier for a sacrifice;
　　　　　　　For pleasures given there's pure delight in store;
　　　　　　　For jewels there's one jewel will be set
　　　　　　　To shine immortal in the Saviour's crown

EVANGELA seats herself on throne, or chair, on raised dais in centre, kneels to WISDOM, and speaks:

　　　　　　　Forgive me, oh I pray, that naught I've done,
　　　　　　　Nothing *could* do like these more gifted ones—
　　　　　　　I had no jewels, and no talents; naught
　　　　　　　To offer but myself. Wilt thou take me?
　　　　　　　My soul has heard the summons; I would go
　　　　　　　To teach the heathen world the name of Christ.
WIS.　　　Daughter, thou hast the blessing. Many well
　　　　　　　Have done, but thou'st excelled them all,
　　　　　　　For she who gives herself can nothing more.
CHIL.　　Though your mission is to earth
　　　　　　　Though to earth is clinging,
GRACES. Beings bright of Heavenly birth
　　　　　　　Help unto your hands are bringing
ALL.　　　Angels lift you up as you go onward, singing.

[*Looking sternly, and pointing to the Powers of Darkness.*]

WIS.　　　Have "missions failed?" Can perish Heaven's light?
　　　　　　　Can God e'er die? And will not Truth prevail?
　　　　　　　Hence! Kneel! for you the chains, O Powers of
　　　　　　　　　Night!
　　　　　　　THE CHRISTIAN MISSION WORK CAN NEVER FAIL!

They retire to rear of stage and kneel, vanquished.
WISDOM *speaks to* EVANGELA:

　　　　　　　Maiden, arise! happy thy way shall be.
　　　　　　　Go forth upon thy holy ministry;
　　　　　　　This Bible take, the lantern of thy course, [*Presents Bible.*]

To bear the light unto the shadowed shores.
Proclaim the love of Christ to lands afar —
I bless the EVANGEL OF THE MORNING STAR!

TABLEAU: THE BLESSING.

```
        S                       G  G
  S  F     C        L           G  G
      A C         W             G  G
        C  C    E
           C
```

W — Wisdom, L — Love, G G — Graces, E — Evangela, C C — other Children of the Church, A — Ashteroth, F — Folly, S S — Sloth and Superstition. The minor characters face different ways to avoid stiffness. Wisdom on throne has one hand on the kneeling Evangela's head, the other raised looking upward to Heaven. Ashteroth and companions kneel in rear. Slow, soft music, which is broken in upon by the hymn which follows.

VOTIVE HYMN.

GIRLS. Sister, rise to your royal call,
    For yours is a high commission.
GRACES. Spirit, be brave! None fall
    Inspired by the Heavenly Vision.
ALL. Eternity will show your labor's full fruition.

[WISDOM *lifts her by the hand, and she rises.*]

EVAN. I must leave the friends loved fondly, scenes of childhood's hallowed charms,
    But your silent prayers will cheer me, and my soul feels no alarms;

God my refuge, and beneath me are the everlasting
  arms.
Once at dawn the bugle sounded over hill-tops'
  castled spires,
When the herald came proclaiming morning in his
  chariot fires .
I would be the Truth-Light's herald to the lands
  that see no sun,
Ere the morn in bannered splendor signals Error's
  night is done.

VALEDICTION.

WIS.   Haste thee on and Heaven befriend thee,
LOVE. Till thy noble worship o'er,
CHIL. Grief and toils are all behind thee,
ALL.   And thy glory all before :

The Powers of Darkness pass out one door, all the others at the opposite in the following manner :. The Graces form the green arch again, under which pass WISDOM, *then* EVANGELA, *then* LOVE, *then the Children of the Church. Lastly the Graces themselves — two at the end pass under the arch, then the next two, the remaining two passing out last of all.*

As they are passing out they sing " *Jesus I my cross have taken,*" *or else to a chant, the valediction given above.*

Temperance Concert Exercise.

BY MRS. C. F. WILDER.

PROGRAMME.

1. SINGING.—Temperance Anthem. . . . . (*By choir.*)
2. PRAYER.
3. RECITATION.—A Ghostly Lesson. . . . (*By a young lady.*)
4. SINGING.—My soul be on thy guard,
   Ten thousand foes arise; . . . (*Tune, Laban.*)
5. DIALOGUE.—The Wine Cup. . . . (*Class of seven boys.*)
6. SCRIPTURE RECITATION.—Water from the Fountain. (*Seven girls.*)
7. SINGING.—Gospel Hymns, No. 10.—
   Whosoever heareth, shout the sound.
8. CATECHISM EXERCISE. . . . . . . (*Boy.*)
9. RECITATION.—Queer Medicines. . . . (*Small boy.*)
10. RECITATION—Only a Stirrup-cup. . . . (*A young lady.*)
11. RECITATION.—Old Rye's Speech. . . . (*Little boy.*)
12. SINGING.—Yield not to Temptation.
13. RECITATION.—Never Begin . . . . . (*By a boy.*)
14. SINGING.—Am I a soldier of the cross,
    A follower of the Lamb?
15. BENEDICTION.

liii.

TEMPERANCE CONCERT EXERCISE.

1. SINGING.— *Temperance Anthem.   By choir.*
2. PRAYER.
3. RECITATION.— *By a girl of fifteen.*

[An eloquent advocate of temperance, lately said that the greatest evil that the temperance cause had to contend with, was the indifference on the part of temperance men.]

A GHOSTLY LESSON.
By B. P. Shillaber.

Mr. Easyman sat in his padded chair
At the close of day, released from care.
Wearied with striving, but well content
That he had gained an ample per cent.
His bosom quiet, his mind at rest,
With wife, and children and fortune blessed,
His cup seemed full, and running o'er,
When there came a sudden ring at his door
And his servant thrust, 'mid his musings warm,
A hand-bill. . . . "*Temperance Reform!*"
"What's that to do with me?" he said,
As its bold heading he carelessly read.
'I'm no drunkard — no drunkard is mine!
This is stretching a point, I opine,
Where a man cannot sit at his evening's ease

Without annoyance from things like these!"
He read the appeal in a petulant mood,
And his anger rose as the case he viewed.
"Raise the fallen!" "Indeed!" said he,
"And what are the fallen ones to me?
Why did they fall? Why not repel
The sensual devils by which they fell?
Had they not guzzled their beer and wine
Their fate would have been as bright as mine.
Their wives and children! Ah, that is true,
What a horrid state they've been brought to!
With homes all ruined, and hopes all fled —
'Twere better for them if the brutes were dead
Well, — well, *'tis* sad; but I fail to see
What earthly concern it is to me."
So he laid himself back in his easy-chair,
His room was silent, and warm its air —
And while he sat in reflection deep
He dropped off into a troubled sleep,
Peopled with dreams of vaguest dread —
One of which was that he was dead;
Deprived of power to do or say,
And that all he'd done was done for aye.
His dreaming bore no semblance of thought,
Began in nothing and ended in naught.
But a voice soon broke the terrible thrall,
And there by his side, gaunt, ghostly and tall,
Stood a figure from hat to boots in gray,
Like a vapory cloud in a misty day.

"Easyman,"— heavily-toned, said he,
"I have a vision for you to see!"
   Easyman gazed
   At the figure, amazed,
   But, ere a single question he raised,

The scene had changed, and older grown;
It seemed that years away had flown,
And his only dear son of yesterday,
A young man grown, o'er the public way
Passed with associates blithe and gay,
Singing a catch as they hurried on:
We are jolly companions every one!"

   His heart grew sick,
   For the voice was thick.
Could this be the son of his love and pride,
With all his wishes and plans allied? —
His son — so firm and immaculate,
That *he* could choose for himself *his* fate,
And fix *his* standard for others weight!
   Then he was aware,
   From the earth or the air,
  Of sounds as of friends invisible there.
 "Wine him and lager him,
  Punch him and stagger him,
  As well for us, as drown him, or dagger him!"
And then he saw with a troubled glance,
A sight that might well his soul entrance;
A scene of revel and riot wild,
And there in the midst his darling child!

He could not speak to the boy of his pride,
But he turned to the figure by his side,
And clasped his garments with fervid grasp
And with choking words and sobbing gasp,
Begged the mysterious one to avert
The ills that threatened *his* boy with hurt.

"And what is the periled one to me?"

The Presence said with mockery:
" I've kept myself in proper trim,
And what have I to do with him?"
Then Mr. Easyman bowed his head,
With a sense of shame, and a sense of dread,
For well he recalled the words he had said,
When he lay back there
In his easy chair,
And for those who were fallen didn't care —
But held them in scorn, and contempt instead.
Then other scenes went hurrying by ;
Shocking the ear, and paining the eye,
And among them all, the wickedest one
Was his dearly-loved, and only son.
He saw a ruined and squalid home,
And a woman waiting for one to come,
'Twas far in the night, and the ember's glare
Shone on a face of sorrow and care —
Revealing children slumbering there
In the chilly breath of the frozen air.
Hark ! there's a step upon the stair,
Which gives new power to her despair!
      That step! — it comes more near !
      'Tis here — 'tis here !
      And fingers catch
      At the rattling latch,
The door swings in, on its hinges wide ;
      While out from the dark,
      By the ember's spark,
The reeling form of a man is descried
That once was a man ; but O, how drear
Doth he now in the dismal light appear !
His blood-shot eyes have an imbecile glare
And his tottering steps reel here and there.

As he sinks o'ercome in the only chair,
And his lips profane breathe a drunkard's prayer,
    With tearful eye
    The wife stands by
    While bitter pangs through her bosom fly!
He starts in anger; his wild eyes gleam;
On the still night air is a fearful scream,
As blows descend on her feeble form;
And the children wake mid a direful storm,
As the fiend in his frenzy rages and roars,
And on wife and children his vengeance pours;
    While, mid the din,
    Steals harshly in
    The chorus of the brood of sin.
    "Batter them! Shatter them!
    Shatter them! Batter them!
O'er the wide world in misery scatter them!"

Then Easyman tore his ghostly hair
In the frenzy wild of his deep despair,
And he turned to catch a pitying ray
From the stony eye of the spectre gray,
    Who shook his head
    And grimly said:
"Better by far that the brute were dead!
What is it to me or to you?" said he;
"He chose his fate — so let it be!"

A sound of strife is heard in the street,
A strife of voices and hurrying feet;
    And then — a flash,
    A pistol crash!
    A hasty crowd in tumult dash;
Then a sudden hush, as with awe replete!
And a voice on the listener's ear doth fall:

"Only a drunken row, that's all?"
While out from the throng,
By muscles strong
A *thing* all stark — is borne along,
And night closes round it like a pall.

"Spare me! spare me!" Easyman cries,
"The sights I have seen shall make me wise.
Let me, O let me, but live again
Let things as they were before remain
And all my heart and all my soul
I pledge to different control.
Let me the wrong I have done undo,
Let me the new-found path pursue,
And, what I most devoutly crave
Are the means and time the fallen to save.
Like letters of fire the dictates shine,
And the sympathy and the work are mine."
Lo! a start! and awake once more,
He felt as he'd never felt before.
The scales had fallen from eyes and heart,
He saw his course as 'twere a chart;
And he breathed a prayer for strength to be
Firm, in his new integrity.
It was with transport almost wild,
He clasped to his heart his darling child,
His boy, the hope and pride of his life,
And shuddered, recalling the recent strife,
Wherein his eyes had been made to see
A dismal fate that still might be.

4. SINGING.— *My soul be on thy guard*
    Ten thousand foes arise; (*Tune, Laban.*)

5. DIALOGUE.— *Class of seven boys.*

THE WINE CUP.

Have a goblet, either Bohemian glass, or a common goblet lined with colored paper, wreathed with flowers and vines upon a prettily decked stand. A boy about fifteen dressed in gay attire, and considerable jewelry. He puts his hand towards the glass, and says:

Jim. "Come on, boys. As Shakspeare has it:
'Good wine is a good familiar creature if it be well used.'
Have a drink?"

John. "Don't drink that sort of thing, Jim. I signed the pledge years ago, and as you quoted Shakspeare, let me try my hand at the same thing. Doesn't he say:
'Oh, that men should put an enemy in their mouths to try to steal away their brains!'"

Edward. "I learned Shakspeare, too, when I was a little shaver, and among other wise words I remember these:
'O thou invisible spirit of wine, if thou hast no name to be known by, let us call thee devil.'"

Henry. "I say, Jim, if I were you I wouldn't quote Shakspeare any more. I too, remember something he says, which is like this:
'To be now a sensible man, by-and-by a fool, and presently a beast. Oh, strange! Every inordinate cup is unblessed, and the ingredient is a devil.'"

Jim. "I'll warrant there's lots in Shakspeare that *I* could quote to some purpose if I only knew it. But here is something a *little* better than Shakspeare:

'Have a little wine for thy stomach's sake.'

What have you to say to that, eh?"

Fred (the smallest boy). "I haven't any stomach's *ache*, and I know some folks that drink wine, and they have stomach's *aches* ever so much more than people who don't drink it. Any way they seem to."

Jim. "I didn't speak to you. Nobody expected a little fellow like you would comprehend. Here's George, he is one of your Sabbath-school fellows and *he'll* know that I quoted from the Bible what Timothy said to Paul and Silas."

Fred. "Well, George *must* be posted, if he knows that."

Jim. "I don't know what you are all grinning about. I tell you that is in the Bible."

George. "Yes, Jim it *is* in the Bible, but it is what Paul said to Timothy. But never mind your mistake. Because Paul said that to Timothy two thousand years ago does not make it that he said it to me. And as I don't know what was the matter with Timothy's stomach I shouldn't dare to take any for *my* stomach which seems all right. But Paul does say to you, and to me, and to all of us:

'It is good neither to eat flesh, nor to drink wine, nor anything whereby thy brother stumbleth, or is made weak.'

and I find in another place that he says:

'Thieves, nor covetous, nor drunkards, enter the Kingdom of Heaven.'

That is plain enough for me."

William. "I find in the Bible, Jim, that it says:

'Woe unto him that giveth his neighbor drink, that puttest thy bottle to him, and makest him drunken.'

And I also find this:

'Woe unto them that call evil good, and good evil; that put darkness for light, and light for darkness; Woe unto them that are mighty to drink wine, and men of strength to mingle strong drink; which justify the wicked for reward, and take away the righteousnes of the righteous from him. Therefore as the fire devoureth the stubble, and the flame consumeth the chaff, so their root shall be as rottenness, and their blossom shall go up as dust; because they have cast away the law of the Lord of hosts, and despised the word of the Holy One of Israel.'

And in another place it says:

'Woe to the crown of pride, to the drunkards of Ephraim, they shall be trodden under feet.'

And Solomon says that:

'He that loveth wine shall not be rich. For the drunkard and the glutton shall come to poverty.'"

Thomas (the oldest boy). "In the Bible I find this, and I say, Jim, we'd better all of us remember it:

'Who hath woe? who hath sorrow? who hath contentions? who hath babbling? who hath wounds without cause? who hath redness of eyes? They that tarry long at the wine. Look not thou upon the wine when it is red, when it giveth its color in the cup, when it moveth itself aright. At the *last* it biteth like a serpent, and stingeth like an adder.'

And let me tell you that the serpent is always there. It is in the cup even though decked with flowers."

They draw nearer the cup, and Thomas ignites a chemical serpent; they all fall back, and the serpent flames up and out on the flowers.

6. SCRIPTURE RECITATION.

WATER FROM THE FOUNTAIN.

Seven young girls dressed in white, rise in a front seat, face the audience, and repeat:

1st. "And the people thirsted for water, and the Lord said unto Moses, thou shalt smite the rock, and there shall water come out of it that the people may drink."

2nd. "And Isaac's servants came and told him concerning the well which they had digged, and said unto him: We have found water."

3rd. "Ho every one that thirsteth, come ye to the waters."

4th. "Jesus stood and cried, saying, If any man thirst, let him come unto me and drink."

5th. "For whosoever shall give a cup of water in my name, because ye belong to Christ, verily, I say unto you, he shall not lose his reward."

6th. "For an angel went down at certain seasons into the water; whosoever then first after the troubling of the water stepped in was made whole of whatsoever disease he had."

7th. "And the Spirit and the bride say, Come. And let him that heareth say, Come. And let him that is athirst say,

Come, and whosoever will, let him take the water of life freely."

7. SINGING. — *Gospel Hymns No. 10. Whosoever heareth, shout the sound.*

8. CATECHISM EXERCISE.— *By two boys.*

CATECHISM EXERCISE.

Who was the first martyr? — Abel.

Who was the first blacksmith? — Tubal-Cain.

Who was the first sea-captain? — Noah.

Who was the first drunkard? — Noah.

Who was the first census-taker? — Moses, when he numbered the children of Israel.

Who was the first strong-minded woman? — Jezebel.

Who was the first theological professor? — Samuel.

Who first took the temperance pledge? — Mother of Samson.

Who first pledged himself? — Daniel.

What is the first prohibitory law? — Look not on the wine when it is red.

Where was the first temperance society held? In the Kingdom of Israel: house of the Rechabites.

What blessing did God promise upon the first temperance society? — Jer. 35: 18, 19:

"And Jeremiah said unto the house of the Rechabites, Thus saith the Lord of hosts, the God of Israel; Because ye have obeyed the commandment of Jonadab your father, and kept all his precepts and done according unto all that he hath commanded you: Therefore thus saith the Lord of hosts the God of Israel; Jonadab the son of Rechab, shall not want a man to stand before me forever."

9. RECITATION.— *By a small boy.*

QUEER MEDICINES.

"I'm dry," says the glutton,
"As dry as a fish;
 So give me a 'bumper'
 To season my dish."

"I'm wet," says the traveler,
"I fain would be dry,
 Prepare for my comfort
 A glass of 'old rye!'

"I'm cold! almost frozen,
 So build up a fire
 In shape of a 'rum-punch'
 To make me perspire."

"I'm hot," says the other
"From toe unto crown;
 I'd fain have a 'julep'
 To cool my blood down."

And so men will swallow,
To patch up their ills
And change their condition,
The devil's worst pills.

10. RECITATION.— *By a young lady.*

ONLY A STIRRUP-CUP.

"Fill up! one glass before you go!
The moon is young, the night is keen,
The creek-ford lies half hid between
The drifting ice, and whirling snow,
And the wind is fierce as a Russian knout,
But here is a draught that will keep it out;
Drain it, and feel how your heart will glow!

"Only a stirrup-cup! now, good-night!
Here's to good luck, 'till we see you again!
The mare only waits for the loosening rein;
She'll make your five miles with the speed of a kite.
Good-bye!" and the horse and his rider were gone.
But the revellers staid 'till the faint winter dawn
Touched the world with its finger of light.

Some miles away, in the morning gray,
A wife looked out o'er the sheeted world,
Weary with heaping the hearth-stone old,
Weary with watching from dark to day,
With hushing the children, who cried in their sleep;
"Listen for father, the snow is so deep,
And he comes through the dark and cold."

When the clock in the corner chimed slowly for three,
And the windows all creaked in the grip of the blast,
A sound, like the neigh of a horse, went past
And a faint, faint voice, as of dread or dree;
But fiercely the wind wrenched the door from her hold
And all she could hear were *its* tones manifold,
And naught but the snow could she see.

Night melted away in the cup of the sun,
The joy of the day made forebodings seem vain;
The tea-kettle bubbled and sung on the crane.
The heart may be heavy, but tasks must be done;
So the cattle were fed, and the platters were laid,
The children went out for a lamb that had strayed,
And the mother's day's spinning begun.

Whiz, whiz, went the wheel, in monotonous round,
And it seemed that its echo beat in on her brain,
'Till a voice calling "Mother!" again, and again,
Pierced her, quick, like a voice that is heard in a swound,
And there, with the ice frozen thick in his hair,
Lay a snow-shrouded form on the ground.

"Who is it?" she cried, and a whinny replied,
For the mare, faithful Polly, stood guard at his feet;
Wan, and pale was his face, and the armor of sleet
Rattled roughly each time when the wind lightly sighed.
Oh, never again, to those lips, or those eyes,
Would the wife, or the child, bring a smile of surprise!
Oh! the dumb parted lips! Oh! the eyes staring wide!

Little fatherless children! The woman bereft!
The pale one, so robbed of his soul in the dark
To your dumb accusations there's One sayeth
    "Hark,
I will drive my sickle from right unto left,
'Till the vine-wreathen pillars shall fall at its stroke,
At the wine-wetted portals the ravens shall croak
And the head of this demon be cleft!"

11. RECITATION.— *Little boy decorated with grain.*

"OLD RYE'S SPEECH."

I was made to be *eaten*,
And not to be *drank*:
To be threshed in a barn,
Not soaked in a tank.
I come as a blessing,
When put through a *mill*;
As a blight and a curse
When run through a *still*.
Make me into *loaves*
And your children are fed;
But, if into *drink*
I will starve them instead.
In bread, I'm a servant,
The eater shall rule;
In drink, I am master,
The drinker a fool.
Then remember the warning,
My strength I'll employ;—
If *eaten* to *strengthen*,
If *drank* to *destroy*.

12. SINGING.— *Yield not to temptation*

13. RECITATION.—*By a boy.*

NEVER BEGIN.

In going down hill on a slippery track,
The going is easy; the task — getting back;
But you'll not have a tumble, a slip nor a stop,
Nor toil from below,— if you stay at the top.

So from drinking, and smoking, and *every sin,*
You are safe and secure if you never begin ;
Then never begin ! *never begin!*
You cannot be a drunkard, unless you begin.

Some boast they can stand on the cataract's brink,
Some do it, but *some* topple over and sink ;
Then I think, to be safe, the most sensible plan
Is to keep from the brink just as far as you can.

So from drinking, and smoking and *every sin*
You are safe and secure, if you never begin.
Then *never begin! Never begin!*
You cannot be a drunkard, unless you begin.

14. SINGING.—*Am I a soldier of the cross,*
 A follower of the Lamb?

15. BENEDICTION.

Exercise for Christmas Day, or Eve.

PROGRAMME.

1. ORGAN SOLO.— Gloria. . . . . *Mozart.*
   Or (if there is no organ in the hall) singing:
   Hark the glad sound the Saviour comes.
2. PRAYER.
3. SCRIPTURAL RESPONSIVE EXERCISE.—
   Israel in need of a Saviour. Arranged by *Miss A. E. Pidgson.*
4. SINGING.— Awake glad heart, get up and sing.
5. RECITATION OF SCRIPTURE.— . . . . (*By twelve little girls.*)
6. SINGING.— When Jordan hushed his waters still.
7. SCRIPTURAL RESPONSIVE EXERCISE CONTINUED.
8. SINGING.— Christmas Carols.
9. RECITATION.— The Overture of Angels. . . (*By seven young girls.*)
10. RECITATION.— Spanish Christmas Carol.
11. SANTA CLAUS FROLIC.— In "Our Boys and Girls Magazine," (Oliver Optic's) for Dec. 24, 1870. . '. . . *By G. M. Baker.*
    Or The Trapping of Santa Claus, in "Adventures of Miltiades Peterkin Paul." Price, 50 cents.
    (D. Lothrop & Co., Boston.) *By John Brownjohn.*

EXPLANATION OF PROGRAMME.

The responses for the children should be written out for them by their teachers, and may be committed to memory and recited by the different classes or may be simply read in concert.

ISRAEL IN NEED OF A SAVIOUR.

SUP. "A voice was heard upon the high places; weeping and supplication of the children of Israel; for they have perverted their way, and they have forgotten the Lord their God."

SCHOOL. "Behold O Lord; for I am in distress, my heart is turned within me, for I have grievously rebelled."

SUP. "Thy ways and thy doings have procured these things unto thee."

SCHOOL. "For these things I weep; mine eye runneth down with water, because the comforter that should relieve my soul is far from me."

SUP. "Go and proclaim these words toward the north, and say, Return thou backsliding Israel, saith the Lord; and I will not cause mine anger to fall upon you."

SCHOOL. "O Lord, our God, how excellent is thy name in all the earth! Blessed is he whose transgression is forgiven, and whose sin is covered!"

SUP. "Speak ye comfortably to Jerusalem, and cry unto her, that her warfare is accomplished, and that her iniquity is pardoned: For a man shall be as an hiding-place from the wind, and a covert from the tempest; as rivers of water in a dry place; as the shadow of a great rock in a weary land."

SCHOOL. "Sing unto the Lord; for he hath done excellent things; this is known in all the earth."

SUP. "The people that dwell in darkness have seen a great light; they that dwell in the shadow of death, upon them hath a great light shined."

SCHOOL. "Cry out and shout thou inhabitant of Zion; for great is the Holy One of Israel in the midst of thee!"

SUP. "Unto us a child is born, unto us a son is given; and the government shall be upon his shoulder and his name shall be called Wonderful Counsellor, The Mighty God, The Everlasting Father, The Prince of Peace."

SCHOOL. "Awake, awake, put on thy strength, O Zion! put on thy beautiful garments, O Jerusalem the holy city."

4. SINGING.—*Awake, glad heart, etc., old carol by Henry Vaughn who lived between 1621 and 1695. Music adapted from "Redcliffe."*

AWAKE, GLAD HEART.

Awake, glad heart! get up and sing!
It is the birthday of thy King;
    Awake! Awake!
    The sun doth shake
Light from his locks and all the way
Breathing perfumes, doth spice the day.

I would I were some bird or star
Flutt'ring in woods or lifted far
    Above this inn
    And road of sin!
That either star or bird should be
Shining or singing still to thee.

5. SCRIPTURE RECITATION.—*For twelve little girls.*

1st. "And there arose in the same country shepherds abiding in the field, keeping watch over their flocks by night. And lo, the angel of the Lord came upon them and the glory of the Lord shone round about them. and they were sore afraid."

2nd. "And the angel said unto them, Fear not, for behold I bring you good tidings of great joy, which shall be to all people. For unto you is born this day, in the city of David, a Savior which is Christ the Lord. And this shall be a sign unto you ; ye shall find the babe wrapped up in swaddling clothes, lying in a manger."

3rd. "And suddenly there was with the angel a multitude of the heavenly host praising God and saying, Glory to God in the highest and on earth peace, good will toward men."

4th. "And it came to pass as the angels were gone away from them into heaven, the shepherds said one to another, Let us now go over unto Bethlehem and see this thing which is come to pass, which the Lord hath made known to us."

5th. "And they came with haste and found Mary and Joseph, with the babe lying in a manger, and when they had seen it, they made known abroad the saying which was told them concerning this child."

6th. "Now when Jesus was born in Bethlehem of Judea, in the days of Herod the King, behold there came wise men from the East to Jerusalem, saying, Where is he that is born King of the Jews? for we have seen his star in the East and are come to worship him."

7th. "And they said, In Bethlehem of Judea, for there it is written by the prophet. And thou Bethlehem in the land of Juda art not the least among the princes of Judah ; for out of thee shall come a Governor that shall rule my people Israel."

8th. "Then Herod sent them to Bethlehem and said, Go

and search diligently for the young child, and when ye have found him bring me word again that I may come and worship him also."

9th. "When they had heard the King they departed; and lo, the star in the East, went before them till it came and stood over where the child was. When they saw the star they rejoiced with exceeding great joy."

10th. "And when they were come into the house they saw the young child with Mary his mother, and fell down and worshipped him: and when they had opened their treasures they presented unto him gifts; gold, and frankincense, and myrrh."

11th. "And behold there was a man in Jerusalem whose name was Simeon; and the same man was just and devout, waiting for the consolation of Israel: and it was revealed to him by the Holy Ghost that he should not see death before he had seen the Lord's Christ."

12th. "And he came into the temple, and when the parents brought in the child Jesus, then took he him into his arms and blessed God and said: Lord now lettest thou thy servant depart in peace according to thy word; for mine eyes have seen thy salvation which thou hast prepared before the face of all people; a light to lighten the Gentiles and the glory of thy people Israel."

6. SINGING. — *By the School. Tune, Migdol.*

>When Jordan hushed his waters still
>And silence slept on Zion's hill,
>When Bethlehem's shepherds thro' the night,
>Watched o'er their flocks by starry light.
>
>On wheels of light, on wings of flame,
>The glorious hosts of Zion came:
>High Heaven with songs of triumph rung
>While thus they struck their harps and sung.

O Zion, lift thy raptured eye!
The long expected hour is nigh,
Renewed creation smiles again
The Prince of Salem comes to reign,

He comes to cheer the trembling heart,
Bid Satan and his hosts depart;
Again the Day star gilds the gloom,
Again the towers of Eden bloom.

7. RESPONSIVE EXERCISE CONTINUED.

SUP. Where are we told of Christ's special love and sympathy with children?

SCHOOL. "Jesus called them unto him and said, Suffer little children to come unto me and forbid them not: for of such is the kingdom of God."

SUP. How are we taught by Christ's example, the duty of submission to parents?

SCHOOL. "And he went down with them and came to Nazareth, and was subject unto them."

8. SINGING.— *Christmas Carols. Star of the East, a carol by Brady E. Backus. This is for two children, to be sung in successive solos, followed by chorus, The Angels sang in the Silent Night, by J. B Marsh; or, Wake ye faithful Christians, a carol for the full school.*

9. THE OVERTURE OF ANGELS.— *The Angels of the Seven Planets, in " Longfellow's Golden Legend," furnishes seven appropriate recitations for Christmas time for girls, if desired. The Wise Men of the East, which follows may be recited by three boys. The girls should be dressed as angels, the central one should hold a wand tipped with a large silver-paper star.*

10. *The following translation of a quaint Spanish Christmas Carol may be recited by a boy.*

>He was born in a hovel
>   Of spider webs full ;
>Beside him there grovel
>   An ox and a mule.
>And King Melchior bade
>   To honor the day,
>And that none might be sad,
>   The musicians should play,
>
>I'm a poor little gipsy
>   From over the sea :
>I bring him a chicken
>   That cries "quiri-qui ; "
>For each of us sure,
>   Should offer his part –
>Be you ever so poor,
>   You can give him your heart.
>
>Good night, Father Joseph ;
>   Madonna so mild,
>We leave with regret
>   Your adorable child,
>With the crown on his locks
>   The symbol of rule ;
>Sleep in peace Senor Ox,
>   God bless you, Sir Mule.

If more recitations or songs are desired, two very good ones may be found in " Rhymes and Jingles," by Mrs. Mary Mapes Dodge; A song of St. Nicholas, page 38, and Christmas Bells, page 10.

SANTA CLAUS FROLIC.

[By G. M. BAKER. From " Our Boys and Girls."]

The rising of the curtain discloses a room with a fireplace, above which are hung stockings of various sizes, from baby's sock to Bridget's long and broad hose. Six or eight children, in nightgowns and caps, stocking feet, with lighted candles in their hands, come straggling in. They move about, looking up the chimney now and then, and singing to the air of " We're all noddin'."

GIRLS. We are all waiting, wait, wait, waiting,
We are waiting for Santa Claus to come,
To catch him we're waiting, he surely will be here
The moments fly quickly, and midnight draws near.

ALL. We're all waiting, wait, wait, waiting,
We're all waiting for Santa Claus to come.

BOYS. We are freezing, freeze, freeze, freezing,
We are all freezing here, waiting in the cold
For Santa Claus to bring us our presents we wait,
Come hurry old fellow, 'tis getting very late.

ALL. We're all freezing, freeze, freeze, freezing,
We're all freezing here, waiting in the cold.

GIRLS. We're all nodding, nod, nod, nodding,
We're all nodding and dropping off to sleep,
To our warm little beds, it is time we should go,
Come hurry, Good Santa, pray don't be so slow.

ALL. For we're all nodding etc.

BOYS. We are all yawning, yaw, yaw, yawning,
We're all yawning so let's go off to bed.

GIRLS. To stay any longer were surely unwise,
We'll wait for the daylight to open our eyes.

ALL. For we're all yawning, yaw, yaw, yawning,
We're all yawning and going off to bed.

[*Exeunt right and left, singing last lines.*]

Santa Claus peeps out from chimney; then enters. Costume: rubber boots with pantaloons tucked into them; heavy fur coat with red comforter tied round it for a sash; red scarf about neck, peaked fur cap, long grey hair and beard, very red face; strapped to his back a basket of toys.

[SANTA, *looking right and left.*]

Ho, ho, my little rogues! You set a trap
To catch me napping: *now*, who takes a nap?
I'm an old schemer; even your sharp eyes
Could never find me in this queer disguise.
Dream on, my darlings, while I treasures heap,
Ho, ho! to fill your *hose* while you're asleep:
Year after year, I drop in on the sly
Through chimneys made for me so broad and high:
To pop down them is made my cheerful duty
It *suits* me too — sometimes almost too *sooty*.

[*Takes basket off back.*]

Let's see, what year is this? why, bless my eyes,
It's 1879! Bless us! how time flies!
And children multiply so fast, 'tis clear
A partner I must have another year.
I'm really getting old; this wrinkled phiz
Of good old age a striking symbol is.
And yet I'm strong, can frolic, dance or play
With young folks yet, for many a Christmas day.
So I'll not grumble: while I can, I'll strive
To let my boys and girls know I'm alive,
That though my head is grey, my heart is young,
And green as Christmas boughs around me hung.

SONG.— *Air, The little brown man. By Santa Claus.*

I am Santa Claus, old as you see;

I drop in once a year, on a Christmas spree;
Plump is my figure, wrinkled is my face;
I'm a jolly little fellow and love the human race.
And I sing and I laugh, and I laugh and I sing,
And I laugh, ha, ha, ha,
For I'm a jolly, jolly, jolly, little, little, little,
Fat, fat, fat Santa Claus.
Hallo, hallo! why this will never do!
Business, old Santa Claus, can't wait for you,
And so to work! Let me first be sure
The children sleep. [*Listens.*] Ha, ha, I hear them snore!

CHILDREN [*outside*].
We are all dreaming, dream, dream, dreaming,
We are all dreaming that Santa Claus has come.

SANTA. Dream on my darlings, unto each and all of you
Morn shall bring joy: your dreams shall be true.
Here are the stockings: bless me, what a row!
Little and big, they make a wondrous show.

[*As he speaks he fills stockings.*]

First comes the baby's, what a tiny thing!
'Twill just hold a rattle, and a rubber ring;
This is a girl's, so very neat and small,
I'll stuff it with candy and a rubber doll;
Ah! here's a boy's. It's very strong and blue
A nice new pair of skates, my lad, for you.
Another girl's! what can I find to please her
Ah! here's a tea-set, don't think that's a teazer!
Another boy's! Ho, this will never do!
Hole in the heel: a present would drop through;
A ball of yarn will make him wiser grow —
'Twill mend his stockings and his habits too.
What monster's this? It must be Bridget's, sure,
'Twould hold all I have brought, I fear much more;

A nice new gingham dress, a good warm shawl
Don't fill it; then here goes a water-fall.
And now I'm off. (*Sees audience.*) Hallo!
Whom have we here?
I really am found out; that's very clear.
Don't expose me, for I did not mean
Upon my annual visit to be seen.
If you are all my children, 'tis not fair
To tell my secrets, even to the air;
So keep them close, don't whisper I've been here,
And shut your eyes; I'm going to disappear.
With Merry Christmas wishes all I greet,
Hoping next year my visit to repeat;
Now, good night, I'm off--yet, ere I go
A little magic I propose to show;
Shut fast your eyes a minute; one, two, three!
Presto! change! behold the Christmas tree.

The Christmas tree, lighted, and hung with ornaments and presents should be arranged on the back of the stage: in front of it should be hung a curtain that will stretch across the stage. This curtain should represent the side of the room, in the middle of which is the chimney and fire-place, a square hole being cut in it, even with which will be the front edge of the mantel-piece. The fire-place may be arranged by setting a large, deep, dry-goods box on end, the front and upper end being removed. Line this with black muslin or paper, nail a narrow board on the front edge covered with lambrequins, this to represent the mantel shelf. As the curtain falls — the upper part of it just behind the back edge of this narrow strip — the open, upper part of the box is left behind the curtain. Andirons and fender should be put in place, and the box held by some one firmly in its place while Santa Claus steps down from a high chair through the box, coming out of the front as from a chimney. As Santa Claus repeats the words, "*Presto, change!*" the box should be removed, the curtains drawn back as quickly as possible, disclosing the tree trimmed with balls, candles, strings of pop-corn, cranberries, bags of candy, etc. Circles of bright cambric, gathered up and tied with ribbon, are more ornamental and more easily made than lace stockings. Pretty cherub faces printed on paper may be made useful by sewing on skirts of tarlatan behind the arms. Appropriate mottoes on the walls add to the beauty of the occasion.

"Children's Day" Service

FOR THE
METHODIST EPISCOPAL SUNDAY-SCHOOL.

LILY-SUNDAY.

[PALM SUNDAY of the Roman Catholic Calendar. See Note.]

PROGRAMME.

1. MUSIC.— Come Gentle Spring. (Instrumental or vocal.) (Haydn.) . . . . *From The Seasons.*
2. PRAYER.
3. SINGING.—Consider the Lilies. . . . . (*Anthem by choir.*)
4. REMARKS—By the Pastor.
5. A RECITATION from the Scriptures. . . . . . (*By a girl.*)
6. SCRIPTURE DIRECTIONS.— How to be a Lady, and how to be a Gentleman. (*Several boys and girls.*)
7. CHORUS.— Spring Song. . . . . *Abt.*
8. RECITATION—What we think of the Bible. (*Supt. Pastor and S. S. Teachers.*)
9. SINGING.— How precious is the book divine, By inspiration given. Tune, Naomi. (*By a boy.*)
10. RECITATION.— Fame. . . . . . (*By a lady teacher.*)
11. RECITATION.—Work. . . . . . *From Mrs. Browning.*
12. PART SONG.— Forest Vales. . . . . . . *Mendelssohn.*
13. RECITATION.— Plants from a Garden of Spices. . . (*Infant class.*)
14. HYMN.— Coronation.
15. BENEDICTION.

NOTE.

"Palm Sunday, the last Sunday in Lent, is so called from the custom of blessing branches of palms and olives. In many countries other trees, as in England, the yew or the willow, and in Brittany the box, are blessed instead. The first writer who expressly refers to it is the venerable Bede. A special service is found for it in the Roman missal. In England, Palm Sunday anciently was celebrated with much ceremonial, but the custom was discontinued in the Church of England in the reign of Edward VI."

THE EXERCISE.

Church to be elaborately decorated with flowers (placing the lilies on the altar) and branches of trees among which hang cages of birds. Place the Sunday-school banner with the Infant school, and give the children the best seats in the church.

1. MUSIC.— *Come Gentle Spring. From the Seasons.* Haydn.
2. PRAYER.
3. SINGING.— *Consider the Lilies. Anthem by choir.*
4. REMARKS.— *By the Pastor.*
5. RECITATION.— *Song of Solomon. The Hope and Calling of the Church. By a girl.*

The voice of my Beloved! behold, he cometh leaping upon the mountains, skipping upon the hills. My beloved spake, and said unto me, Rise up, my love, my fair one, and come away, For lo, the winter is past, the rain is over and gone: the flowers appear on the earth; the time of the singing birds is come, and the voice of the turtle is heard in our land. The fig-tree putteth forth her green figs, and the vine with the tender grapes give a good smell. Arise, my love, my fair one, and come away. Awake, O north wind, and come thou south, blow upon my garden, that the spice thereof may flow out. Let my beloved come into his garden, and eat his pleasant fruits.

6. SCRIPTURE DIRECTIONS.—*How to be a Lady and how to be a Gentleman. Copied on separate slips of paper and given to twelve girls in different parts of the audience, who rise and read; also to twelve boys who do likewise.*

1st. For the Lord taketh pleasure in his people: he will *beautify* the *meek* with salvation. Psa. 149 : 4.

2nd. Favor is deceitful and beauty is vain: but a woman that feareth the Lord, she shall be praised. Prov. 31 : 30.

3rd. *Pride* goeth before *destruction*, and a *haughty spirit* before a fall. Prov. 16 : 18.

4th. He that loveth *pureness of heart*, for the grace of his lips, the king shall be his friend. Prov. 22 : 11.

5th. He that hath a *bountiful eye* shall be blessed: for he giveth of his bread to the poor. Prov. 22 : 9.

6th. The *ear* that heareth the reproof of life abideth among the wise. Prov. 15 : 31.

7th. A wholesome *tongue* is a tree of life; but perverseness therein is a breach in the spirit. Prov. 15 . 4.

8th. Righteous *lips* are the delight of kings, and they love him that speaketh right. Prov. 16 : 12.

9th. Pleasant *words* are as an honey-comb, sweet to the soul and health to the bones. Prov. 16 : 24.

10th. The hand of the diligent maketh rich. Prov. 10 : 4.

11th. Ponder the path of thy *feet*, and let all thy ways be established. Turn not to the right hand nor to the left; remove thy *foot* from evil. Prov. 4: 26, 27.

12th. (*An older girl than the others.*) Wherefore, seeing we are also compassed about with so great a cloud of witnesses, let us lay aside every weight, and the sin that doth so easily beset us, and let us run with *patience* the race that is set before us. Looking unto Jesus, the author and finisher of our faith. Heb. 12 : 1, 2.

[*Boys now recite.*]

1st. Be kindly affectioned one to another. Rom. 12 ; 10.

2nd. If thine enemy hunger feed him, if he thirst give him drink. Rom. 12 : 20.

3rd. Let your conversation be without covetousness: and be content with such things as ye have. Heb. 13 : 5.

4th. It is good neither to eat flesh nor to drink wine nor anything whereby thy brother stumbleth. Rom. 14: 21.

5th. Abhor that which is evil, cleave to that which is good. Rom. 12 : 9.

6th. Comfort the feeble minded ; support the weak. I. Thess. 5 : 14.

7th. Mind not high things but condescend to men of low estate. Rom. 12 . 16.

8th. Let patience have her perfect work. Jas. 1 : 4,

9th. Be not hasty in thy spirit to be angry. Eccl. 7 : 9.

10th. Be courteous. I. Peter 3 : 8.

11th. As ye would that men should do to you, do ye also to them likewise. Luke 6 . 31.

12th. Jesus said unto him, Thou shalt love the Lord thy God with all thy heart, and with all thy soul, and with all thy mind. This is the first and great commandment. And the second is like unto it, Thou shall love thy neighbor as thyself. Matt. 22 : 37,38,39,

7. CHORUS.— *Spring Song.*

8. RECITATION.—*What we think of the Bible!* *Superintendent repeats first answer, the Pastor the second and seventh, and the S. S. Teachers the others.*

1st. SUPT. Give me understanding and I shall keep thy law, for therein do I delight, O Lord my God.

2nd. PASTOR. Thy word is a lamp unto my feet and a light unto my path.

3rd. S. S. TEACHER. How sweet are thy words unto my taste, yea sweeter than honey to my mouth.

4th. S. S. Teacher. Thy word have I hid in my heart that I might not sin against thee.

5th S. S. TEACHER. The entrance of thy word giveth light.

6th. S. S. TEACHER. Thy statutes have been my song in the house of my pilgrimage.

7th. PASTOR. All Scripture is given by inspiration of God and is profitable for doctrine, for reproof, for correction, for instruction in righteousness.

9. SINGING.—*How precious is the book divine
By inspiration given. Tune, Naomi.*

10. RECITATION. —*By a boy.*

FAME.

What shall I do lest life in silence pass?
    And if it do,
And never prompt the bray of noisy brass,
    What need'st thou rue?
Remember, aye the Ocean's deeps are mute;
    The shallows roar;
Worth is the Ocean — Fame is but the bruit
    Along the shore.

What shall I do to be forever known?
    Thy duty ever.
This did full many who yet sleep unknown.
    Oh! never, never —
Think'st thou, perchance, that they remain unknown
    Whom *thou* know'st not?
By angel-trumps in heaven their praise is blown,
    Divine their lot.

What shall I do to gain eternal life?
    Discharge aright
The simple dues with which each day is rife;
    Yea, with thy might.
Ere perfect scheme of action thou devise
    Will life be fled;
While he, who *ever* acts as conscience cries,
    Shall live, though dead.

11. RECITATION.— *By a lady teacher.*

WORK.

What are we set on earth for? Say, to toil;
Nor seek to leave thy tending of the vines,
For all the heat of the day, till it declines,
And Death's wild curfew shall from work assoil.
God did annoint thee with his odorous oil,
To wrestle, not to reign; and He assigns
All thy tears over, like pure crystallines,
For younger fellow-workers of the soil
To wear for amulets. So others shall
Take patience labor to their heart and hand
From thy heart and thy hand; and thy brave cheer
Shall God's grace make fruitful through thee to all.
The least flower with a brimming cup may stand
And share its dew-drop with another near.

12. PART SONG.—*Forest Vales.   Mendelssohn.*
13. RECITATION.—*Plants from a Garden of Spices.*

All the children in the Infant classes; the girls in white with branches in their hands, the boys also with larger branches. All march to the platform. Arrange row of smallest children in front, then shorter row of taller children behind these, and so on, until you have a pyramid of heads and branches. Have the arranging practiced so that the places can be taken without confusion. When arranged they may recite the following texts and verses:

1st. Whose glorious beauty is a fading flower. Isa. 38: 13.

2nd. Because as the flower of the grass he shall pass away. Jas. 1: 10.

3rd. All thy garments smell of myrrh, and aloes, and cassia. Psa. 45: 8.

4th. And the house of Israel called the name thereof manna: and it was like coriander-seed, white. Ex. 16: 31.

5th, A branch with one cluster of grapes and they bare it between two upon a staff. Num. 13: 23.

6th. And they brought of the pomegranites and of the figs. Num. 13: 23.

7th. The desert shall blossom as the rose. Isa. 35: 1.

8th. He shall grow as the lily. Hosea. 14: 5.

9th. Who is he that cometh out of the wilderness like pillars of smoke, perfumed with myrrh and frankincense? Cant. 3: 6.

10th. Thy plants are an orchard with pleasant fruits; camphire with spikenard and saffron, calamus and cinnamon. Cant. 4: 13, 14.

11th. Instead of the thorn shall come up the fig tree and instead of the brier shall come up the myrtle tree. Isa. 55: 13.

12th. Tell me, gard'ner, dost thou know
       Where the rose and lily grow?
       Rude is yet the opening year
       Yet their sweetest breath is here.
13th. I am the rose of Sharon
       And the lily of the valley.
14th. Seek we then the Lord above
       See his face and know his love;
       If we love Him we shall know
       Where the rose and lily grow.
                        —*Bishop Coxe.*

14. HYMN.— *Coronation.*

15. BENEDICTION.

Sunday Evening Exercise.

DEATH AND RESURRECTION.

[Suitable for EASTER.]

PROGRAMME.

1. MUSIC.— Bright shines the golden sun.
2. SCHOOL.— Repeat in concert, Rom. 14: 8.
3. READING.— A parable about a dewdrop. (From Children's Church at Home, and National Sunday-School Teacher, Oct. 72.)
4. RECITATION.— The Reaper and the Flowers. By Longfellow. (Bryant's Library of Poetry and Song, p. 184.)
5. MUSIC.— There is a happy land.
6. READING.— Little Dora. (Nat. S. S. Teacher, April, 73.) Rev. John Todd.
7. SCHOOL.— Repeat in concert, John 11: 25.
8. RECITATION.— Texts by an older pupil, illustrated by living plants if possible. John 12: 24. I. Cor. 13: 35-38.
9. SERMON.— On Death. (From Children's Sermons. A little pamphlet by J. G. Merrill, Davenport, Iowa.)
10. RECITATION.— By a very little child. Good night and good morning. (Child Life, p. 62.)
11. SOLO.— My Ain Countree.
12. RECITATION.— An Eastern Carol. (St. Nich. 1876, April, p. 385.)
13. RECITATION — "When with one foot on the water,
    And one upon the shore,
    The angel of sadness gives warning
    That day shall be no more.
    Happy is he that heareth
    The signal of his release,
    In the bells of the Holy City,
    In the chimes of eternal peace."
14. MUSIC. — Only waiting.

xc.

(Additional.)

LIFE AND DEATH.

[By Kate Cameron.]

The following poem may be recited in alternate lines or verses, as indicated, by two little girls, Life and Death; one, Life, holding roses, and the other, Death, holding a stalk of lilies.

BOTH.   Two angels standing by our side:
        Ah! which will prove the better guide?

LIFE.   Fair Life, adorned with roses bright.

DEATH. Pale Death, arrayed in lilies white.

LIFE.   We speak of one with joy and cheer,

DEATH. The other we forget, or fear.

LIFE.   One leads us up the flowery slope
        Where bloom the buds of earthly hope.

DEATH. The other lays those flowers in dust,
          And tramples on our fondest trust.

LIFE. One calls dear friends to cheer our way,
          And gives the sunshine to our day.

DEATH. The other in the gloom of night,
          Brings out the stars to yield us light.

BOTH. Oh Life! Oh Death! which is the best?
          The toil of earth, or Heaven's rest?

LIFE. The loved ones present at our side,

DEATH. Or sainted spirits, sanctified?

LIFE. 'Tis well we are not left to say
          Which we will choose to lead the way;
          With Life we now walk hand in hand.

DEATH. But Death will come at God's command,
          E'en now there's but a step between!
          For he is near us tho' unseen.

LIFE. Sweet Life, with thee there's much of joy
          Tho' mingled all with grief's alloy.

DEATH. But Death a better portion gives,
          The pleasure that in Heaven lives.

BOTH. O! if our faith be not in vain,
          "To live is Christ, to die is gain."

(Additional.)

The following quaint device by the ancient writer, George Herbert, may be made use of in decoration. These lines should be printed, or painted, in old English text:

EASTER WINGS.

My tender age in sorrow did begin:
And still with sicknesses and shame
Thou didst so punish sin,
That I became
Most thin ;

With Thee
Let me combine
And feel this day thy victory—
For if I lean my wing on thine
Affliction shall advance the flight in me.

Lord, who createdst man in wealth and store,—
Though foolishly he lost the same,
Decaying more and more
'Till he became
Most poor,

With Thee
Oh! let me rise,
As larks harmoniously,
And sing this day thy victories —
Then shall the fall further the flight in me.

FLOWER CONCERT.

A flower concert given at the last of May or first of June, may be very beautiful. The hall and stage should be elaborately decorated with boughs and blossoms of all kinds, especially the stage, which should represent a garden. The performers and singers should ornament themselves with flowers as far as possible. The following is an entertaining programme, in which the solos and duets may be taken by the older members of the school, while the recitations and the little drama are for the younger ones, and are extremely pretty when rendered with spirit.

PROGRAMME.

PART I.

OPENING.—Piano Solo.
1. CHORUS.— In the beauty of the Lilies, etc. (Mrs. Howe's Battle Hymn of the Republic.) Tune, John Brown's body.
2. DUET.—There's a sweet wild rose. . . . . *Glover.*
3. SOLO.—Won't you buy my pretty flowers? . . . *Persley.*
4. RECITATION.— Jack in the Pulpit.
5. SOLO.—'Tis the last rose of summer. . . . . *Flotow.*
6. PRAISE meeting among the flowers; sixteen varieties being present.

PART II.

1. TRIO.—Down among the lilies. . . . . . *Glover.*
2. SOLO.— The rose bush. . . . . . *Hodges.*
3. DUET.— Maybells and the flowers. . . *Mendelssohn.*
4. SOLO.— The last violet. . . . . *Mendelssohn.*
5. DUET.— Rosebud, dainty and fair to see. . . *Pease.*
6. RECITATION.— You must wake and call me early. . *Tennyson.*
7. RECITATION.— Little drama; May-day in-doors. . *Mrs. Dias.*

PRAISE MEETING AMONG THE FLOWERS.

[ANONYMOUS.]

The Praise Meeting among the Flowers should be represented by sixteen little girls who shall each recite one stanza, while the first and last stanzas are recited in unison. They may be dressed in white, with wands twined with the flowers they represent. They may enter in line, describing a double curve, in serpentine fashion, or in any other form that will add motion and spirit to the performance. When the Rose reaches the centre of the platform for the second time, all should halt and repeat the first verse in unison. The Rose then advances, looks at her wand, and repeats her verse, the others following in turn, till the last verse is reached, which should be repeated in concert.

>The flowers of many climates,
>   That bloom all seasons through,
>Met in a stately garden,
>   Bright with morning dew.

>For praise and loving worship
>   The Lord they came to meet;
>Her box of precious ointment
>   The Rose broke at his feet.

The Passion-flower, His symbol
    Wore fondly on her breast;
She spoke of self-denial,
    As what might please him best.

The Morning-glories, fragile
    Like infants soon to go,
Had dainty toy-like trumpets
    And praised the Master so.

"Thy words are like to honey,"
    The Clover testified;
"And all who trust Thy promise,
    Shall in Thy love abide."

The Lilies said, "Oh trust Him!
    We neither toil nor spin,
And yet his house of beauty
    See how we enter in."

The King-cup and her kindred
    Said, "Let us all be glad!
Oh, his redundant sunshine!
    Behold how we are clad."

"And let us follow Jesus,"
    The Star of Bethlehem said;
And all the band of Star-flowers
    Bent down with reverent head.

The glad Sun-flower answered,
    And little Daisies bright,
And all the cousin Asters —
    "We follow toward the light."

"We praise Him for the mountains,"

The Alpine roses cried ;
"We bless Him for the valleys,"
The Violets replied.

"We praise Him," said the Air-plants,
"For breath we never lack ;"
"And for the rocks we praise Him,"
The Lichens answered back.

"We praise God for the water,"
The salt Sea-mosses sighed ;
And all His baptized Lilies
"Amen ! Amen !" replied.

"And for the cool green woodlands
We praise and thanks return,"
Said Kalmias and Azalias,
And graceful, feathery Fern.

"And for the wealth of gardens,
And all the gard'ner thinks,"
Said Roses and Camelias,
And all the sweet-breathed Pinks.

"Hosanna in the Highest,"
The Baby Bluets sang;
And little trembling Harebells,
Their softest music rang.

'The winter hath been bitter,
But sunshine follows storm !
Thanks for His loving kindness,
The earth's great heart is warm:"

Thus spoke the Pilgrim May-flower,
That cometh after snow,

Entertainments.

The humblest and the sweetest
    Of all the flowers that blow.

" Thank God for every weather,
    The sunshine and the wet,"
Spake out the cheery Pansies,
    And darling Mignonette.

" And so our love and worship,
    Our praise we here would bring
For our Maker ne'er forgets us
    Nor can we forget him."

MAY-DAY IN DOORS.

[Reprinted by permission.]

CHARACTERS.

ARTHUR, *William Tell;* NED, *the Tyrant;* TOMMY, *Tell's son;* GEORGE, CAROLINE, LUCY, ANNA, POLLY, KATE. *Girls are all dressed in white, and have little flags, George has a larger flag.*

SCENE.— *Room in home of* NED, POLLY *and* TOMMY. *Lunch baskets, etc., on chairs;* POLLY *sits holding her hat, shawl and sack.* TOMMY *is seated on floor, playing with marbles; and a much larger boy leans over the back of a chair.*

Ned (dolefully). "We shall have to give it up, Polly. No May-party to-day." (*Goes to window.*)

Polly (earnestly). "Oh! don't you think the clouds will blow over?"

Ned. "The whole sky will have to blow over. It's all lead color."

Polly (sighing). "Oh dear, dear, dear!"

Voices heard outside. Enter, with a rush, CAROLINE, LUCY, ANNA, KATE, GEORGE, *and* ARTHUR, *with baskets, tin pails, etc. The boys' hats are trimmed with evergreen, the girls, with flowers.* TOMMY *leaves off playing with marbles, to watch new comers.*

George (throwing down long coil of evergreen). "Here we come!"

Lucy (speaking fast). "Yes, here we come, pell mell! It's going to pour!"

Caroline (in haste). "Oh, how we have hurried! I felt a great drop fall on my nose!"

Anna (out of breath). "And think of our dresses, our span clean, white dresses!"

Kate (in haste). "No procession to-day! No dancing around the May-pole!"

ARTHUR *throws up hat and catches it.* GEORGE *does the same.*

Lucy. "They got all that evergreen to trim the May-pole, and George brought his flag."

Ned. "If it had been pleasant to-day I'd have let it rain a week afterward!"

George (stepping to window). "There! it pours. It's lucky we hurried."

Polly. "Now all of you stay here and keep May-day with us *(clapping hands).* Do! do!"

Caroline. "Will your mother like it?"

Polly. "I'll go and ask her." *(Goes out.)*

Ned. "Any way you can't go till it holds up."

[*Girls go to window.*]

Arthur. "That may not be for a week."

[*Enter* POLLY *in haste.*]

Polly. "She says we may do any thing but make 'lasses candy."

Ned. "The last time we made it, father said he found some in his slipper-toes."

Girls take off hats and shawls, which with baskets are placed in a corner; some take seats, some stand.

Arthur. "Now what shall we do with ourselves?"

Ned. "Let's get up some entertainment. Tickets, ten cents; grown folks, double."

Kate. "So I say, and call ourselves a 'troupe,' or 'family,' or something."

George. "Something that has a foreign sound."

Arthur. "How would Totopski do?"

Caroline, Lucy and Anna. "Splendid!"

Anna. "Let us call ourselves the Totopski Family."

Lucy. "But what shall we have for our entertainment?"

Polly. "I think *tableaux* are perfectly splendid."

Anna. "Oh, I tell you; have the kind that winds up."

George. "Why, all entertainments wind up when they are done."

Anna. "I mean have each one wound up with a key, and then they move."

Arthur. "She means Mrs. Jarley's Wax-works."

Ned. "All right, we'll have the winding kind."

Caroline. "What wax-works shall we have?"

Ned. "We might have William Tell shooting the apple, for one."

Tommy. "I've seen that. It will take three to do that. Mr. Tell and his son, and the cross tyrant."

George. "And the apple makes four."

Anna. "Who'll be Mr. Tell? You, Ned?"

Ned. "No, I'd rather be the cross tyrant. I feel just right for that. Arthur'll be Mr. Tell."

Arthur. "Oh, yes, I'll be Mr. Tell; and Tommy can be the boy. (*Tommy moves toward the door.*) Where are you going, Tommy?"

Tommy (*going out*). "After my bow an' arrow."

Lucy (*bringing an apple from her basket*). "Here's the apple!"

Caroline. "What shall we do for a feather? Mr. Tell's hat must have a feather."

Kate. "Twist up a piece of newspaper." (*Turns Arthur's hat upon one side, fastens in a piece of twisted paper loose at the top.*) There you have it! and Polly's sacque turned inside out, will do for a tunic."

ARTHUR *puts on hat and sacque; the sacque is lined with a bright color.*

Polly. "He ought to have a wide sash."
Lucy (taking off hers). "Here, take mine."
Polly. "Not that kind of a sash!"
Anna. "Oh, that won't do!"
Caroline. "It should be a scarf."
Ned (tying the sash at the side, around Arthur's waist). "Oh, never mind, we're only rehearsing."
Lucy. "How must the cross tyrant be dressed? Who knows?"
Anna. "The tyrant I saw had a cape hung over one shoulder. A shawl will do for that. (*Brings shawl, which Ned hangs over his left shoulder.*) Now what must he wear on his head?"
Lucy. "I should think a tyrant ought to wear a tall hat."
Polly (going). "I'll get father's."
Anna (to Polly). "And something bright to put on it. I remember that part, plainly."
George (calling after Polly). "And something long for a sword."

[*Exit,* POLLY.]

Caroline. "If the boys do that, can't we make ourselves into wax-works?"
Anna. "Let's be a May-day wax-work, singing and dancing around a pole."
George. "I'll be the pole."
Caroline. "But you are not long enough."

George (mounting a chair). "Now I am!"

Girls (laughing and clapping). "Oh yes! oh yes! He'll do! trim him up, trim him up!"

Ned (to George). "Yes, come down, and be trimmed up."

GEORGE *steps down, stands erect, arms close to his body. Girls hand garlands;* NED *winds them around* GEORGE.

Kate. "Shall we hoist the flag?"

Ned. "Oh yes! bring me the flag. And here's a string (taking a ball of string out of his pocket), to fasten it on with."

NED *fastens the flag to* GEORGE'S *head by winding the string around, then helps him to mount the chair.*

"Three cheers for the flag! Now — one, two, three! (*All cheer and clap.*)

[*Enter* POLLY *with an old hat and a poker.*]

Polly. "Won't this hat do? Mother couldn't have father's good one banged about."

George. "Oh, that's good enough! we're only rehearsing. Did you get something bright?"

[NED *puts on hat.*]

Polly (taking out yellow bandanna handkerchief). "Mother said this was quite bright."

Anna. "Why, I meant something shiny, like a clasp or a buckle."

Kate. "No matter, we're only rehearsing."

[NED *ties handkerchief round hat so the corners hang down.*

Polly (hands the poker). "Here's your sword. That's the longest thing I could find."

All laugh. NED *seizes poker, and strikes a military attitude. Enter* TOMMY *with bow and arrow.*

Tommy. Where shall I stand up?"
Arthur. "Come this way (*leads Tommy to one side of stage, Ned follows*). Ned, you must scowl and look fierce. Tommy, fold your arms, and stand still as a post."

Puts an apple on TOMMY'S *head, and takes aim with bow and arrow.*

Tommy. "Oh, I'm afraid! Look out for my eyes! The arrow might go off."
Arthur. "I'll put the apple in the chair."

TOMMY *stands motionless.* ARTHUR *aims at apple on chair;* NED *stands by with drawn sword; then all three resume their former positions.*

Kate. "Now we girls must stand round the May-pole. (*They gather round the pole.*) Who'll wind?"
The Girls. "You, you, you!"
Polly. "What a little circle; wish we had more girls —"

Kate (to Anna). "How shall I wind up the wax-works?"

Anna. "The ones I saw all stood on a string, and the string led to a box, and when the box was wound up, the wax-works began to act their parts. A door-key will do to wind with."

Kate. "We'll manage the same way."

KATE *lays a long string on the floor, passes it under the feet of the wax-works, drops the end of it in a work-box upon the table.*

Arthur. "Don't you girls think you ought to be wearing your wreaths, and holding your baskets and your flags, and your posies? They'd make your wax-works look handsomer."

Caroline. "So they will."

Girls get the flowers, flags and baskets, taking the wreaths from their hats and putting them on their heads.

Anna. "You must take the key and pretend to wind up the machinery. What song shall we sing?"

Lucy. "'The Merry Month of May,' is perfectly splendid."

Caroline. "I wonder if we know the words Let's try."

[*They sing. Tune, The Poacher's Song, or any lively tune.*]

We come, we come with dance and song,

With hearts and voices gay;
We come, we come, a happy throng;
For now it is beautiful May.

We've lingered by the brookside,
    To find the fairest flowers;
We've rambled through the meadows wide,
    These sunny, sunny hours.

[*All move around.*]

Chorus.   Oh, we'll dance and sing around the ring,
        With footsteps light and gay,
    Oh, we'll dance and sing around the ring,
        For now it is beautiful May.

Kate. " That's a good song. Now then! All ready! Stand in your places. (*Gets the door key.*) Arms folded, Tommy. When I've done winding up Arthur must begin to take aim, Ned begin to scowl and to hold up his sword, and you girls begin to sing and dance round. Can't you hold your hands high, so the flowers and flags will show? (*Girls raise their hands.*) That's prettier. Now all stand as still as real wax-works till the machinery is wound up, then begin."

KATE *winds up machinery, the actors remaining quiet. When the winding stops they begin to perform their parts and while the dancers are still singing, the curtain falls.*

(Additional.)
MAY BASKETS.

It is a pretty custom, that of hanging baskets of flowers upon the handles of doors, on the evening of May-day. They may be nothing more than tiny white paper boxes filled with violets. They are simple gifts, but may give much pleasure. If they have a bit of poetry added, so much the better. Here is something for one:

    May the fates propitious be,
    While I this basket hang for thee;
    Freighted only with May-flowers
    Born of sunshine, wind and showers;
    Gathered from the sunniest nooks
    On the hill sides, by the brooks,
    Where they bloomed in beauty bright
    Just for me — and you — this night.
    And I know you will not mind
    If no bon-bons here you find,
    As you search with curious eye,
    Where only these fair blossoms lie.
    And now my simple lay is sung,
    My basket on the door is hung,
    I know you for a spry young man,
    But catch, oh, catch me if you can!

THE FAIRY QUEEN.

A MAY-DAY CANTATA.

BY W. EUSTIS BARKER.

DRAMATIS PERSONÆ.

WANDA, *a beggar, afterwards Fairy Queen;* LUCIE, *her attendant;* ALICE, *May Queen;* MABEL, NELLIE, FRANCIS, MAUD, LAURA, *and other children, fairies.*

Long ribbons of different colors should be attached to the May-pole. After the curtain rises a chord should be struck as a signal for each child to grasp the end of one of these ribbons. They stand facing the audience. A second chord, and they separate into alternate couples, facing each other. Then as the music begins they skip around the pole in two lines, moving in opposite directions, as in the "Ladies Chain," in dancing. They wave the ribbons under and over, as they move, alternately lifting it above the heads of those they meet, and alternately stooping and passing under. On WANDA'S *first appearance she wears an old waterproof over her fairy costume; this can be twitched into the wings, by unseen lines with fish-hooks attached.*

If colored fire flashes upon the stage at this instant and the fairies run in briskly and group prettily, the effect will be very pretty. A simple square dance should be introduced during the singing of Air No. 2, "Fairies join us hand in hand," the two queens, with arms entwined, standing in the centre.

SCENE 1st. *Children dancing round May-pole:* ALICE *in centre, uncrowned. Children dance and sing:*

>Welcome, welcome genial May,
>   Stay your passing feet;
>Listen to the children's song,
>   Rising full and sweet.
>
>Birds are singing in the trees,
>   There, too, sunbeams play;
>And the wild flowers of the spring,
>   Kiss thy feet, sweet May.
>
>In the fragrant meadows green,
>   Hear the melody
>That the rippling brooklet sings
>   All for love of thee.
>
>We will laugh and dance and sing,
>   'Tis the children's day;
>And we'll crown with blossoms sweet
>   Alice — Queen of May.

RECITATION.

LAURA.   Alice dear, you know that we
         All agreed that she should be,
         Who excelled in everything,
         Crowned our May-Queen in the spring.
         Playmates, who has gentlest been?
CHIL.   Alice — she shall be our Queen.

RECITATION.

LAURA. Sweetest heart and most unselfish,
When the Autumn days fell darkly,
'Twas the sunshine of thy presence
Brought the spring-time back again.
Upon thee, who all excellest,
In thy gentleness and goodness,
Do we place this flowery crown.
CHIL. Fairer queen was never known.

SONG [*Tune, Upidee.*]

Whate'er Queen Alice of us asks,
We'll obey, we'll obey;
If she gives us all hard tasks,
Yet we must obey.
O'er our hearts long may she reign,
No harsh word shall cause her pain,
But punished shall that subject be,
Who refuses to obey;
But punished shall that subject be
Who will not obey.

RECITATION.

ALICE. Oh playmates dear, I have not been
And am not worthy to be Queen !
I've done my best ; yet every day,
In something, I have gone astray :
But since your love has so crowned me,
A loving Queen I'll try to be.

[*Thunder afar off.*]

Hark ! a tempest gathers near,
Thunders' muttering I hear. [*Thunder.*]

Come with merry roundelay,
Let's drive the coming storm away.

[All dance and sing.]

Rain, rain, jewel the grain,
   Hide in the hearts of the violets blue ;
Or when the rainbow bridge shineth again,
   Pass back to heaven, like uplifted dew.

Enter WANDA *and* LUCIE R. *Children gather round them.*

MABEL. Who are these, that hither stray?
NELLIE. Why they're beggars come to play
MAUD. See their ragged clothing too!
FRAN. With no sign of hat or shoe!
LAURA. Come, let's drive them quick away.

[They hustle WANDA *and* LUCIE.*]*

ALICE. Shame, my subjects! Children, stay!

[Children seem afraid.]

ALICE (*to W. & L.*).
  Fear them not, for they are kind ;
  I am their queen, and you shall find
  They'll reach you forth a loving hand
  To join our play, if I command ;
  Come with me, my throne is yonder ;
  Tell us why you hither wander.

RECITATION.

WANDA.   Weary and way-worn,
       We've journeyed on,
     Fatherless, motherless,

Dear ones all gone,
Poor little waifs are we,
   Drifting on life's great sea,
Oh, heed our piteous plea,
   And sad heart's moan.

Food we have eaten none,
   Throughout the day —
Our childhood's home we've left,
   Far, far away.
You whom the years but bless
   With added happiness,
Feel for our sore distress
   We humbly pray.

Let us a moment rest
   Then we will go,
Though whither
   We do not know;
Our eyes are dim with tears,
   Our hearts are filled with fears,
Hope's promise disappears
   In clouds of woe.

[*They hesitate and turn as if to go.*]

ALICE. Stay, this is a day of pleasure!
You shall share its joy complete,
You shall watch our dances' measure,
While you rest your weary feet.
On the turf, so green and fragrant,
Seat yourselves and have no fear;
Listen to our words of comfort,
Love and tenderness are here.
Playmates, subjects who have been

Faithful to your little Queen,
Here are children, poor, distressed,
With no parents' dear love blessed;
Shall we turn them from our door?
Are they not the Saviour's poor?
Would your Queen deserve to wear
This bright crown of flowers fair,
If she gave from out her store
Nothing — to the Saviour's poor?

All shout "good Queen Alice," and gather around beggars with sympathy.

ALICE (*to beggars*).
    Rest here while we sing a song,
    It will not be very long.

[*Song, during which* WANDA *and* LUCIE *disappear.*]

Tune, Kind words can never die.

    Kind deeds can never die;
      Nurtured in Heaven,
    They live eternally,
      Like mercy given.
    So let us always be
    Kind, and give willingly,
    Whilst we to Heaven yield
      Praise evermore.

[*Heavy thunder: children startled.*]

ALICE. Haste, oh haste, the storm comes on!
    Where are the beggers? they are gone —
    The thunder's moan and the falling rain
    Have frightened them. Haste, we may find them again.

Exeunt omnes singing; song dies away, with low thunder; and scene closes.

   Oh, we have been a-Maying
    And crowned our Queen of May!
   And with a deed of kindness
    We've closed the happy day.

  [SCENE 2d. *Enter* ALICE.]
    RECITATION.

The wrathful storm has spent itself at length,
And now o'er Earth has fallen a hush of peace.
Here in the forest lonely, where shadows of the night lie
   darkly brooding,
Alone and lost, upon a pathless way, I grope bewildered.

   Mother and father dear
    My voice ye cannot hear —
   I'm weary of the way,
    Here let me kneel and pray. [*Kneels.*]

  [WANDA *and* LUCIE *enter.*]

Father, listen to my prayer!
  Thou who marks't the sparrow's fall,
Thou whose love is everywhere,
  Wilt thou hear my feeble call?

I am but a little child;
  Wilt thou bid thine angels keep
Close beside me all the night,
  When I lay me down to sleep?

Father — thou art very high,
  But thy tender face I see;

Thou cans't bend to me so low;
 Lord, I sleep in peace and Thee. [*Sleeps.*]

RECITATION.

WANDA (*coming forward*).
 Hush! very softly tread, for see, she sleeps.
 How sweet and peaceful is her quiet rest!
 Such dreams as have the pure in heart are hers,
 And of the night's alarms she feareth naught.

WANDA (*to* ALICE).
 Wake, gentle maiden! we will guide
 You safely down the mountain side;
 Your companions are not sleeping,
 All are searching, all are weeping,
 Each one blames herself the most,
 That her loving Queen is lost. [*Alice wakes.*]

WANDA *strikes with staff; her dress falls back disclosing Fairy Queen. Enter fairies on all sides. Form circle round* ALICE *and sing, Air No.* 1.

 Merry mountain nymphs are we;
  Down below's our fairy glen;
 This place is our magic mountain,
  Far away from haunts of men.
 When the moonlight's silvery arrows
  Through the forest leaves are seen,
 There we meet for song and dancing,
  With our gentle Fairy Queen.
 You shall hear the fairy music,
  You shall hear the echoes ring

With the fairies happy laughter,
    And the melodies they sing.

[*Join hands and dance, singing Air No. 2.*]

Fairies join us hand in hand,
Nymphs from sea, and elves from land,
Quickly form the magic ring,
Gaily dance, and softly sing
    Praises of our Fairy Queen.

Hair like twilight's golden sheen,
Marble brow and hazel een,
Coral lips from which between
Glimpses as of pearl are seen —
    Such is she our Fairy Queen.

Form divine, and light as air,
Velvet cheek — how soft and fair!
Blushing to the gentle pink
Of dawn on heights of Neversink —
    Who is like our Fairy Queen!

So guileless is her loving heart,
So gentle, free from every art,
So pure, unstained by taint of earth,
Her spirit claims a heavenly birth;
And only those, the pure and good,
Can wander through this fairy wood,
    Fearless of our Fairy Queen.

Then fairies join us hand in hand,
Nymphs and sprites from sea and land;
Quickly form the magic ring,
Gaily dance, and softly sing
    Of our lovely Fairy Queen.

WANDA (*speaking earnestly*).
>Dear Alice, thou hast won the love of fairies!
>Within their hearts a shrine to you is builded,
>Decked with forget-me-nots and rosemary,
>And tended sacredly forevermore.
>Thou hast been tried by us and not found wanting,
>And all good fairies' wishes follow thee.
>When·I, their Queen, in garb of wretchedness,
>Came to thy May-day festival unasked,
>With tale most piteous of wandering long
>In hunger and distress ———
>Thou gave'st to me and my poor companion,
>With tears that deepened all thine eyes' soft blue,
>The gracious sympathy of thy young heart.
>Thou gavest food and drink and tender care,
>And so hath won a fairy recompense.
>Safely unto thy home, with music sweet,
>And to thy parents' arms, shalt thou be borne;
>Thy playmates, too, who near and far have sought
>   thee
>With sorrowing hearts, our messenger shall call.
>Go, Lucie, bring the children quickly hither,
>And fairy sprites shall lead them, singing, home.

[*Children enter and gather around* ALICE.]

>>Fairy hour is almost done,
>>   Let us speed, then, on our way,
>>Home we'll bear the gentle one,
>>   Little Alice, Queen of May.

[*Exeunt omnes, singing "Home Again."* Curtain falls to music.]

FOUR ODES FOR DECORATION DAY.

[By Kate Cameron.]

I.

The young, the noble and the brave,
Who fill for us the soldier's grave,
Who will have earned the hero's fame,
To-day our fond remembrance claim.

A loving tribute now we bring,
The fair and fragrant flowers of spring,
And while we deck each hallowed mound,
We feel we tread on holy ground.

They are not dead, these martyred ones,
Our sires, our brothers, and our sons;
Within our grateful hearts they live,
The truest life that God can give.

Our country claims them for her own;
Their deeds of valor oft are shown,
And coming years will serve to make
This day more bright for their dear sake!

II.

Flowers from the garden and wildwood,
  Eager we pluck from the stem;
Fair as our brave in their childhood,
  Early to perish like them.

Over their dear graves we scatter
    Blossoms of every hue,
Soon will they fade, but what matter?
    Tears can refresh them like dew.

Oh! for our sires and our brothers,
    Oh! for our husbands and sons,
Oh! for the widows and mothers,
    Oh! for the desolate ones.
Thus for the dead and the living
    Mourn we, as hither we bring
Treasures of memory's giving,
    Blossoms of beautiful spring.

Fondly the tribute we render!
    Hallow this day through the years,
Fraught with such thoughts deep and tender,
    Christened with holiest tears;
Tho' names from marble may vanish,
    Graves of our soldiers shall stand —
Altars whence time can not banish
    Thanks of our purified land!

III.

Again we bring an off'ring meet,
The buds and flowers fair and sweet,
Our Hero's praises to repeat,

Again we tread on holy ground,
Again we deck each hallowed mound,
Wherein a soldier's dust is found.

Our voices speak with loud acclaim
Each well-remembered, honored name,
Deep-graven on the roll of Fame.

And as with grateful pride we view
Our chosen colors, Red, White, and Blue,
Our loyal faith would we renew.

A fitting emblem is the Red
Of precious blood that has been shed,
When noble hearts for Freedom bled.

The White forever shall endure
A type of all that's true and pure,
Our country's honor, staunch and sure.

The Blue reminds us of the skies
That smile upon our high emprise,
And bid us ever upward rise.

Baptised within War's deep Red Sea,
Henceforth the Country of the Free
Must worthy of her Martyrs be!

IV.
OUR HEROES.

Again we sing our simple lay,
  And bring our floral token;
Forever on this hallowed day,
  Shall heroes' praise be spoken,
And not till time shall pass away,
  This sacred trust be broken.

The names so bright on Fame's fair leaf,
  We in our hearts are keeping;
With loyal pride, not selfish grief,
  We leave them to their sleeping;
They sowed the seed — the golden sheaf,
  Was left for others' reaping.

The harvest of their deeds is ours,
    Well won in fight and foray,
And as we crown their graves with flowers,
    We tell the oft-told story;
Thus year by year, through sun and shower,
    We keep undimmed their glory!

The following poem by the same author, though not written for Decoration Day, may be used by omitting the fifth stanza. As it stands it is beautifully appropriate for a memorial exercise on the death of any member of the Sabbath-school.

THE DEPARTED.
[By Kate Cameron.]

Down the dim vista of the vanished years
    I gaze sad-hearted,
And see, through gathering mists of blinding tears,
    Loved ones departed.

Brows on which mem'ry's radiance is cast
    In fadeless splendor,
And voices that whisper of the past
    In accents tender;

Hands that have laid confidingly in mine,
    As loth to sever;
Eyes that upon my darkened pathway shine
    No more, forever;

Hearts on which mine was ever wont to lean
    With trust unshaken,
While not a single cloud could flow between,
    Doubt to awaken.

And dearer than all others to my sight,
        Sweet childish graces ;—
How dark the world grew when death's solemn night
        Hid those dear faces!

I sometimes wonder I can ever smile,
        Or speak with gladness;
But God is good, and present joys beguile
        The past of sadness.

And the fair future stretches far away,
        From our weak vision,
And thinking of its sunny days I stray
        In fields Elysian.

Yet earthly futures are but dark and dim
        Beside that Heaven.
To which God hath, to all that follow Him,
        Free entrance given.

And then I know my loved ones are at rest
        Mid beauty vernal,
And ne'er can sorrow, care nor sin molest
        Their peace eternal.

And I will wipe away my selfish tears ;
        Death cannot sever
The ties that bind our souls thro' mortal years,
        They last forever !

UNKNOWN.

[By Dr. Francis O. Ticknor of Georgia.]

The world is bright with other bloom ;
    Shall the sweet summer shed

>   Its living radiance o'er the tomb
>   That shrouds the doubly dead?
>
>   UNKNOWN! Beneath our Father's face
>   The star-lit hillocks lie;
>   Another rosebud! lest His grace
>   Forget us when we die!"

DECORATION DAY.

[Words by H. S. THOMPSON. Music "Good Night," from "Martha."]

>   Once again a floral offering
>   To the memory of the brave!
>   Sweetest flowers of earth's fair bosom
>   Bring we to the hero's grave.
>
>   Tho' the flowers may droop and perish,
>   Patriot deeds shall never die;
>   By a grateful country cherished,
>   Time and wreck they may defy.
>
>   Thus as long as our loved banner
>   In the breeze of Heaven shall wave,
>   Year by year will we bring garlands,
>   To bedeck the hero's grave.

FORGIVENESS.

[By WHITTIER.]

    With faces darkened in the battle flame,
    With banners faded from their early pride,
    Through wind, and sun, and showers of bleaching
            rain,
    And red in all their garments doubly dyed;
    With many a wound upon them, many a stain,

With steps that never faltered, thus they came.
Through water and through fire
They came to Thee, and not through these alone —
They came to Thee by blood! Thou didst require
A living sacrifice, and like Thine Own,
The life Thou gavest us Thou didst desire.
And all are ready for thee! Lo, the knife
And cloven wood were waiting.
They, too, were ready! In the battle strife,
Or by the lonely fireside, unto Thee
We offered love for love, and life for life;
And as they came to Thee, a sound of war
Ran after them from distant fields; the jar
Of shield and sword, and battle bow; a cry,
Confined and harsh, that rolled to "Victory,"
And seemed upon the darkening heavens to cease;
For as they neared the city, morning broke,
And all around its lofty ramparts woke
One word of greeting, flooding all the ear,
And all the heart, with solemn music, clear,
As of a trumpet talking with us — "Peace."

— Adapted by Dora Greenwell.

MRS. JUNE'S PROSPECTUS.

[From the "Little Corporal"— A good Recitation for any Spring Festival.]

Mrs. June is ready for school,
   Presents her kind regard,
And for her measures and rule
   Presents the following
        CARD
To Parents and Friends.
        Mrs. June,
Of the firm of Summer and Sun,
Announces the opening of her school
   (Established in the year one).
An unlimited number received ;
   There is nothing at all to pay,
All that is asked is a merry heart,
   And time enough to be gay.
The Junior class will bring,
   In lieu of all supplies,
Eight little fingers and two little thumbs,
   For the making of pretty sand-pies.
The Senior class, a mouth
   For strawberries and cream ;
A nose apiece for a rose apiece,
   And a tendency to dream.
The lectures are thus arranged :
   Professor Cherry Tree
Will lecture to the climbing class,
   Terms of instruction — free ;

Professor Dr. Forest Spring
  Will take the class in drink ;
And the class in titillation,
  Sage Mr. Bobolink ;
Young Mr. Ox-Eye Daisy
  Will demonstrate each day
On "botany," on "native plants,"
  And the " properties of hay ; "
Miss Nature, the class in fun
  (A charming class to teach);
And the swinging class, and the birdsnest class,
  Miss Hickory and Miss Beech ;
And the sleepy class at night,
  And the dinner class at noon,
And the fat and laugh and roses class,
  They fall to Mrs. June ;
And she hopes her little friends
  Will be punctual as the sun,
For the term, alas ! is very short,
  And she wants them every one.

FOURTH OF JULY EXERCISE.

Fourth of July can be celebrated in no better way than by an Old Folks' Concert. The Centennial is in so recent a past that no hints as to costume or furniture, are necessary. Almost every family has dragged from the garret some heirloom in the shape of tall, narrow-backed chairs, spinning wheels, old china, a limp brocade that on great grandmother's wedding-day stood stiff and lustrous —

"In teacup-times of hood and hoop,
Or when the patch was worn."

Some one can probably be found who will teach the Minuet, or Sir Roger de Coverly, to a set of young dancers, and we must have an old-fashioned choir to give us the dear old fugue tunes such as: Sherburne, Lennox, Russia, New Jerusalem, Bridgewater, Anthem for Easter, Complaint, David's Lamentation, Majesty, Invitation, Exhortation, China, Grafton, Northfield, Denmark, Ode on Science, and St. Martin's, all of which are found in "Ancient Harmony Revised." Then, there are the sentimental songs, a few of which are mentioned in the following poem, which might itself be sung with perfect appropriateness:

OLD FASHIONED SONGS.
[By Kate Cameron.]

Her fingers swept across the keys,
    And swift as birds they flew ;
The music floated on the breeze
    Our hearts went with it, too.

We heard again the simple lays,
    Each sweet, familiar tune,
That won our ardent love and praise,
    When life was in its June.

Once more we saw on flower and tree,
    The morning sunlight shine ;
Our hearts were joyous, blithe and free
    " In days of Auld Lang Syne."

And while we shed a silent tear
    For happy hours gone by,
We met a friend so true and dear
    Still " Coming thro' the Rye."

That vanished dream was in our thoughts,
    We breathed a once loved name,
When with a tender sadness fraught,
    " Last Rose of Summer " came.

And then we found the refuge blest,
    Of hearts that widely roam,
And owned the dearest and the best
    Of all was " Home, Sweet Home.

Some other old-fashioned favorites are Annie Laurie, Ivy Green, The Mistletoe Bough, The Scotchman's Wallet, The Rose that all are Praising, The Old Kirkyard, My Old Kentucky Home, Days of Absence, Oh no! we never mention her, Slowly wears the day, love, I won't be a Nun, Oh what can the matter be? Nid, nid, noddin, Auld Robin Gray, Dark-eyed one, dark-eyed one, Bonny Doon, and My Heart's in the Highlands. There is scope for unnumbered tableaux to accompany the reading or singing of such selections as Zekle's Courtship, and the following, which admits of richer costumes:

>In teacup-times!" The style of dress
>Would suit your beauty, I confess;
>   Belinda-like the patch you'd wear;
>   I picture you with powdered hair—
>You'd make a charming Shepherdess!
>
>And I no doubt --- could well express
>Sir Plume's complete conceitedness ---
>   Could poise a clouded cane with care
>   " In teacup-times!"
>
>The parts would fit precisely --- yes;
>We should achieve a huge success;
>   You should disdain, and I despair,
>   With quite the true Augustan air;
>But * * * could I love you more, or less,
>   In teacup-times!
>   —*Austin Dobson, in Blackwood's Magazine.*

PROGRAMME.

(This programme, which was used at Marquette, Mich., should be printed on coarse brown paper in imitation of time-stained documents; and if practicable, the old-style " s " should be used by the printer.)

A LYSTE

of ye olden tyme Sacred Hymns, and likewise Worldlie Songs which shall be sung by ye

ASSOCIATION SINGIN SKEWL,

at ye great

PUBLICK CONCERTE,

to be attended at ye Big Meetin Room in ye large stone Bank Building in ye

CITYE OF MARQUETTE, MICH.,

on Friday, ye Eighth Day of ye Month of December. N. S., in ye year of our Lord MDCCCLXXVI.

Ye doors shall be open at earlie candle lighte, and ye musick will commence at 8 by ye Timist's watch.

Ye men and ye women will be suffered to sit together. N. B. — This refers to married couples; ye young men and ye maidens must occupy separate chairs.

Ye price to enter in at ye greate door is Four Yorke Shillings, or ye lesser door Two Yorke Shillings. Tickets may be bought of Hezekiah Holon Stafford, or at any of ye stores or taverns who may have them to sell.

A LYSTE OF YE SINGINGE CLASS,
to witte:
Timeist — HODIJAH SYNO TOMPERSIN;

WOMEN SINGERS.

HEPZIBAH VON DRUM.
  PEACE AND HOPE SLIMMER.
    MARIAM JORDON (ye seamstress).
      COMEFORT CAREFUL BROADCAST
        (she that was a Goodenough).
      EXPERIENCE BERRY.
        LOVEGOOD CHRISTY (ye widow).
      SERAPHINE BURDEN.

MEN SINGERS.

TIMOTHY TIBBALLS.
  ZEDEKIAH PERKINS.
    OBED HAGADOW.
      JACOB SHEPARD (ye parish sexton).
        MIRACULOUS ORDINARY.
          SOLOMAN BRAGG (ye pedagogue).
        ABSALOM BEEDER.

Also a good many other discreet persons and good singers who did not wish their names to appear in print.

Harpsichorder — EDESSA EMMER MCCUMLEY.

Ye Class will sing ye following Tunes, to witte:

(The names in the programme should be recognizable through their disguise, as belonging to the singers.)

YE FIRSTE PARTE.

1. ODEON SCIENCE.—All ye men and women singers.
   Swan.
2. SCHOOL-BOY DAYS.— II. of ye men singers.
   Thompson.
3. INVITATION.— Ye whole companie.
   Kimball.
4. AULD LANG SYNE.— IV. of ye men singers.
   Burns.
5. RUTH AND NAOMI.—II. of ye women singers.
   Glover.
6. STAR SPANGLED BANNER.---Ye whole companie.
   National.
7. THE NIGHTINGALES SISTERS— Seraphina Burden.
   Everet.
8. A WORLDLYE INSTRUMENTAL PEECE.—Ye Harpsichorder.
   Lysbay.
9. MARSEILLES HYMN.—All ye men and women singers.
   French Air.

YE SECOND PARTE.

1. HALLELUJAH CHORUS—Ye whole companie.
   Messiah.
2. HAIL COLUMBIA.—Ye town fiddler
   National.
3. SOUND THE LOUD TIMBREL.---Eponine Perkins and the Skewl. *Avidon.*
4. EMIGRANT'S LAMENT.-- Ye Timeist.
   Dumpster.
5. PSALM TUNE *St. Martins.*— All ye singers.
6. QUAKER COURTSHIP.— Hezekiah Sunlight and Careful Charity. *Parry.*
7. SALVE REGINA.— Bobodil Downright.
   Dudley Buck.
8. SHERBURNE.—Ye whole companie,
   Read.
9. A WORLDLYE AND PARILOUS PEECE.— II. of ye men and II. of ye women singers. *Bliss.*
10. AMERICA.— All ye men and women singers.
    National.

Ye following remarks will help ye audience.

N. B. — Forasmuch as ye children are sometimes troublesome, ye mothers are requested to bring peppermint to soothe them, and to place them under the seats if so be they cry obstrepolously.

N. B. — Ye tithing man, Philistine Ferguson, who is of mighty strength, will summarilie chastise and send home all ye small boys who break ye chairs or otherwise disturb ye meetinge.

N. B. — All ye discreete women who fryed cakes to eat, are requested to eat them between ye first and second partes.

N. B. — Ye Beadle will hand up apples and nosegays, and all such tokens of approbation to ye singers.

N. B. At ye singin in the last peece ye whole assemblie is expected to stand and help singe ye last tune withe their whole heart.

Printed at ye Printing Shoppe of Len Crary, in ye big City of Marquette, Mich.

A very comical performance suitable to the day is arranged in this way. The stage represents a New England kitchen. It contains a number of persons in ancient costumes, each one occupied in some domestic industry. Their activity keeps pace with the tune, Yankee Doodle, which is played very slowly at first, and is gradually accelerated, till at last they are churning, washing, ironing, spinning, rocking baby, quilting, chopping mince-meat, paring apples, knitting, sawing wood, husking corn, etc., in a jolly frolic.

Recitations suitable for Fourth of July may be found in the St. Nicholas for 1876, pages 553 and 582; also One Hundred Years, page 103; and in Wide Awake for July 1878.

Thanksgiving Exercise.

PROGRAMME.

1. SINGING.—Let us with a gladsome mind.
2. SINGING.—When spring unlocks the flowers. . . . *Heber.*
3. THE LESSON OF THE WHEAT.—For five boys   (From Wide Awake.)
   Mrs. M. B. C. Slade.
4. THANKSGIVING HYMN.—For little children. Can a little child like me? . . . *Mary Mapes Dodge.*
5. RECITATION.
6. SCRIPTURAL RESPONSIVE EXERCISE.—A Thanksgiving Dinner of Bible Texts. . . . .
7. MUSIC.
8. READING.—The coming of Thanksgiving and the season of Pumpkin Pie. (Chap. 8 and 9 of "Being a Boy.")
   Charles Dudley Warner.
9. RECITATION.—The Pumpkin. . . . . . *J. G. Whittier.*

EXPLANATION OF PROGRAMME.

The first scholar holds and shows some blades of wheat, the second a handful of wheat-stalks, the third an ear of wheat in blossom, the fourth some full, ripe ears. Teacher reads Mark. 4 : 28.

THE LESSON OF THE WHEAT.

[By Mrs. M. B. C. Slade, in Wide Awake.]

1st Scholar.　　First the blade :
　　　　　　　Out in the field I found,
　　　　　　　Shooting above the ground,
　　　　　　　Just down beside my feet,
　　　　　　　These two small blades of wheat.

In Concert.
　　　　　　　And don't you surely know,
　　　　　　　When these begin to grow,
　　　　　　　It is because the seed was planted down below?

2nd Scholar. "So is the kingdom of God, as if a man should cast seed into the ground, and the seed should spring and grow up, he knoweth not how."
　　　　　　　I found beside my walks
　　　　　　　These higher stems and stalks;
　　　　　　　The sap within supplied
　　　　　　　Long leaves on either side.

In Concert.
　　　　　　　And don't you surely know,
　　　　　　　As fresh and green they grow,
　　　　　　　It is because the seed was planted down below?

3rd Scholar. "Then the ear :"
　　　　　　　I found and bring you here,
　　　　　　　This young and tender ear;
　　　　　　　Each perfect grain beneath
　　　　　　　Its nice, protecting sheath.

In Concert.
　　　　　　　And don't you surely know,

>   As strong and full they grow,
>   It is because the seed was planted down below?

4TH SCHOLAR. "After that the full corn in the ear,"
>   I bring the full ripe wheat;
>   Dew, rain, and summer heat,
>   Whether we rose or slept,
>   O'er them their care have kept.

In Concert.
>   And don't you surely know,
>   Though these have made them grow,
>   It is because the seed was planted down below?

5TH SCHOLAR. "The seed is the word of God. He that soweth good seed is the Son of God."
>   Lord, in our tender youth,
>   Sow precious seeds of truth
>   Deep in these hearts of ours,
>   Then send thy sun and shower.

In Concert.
>   And we shall surely know,
>   When Heavenly graces grow,
>   It is because the seed was planted down below!

4. *Can be found set to music in St. Nicholas for Nov. '77.*

5. RECITATION. *See Whittier's Child Life, page 192.*

6. SCRIPTURAL RESPONSIVE EXERCISE.

7. *A Thanksgiving Dinner of Bible Texts may be introduced by singing the following stanza:*

>   In autumn a rich feast
>   Thy common bounty gives

> To man, and bird, and beast,
>   And everything that lives.
> Thy liberal care at morn and noon,
> And harvest moon, our lips declare.

The Superintendent may read the bill of fare, the School responding with the texts.

BILL OF FARE.

SOUP. Pottage of Wild Gourds. II. Kings 4 : 38-41.
SHELL-FISH. Oysters and clams. Deut. 33 : 19.
FISH. Broiled, with sauce. St. Luke 24 : 42.
BIRDS. Quails on toast. Psalms 105 : 40.
BIRDS. Pigeons. Numbers 6 : 10, "Two turtles or two young pigeons."
VENISON (stuffed). Genesis 27 : 14, 19.
WILD TURKEY. Ezekiel 17 : 23.
MEATS (roast and fried). Leviticus 7 : 9.
WAFFLES and Bread. Leviticus 7 : 12, 13.
THE CASTOR. 1. Salt, Leviticus 2 : 13. 2. Vinegar, Ruth 2 : 14. 3. Oil, I. Kings 17 : 12. 4. Catsup, I. Chronicles 9 : 30.
VEGETABLES. Numbers 11 : 5.
GREEN CORN. Leviticus 2 : 14.
LENTILS. Genesis 25 : 34.
BEANS, peas, etc. II. Samuel 17 : 28.
BUTTER. In handsome silver butter dish. Judges 5 : 25.

DESSERT.

And *honey* and *cheese* of kine, etc. II. Samuel 17 : 29.

APPLES. The Song of Solomon 2 : 5.
GRAPES, pomegranates and figs. Numbers 13 : 23.
NUTS. Genesis 43 : 11.

8. READING. *From Chapters 8 and 9 of "Being a Boy." By Charles Dudley Warner.*

9. RECITATION.

THE PUMPKIN.
(By J. G. Whittier.)

Oh! greenly and fair in the land of the sun,
The vines of the gourd and the rich melon run,
And the rock and the tree and the cottage enfold
With broad leaves all greenness, and blossoms all gold,
Like that which o'er Nineveh's prophet once grew,
While he waited to know that his warning was true
And longed for the storm cloud, and listened in vain
For the rush of the whirlwind and red fire of rain.

On the banks of the Xenil the dark Spanish maiden
Comes up with the fruit of the tangled vine laden;
And the Creole of Cuba laughs out to behold
Through orange leaves shining the broad spheres of
    gold;
Yet with dearer delight from his home from the north,
On the fields of his harvest the Yankee looks forth,
Where crook-necks are circling and yellow fruit shines,
And the sun of September melts down on his vines.

  Ah! on Thanksgiving day, when from East and from
    West,
    From North and from South, came the pilgrim and
      guest,
    When the gray-haired New Englander sees round
      his board
The old broken links of affection restored
When the care-wearied man seeks his mother once more,

And the worn mother smiles where the girl smiled
    before —
What moistens the lip and what brightens the eye?
What calls back the past like the rich pumpkin pie?

Oh, fruit loved by boyhood! the old days recalling,
    When wood-grapes were purpling and brown nuts
        were falling!
When wild, ugly faces we carved in its skin,
Glared out through the dark with a candle within!
When we laughed round the corn heaps, with hearts
        all in tune,
Our chair a broad pumpkin, our lantern the moon,
Telling tales of the fairy who travelled like steam,
In a pumpkin shell coach with two rats for a team,

Then thanks for the present! none sweeter or better
E'er smoked from an oven or circled a platter!
Fairer hands never wrought at pastry more fine;
Brighter eyes never watched o'er its baking than thine
And the prayer which my mouth is too full to express,
Swells my heart that thy shadow may never grow less,
That the days of thy lot may be lengthened below,
And the fame of thy worth like the pumpkin-vine grow,
And thy life be as sweet, and its last sunset sky
Golden-tinted and fair, as thy own pumpkin pie!

THE SECOND PART OF

THE PILGRIM'S PROGRESS.

[As Dramatized by Mrs. Geo. MacDonald.]

A letter by the author of "An Art Student in Munich," quoted by permission from the Hartfort Courant.

In the year 1850, I witnessed the celebrated "Passion Play of Ober-Ammergau," little knowing what I was about to behold, for at that time the far-famed performance was a mystery as yet scarcely revealed at all to the big world outside the little world of the Bavarian mountains. That was a never-to-be-forgotten experience. Thrilled by the mingled tenderness and sternness of the strange drama, by the guilelessness and piety of the actors, by the novel beauty of the whole spectacle, I wrote a description, seeking to embody the sentiment of that which had so profoundly and unexpectedly touched my heart. Hundreds of hearts responded to the words. Some hundreds, nay, I may say thousands of visitors from all parts of England and America, have hastened to Ammergau to witness the performance, and countless writers have united with one accord to spread the fame of the Bavarian Passion-Play and of the Peasant Players. My emotion truly had been prophetic.

This Easter I have unexpectedly experienced, though it may be in somewhat minor degree, a similar emotion in witnessing — what, if not a Passion-Play, assuredly may be called a "Mystery-Play." The stage was erected in the Town Hall of a little town in the south of England — the actors were the wife and children of a poet — the play was the second part of "Pilgrim's Progress," that lovely old allegory of the progress of the soul towards the life eternal.

The wife of George MacDonald, the popular author, has dramatized the history of the Pilgrimage of Christiana and her Children, and the corps dramatique were the members of one large and loving family — an unique corps dramatique to enact an unique drama.

Come with me in imagination to the little improvised theatre, and let us take our seats waiting the drawing up of the curtain, where the stage is made beautiful and rural by banks of primroses, whereon bloom real flowers, shining and star-like behind the foot-lights. The play is called

THE PILGRIMAGE OF CHRISTIANA — A MYSTERY PLAY.

As the curtain rises, we behold Christiana, the comely young Puritan widow, arrayed in a black dress, stiff white muslin cuffs, 'kerchief, and long white apron. She is seated beside a table, over which she leans with bowed head, weeping and lamenting. Ever and anon she exclaims, "Oh, what shall I do to be saved?" Clinging around her are her four young children, Matthew, James, Samuel, and Joseph, clad all in crimson, their chubby little faces beautiful with the innocence of childhood; quaint, withal are they, as a group of angels in some picture by Sandro Botticelli. Bursting into tears as they hear their mother's words, they cry aloud in their shrill, childish voices, "Oh, woe the day!" Then Christiana relates to her "sweet babes" her portentous dream, regretting even more that she "sinned away their dear father, who would have had them all with him when he went on his long pilgrimage — he, who now was gone to high places, and well thought of, yea, high in favor, with his dear Lord and King."

Even as they are thus conversing, a loud knocking is heard upon the door of the chamber, and the visitor being bidden "in God's name to enter," there steps forth a yet older angel of the Botticelli type — a messenger-youth from the King, wearing white raiment girded around him with an embroidered sash, and his pendent sleeves of a celestial blue falling almost down to his feet.

"Christiana," he cries, "my King will have thee know that He inviteth thee to come into His presence, to His table, and here is a letter to thee from thy husband's King."

Whereupon the angelic youth presents a scroll, inscribed with golden characters, to the awe-struck woman, who, kneeling, receives and unrolls the precious document, her children looking on with amazement as she reads the sweet words of invitation to the city of her Lord.

Upon this Christiana and her children unanimously elect to set forth on a pilgrimage to the celestial city. The children commence making up their little bundles, and prepare at once to start upon their long journey, in imitation of their father. Meanwhile, the news of their sudden determination spreading abroad, three neighbors of Christiana, Mrs. Timorous, Mrs. Bat-eyes, and Mercy, come to see and seek to dissuade her from so extraordinary an enterprise. But Mercy, the gentlest and youngest of the three, finally determines at least to give her friend and her children convoy for a short distance upon the way. Christiana, accompanied by Mercy, arrayed in her pilgrim's cloak and with her staff in her hand, goes forth, singing softly:

> Let the Most Blessed be my guide,
>   If't be His holy will;
> Unto His gate, unto His fold,
>   Up to His holy hill,

while the four little ones, shouldering their bundles, join in the singing of the hymn with their silvery, piping voices; and as they depart, the curtain falls.

When again the curtain raises, the women and the children have already crossed the plain, and have just arrived in front of the "Wicket Gate." Before them rises at the back stage a pair of tall grey gates, covered over with black, scrolly iron-work; on either side a weather-stained red brick gate-post. Trees grow around, and on one side of the gate is a wooden fence. On one of the doors is painted upon a white ground, in large old English letters, "Knock, and it shall be opened unto you." Beneath these words is a smaller door cut in the larger one — this is the "wicket gate."

"Knock, and it shall be opened unto you," read the little children, and forthwith beseech vehemently their mother to boldly knock at the "wicket"— "yea, and continue knocking, sweet mother, until the porter openeth unto thee." Christiana, in fear and trembling, knocks repeatedly, until at length the little door flying back, reveals in its dark, narrow opening the face and figure of the angelic Youth-Messenger from the King. Christiana, making a low obeisance, says, "Let not our Lord be offended with his handmaidens, for that we have knocked at His princely gate," and the angel stretches forth his hand, saying, "Suffer little children to come unto me," and draws within the gate the mother and her children. Then, shutting it again, leaves Mercy standing without, in humility and grief — such bitter grief that she swoons and falls prostrated upon the earth before the very threshold of the gate.

"But," as says Bunyan, "when Christiana had gotten admittance for herself and her boys, she began to make intercession for Mercy." Ere long the little gate once more flies open, and the loving hand of the angel draws upwards and inwards the fainting maiden, whilst Christiana and her children watch anxiously the reception of their fellow Pilgrim, as they stand secure behind the wooden enclosure. Then, all again united within the "wicket gate," singing and giving God praises, the Pilgrims are seen passing onward to further experiences of the Christian life, as the curtain falls.

Now commences the third act; perhaps, as regards scenic effect, the most beautiful of all. The Pilgrims are here received into the calm resting place of the House of Prudence and her daughters, Piety and Charity; and thankful they are here for a season of refreshing to repose themselves after their dire encounter with the lions on the King's Highway. Much converse is there held regarding their past dangers, as the ladies are seated together in the fair chamber assigned to the Pilgrims; the children with much simplicity adding their little details to the description of the terrific encounter with the lions by the way, and of Greatheart's valiant defense of the Pilgrims. Beautiful draperies and beautiful blossoming plants had been sent from B—— (truly an earthly " Home Beautiful ") to adorn this similitude of a spiritual " mansion "— here represented with true artistic feeling upon the little stage. Pieces of " art needle work, with pomegranate, orange, and sun-flower," designs wrought upon fair linen, were tastefully displayed, whilst lovely and fragrant exotics, standing in pots, made a background to the whole chamber.

Prudence, the lady of the mansion, was represented by Mrs. MacDonald, the mother, in fact, of the whole little drama, since the actors and actresses were her children, and the piece was her own adaptation of the old tale of Bunyan's. She was arrayed in a semi-classical robe of a creamy coffee-color, bound round the waist by a scarlet girdle, into which was stuck a bunch of "fair daffodils," her head being covered by a long and matronly white veil. Piety and Charity, her daughters, wore robes of a similar color and fashion, but no veils; their black hair was knotted up in a classic style, and bound about the head with fillets of scarlet. Fresh flowers were also stuck within their scarlet girdles. The whole *misé en scene* was rich in color in the extreme, yet full of a quaint simplicity. The groups of the Pilgrim women in their black, blue and white garments, with the three elder children in their crimson dresses, seated at the women's feet, whilst the youngest child, of some seven years, lay in Christiana's lap with his little arms around her neck, fed the eyes of the spectators with harmony of color and graceful forms; the mind being fed likewise by the beautiful words of the sweet old parable, as they fell in silvery accents from the gentle lips of the women and the "babes"—"perfecting praise;" and, exquisite as at all times is Bunyan's strange and painful imagery, it seemed, as one thus looked and listened, to kindle with yet even greater beauty and significance.

Whilst in the house of Prudence, the maiden Mercy, ever occupied with her charitable labors of garment-making for the poor, receives an elegant and unexpected visitor, a Mr. Brisk by name, "a man of some breeding," indeed, a very fine gentleman of the quasi-Puritan school, who, admiring Mercy's pretty, modest face, and having at the same time "an eye to the main chance," since he believes her to be a good housewife and an earner of much money by her labors, offers Mercy his hand, proposing that thus as Pilgrims they shall walk together through life. But Mercy having taken counsel with the maidens of the home, Charity and Piety, learns from them that though he pretends to be religious this Mr. Brisk is, they fear, "a stranger to the power of that which is good."

Therefore Mercy, when Mr. Brisk continues to pay his compliments to her, offering her all manner of service, tests his love and his nature by requesting him as a favor to carry for her to a poor widow in the next lane a bundle of her needlework, a loaf and a patchwork quilt — a commission which Mr. Brisk finds extremely embarrassing, finally declines, thereupon feeling himself injured and insulted by Mercy and takes his leave of her abruptly, with many graceful but rather sulky congees. This trial of Brisk is an addition by Mrs. Mac-Donald to the old text, but is in entire harmony with the spirit of Bunyan, and told well on the stage, especially with the refined comic acting of the artist who embodies the character. The character of Brisk was as a little touch of comedy in the midst of so much of sentiment and pathos, and made a wholesome pause and refreshment.

But not even in the Home of Prudence may Christian Pilgrims find rest for long. The curtain falls upon them as they are about once more to set forth on their weary way.

When it again rises we find them arrived in the valley of Humiliation, " the best and most useful piece of ground in all these parts." And here, as the Pilgrims are conversing together, they espy " a boy feeding his father's sheep." The sheep are not made visible upon the stage, but you see the pretty shepherd-lad slowly walking along, dressed in his embroidered blue smock-frock, his hat wreathed with roses, and a tall crook in his hand. Hark, too, how sweetly the boy sings! The Pilgrim women and the children, together with their guardian, Greatheart — half man, half angel — clad in his shimmering coat of mail, with his large shield emblazoned with its big crimson heart hanging at his back — and his two-handed sword in his hand — all stop and listen to the song of the Shepherd. "Hark! what he says," exclaims Greatheart: —

> "He that is down, need fear no fall;
> He that is low, no pride;
> He that is humble, ever shall
> Have God to be his guide."

It is even sweet as the warbling of the "merle and the mavis," this song of the shepherd boy in the green vale of Humility.

"I will dare to say that this boy lives a merry life, and wears more of that herb called Heartsease in his bosom than he that is clad in silk and velvet," says Greatheart. And now the shepherd-lad distributes to the Pilgrims, small and great, little slips of his sweet herb of blessing.

But alas! Not even in this calm green valley of Humility may Pilgrims long abide. Neither may any who hasten towards the Celestial city find much peace upon the road. They must hasten onward. They must pass the spot where Christian had his dread encounter with Apolyon, and where the ground remains still muddy, blood-stained and betrampled from the conflict. And now, defended by Greatheart, they enter the valley of the Shadow of Death. Terrible shadowy sights of great horror are here beheld in the distance by the Pilgrim women; especially by Christiana, in whose countenance as in a mirror the spectator sees reflected the shadow of the anguish of death, as she gazes, paralyzed with terror, by the, to him, invisible horror.

This rendering of the terrors of the valley was specially poetic, and tragic in a high degree. The children and Mercy catch the infection of the terror, as they gaze on Christiana, and cling affrighted around her as she, held and supported by the valiant knight, Greatheart, appears ready to fall into the swoon of death. "Now I see what my poor husband went through," murmurs Christiana, as in a dream. "Many have spoken of it, but none can tell what the Valley of the Shadow of Death should mean, until they come unto it themselves."

Whilst yet in the Valley of the Shadow, strengthened ever by the valiant words and strong power of Greatheart, and saying ever holy words, the curtain falls upon the pilgrim band.

When next the curtain rises, the Pilgrims have arrived in the blessed land of Beulah. It is a region of mountain and wide valley. Near at hand, not yet visible to the spectator, you are told runs the river that divides the land from the Celestial city of Eternal Rest. Here, lying upon the ground asleep, is found by the children a very aged man clad in Pilgrim's weeds, and with a long snow-white beard. He is Mr. Honesty; and aroused from his sleep by Greatheart he joins the pilgrim band. The four little boys run about merrily, gathering flowers and binding them into nosegays — and the talk of all, great and small, is of the gladness of this happy land, where troops of Pilgrims daily come to await their passage over the river to the Celestial city, and where, ever and anon, "a legion of shining ones" arrives, by which it is known that more Pilgrims are upon the road; for the "shining ones" assemble to comfort the Pilgrims after their long sorrows on the road. Here two children come forth from the King's garden, which is near at hand, with bundles of camphire and spikenard, saffron, calamus and cinnamon, and every manner of sweet spice in their little hands, to give to the weary Pilgrims.

Here, as the Pilgrims converse regarding these joyous matters, behold once more the messenger of the King — the youthful angel who has ever and anon presented himself to Christiana on the road. He stands once more with them. He gives to each a branch from some sweet spice tree growing in the garden of his King. From the King to Christiana he brings a special letter of good tidings, bidding her within ten days to stand within the presence of her Lord; and, in sign that he is a true messenger, he gives to her a small silver arrow, "sharpened with love, that should easily enter into her heart and which should work so effectually there that by the appointed time she must be gone." Having thus received these tokens of the love of her husband's King, Christiana, filled with a solemn joy, calls unto her boys, and, tenderly blessing them, confides them as little lambs into the hands of the Shepherd Boy, who with his hat crowned with roses and his long shepherd's crook once more appears amidst the Pilgrims. He, lovingly and carefully, leads them away with him; all saying that "the sheep know their own shepherd and follow him." Then Mercy, the ever faithful friend, the old man Honesty, and valiant Greatheart, give Christiana convoy towards the banks of the unseen mysterious river. She, chanting solemnly a holy hymn as she slowly departs, with upraised, joyful countenance, and arms folded over her breast, you see no more, but hear the joyous ringing of the bells of the Celestial City to welcome her safe arrival in the place of Eternal Rest.

Again comes the King's Messenger to summon venerable Mr. Honesty to his King. And yet again he comes, bearing in his angel hands to Mercy, as a sure token of the love of her King, a shattered "golden bowl" and a loosened "silver cord." And Mercy, solemnly chanting words of praise, supported by the strong arm of Greatheart, passes slowly from the land of Beulah towards the shores of the invisible river, and is seen of us no more.

Now alone is left in the land of Beulah, of all our group of friends, Greatheart, the shining warrior, half mortal, half angel. The curtain falls — this time not to rise again — as Greatheart stands fixedly gazing upon the retreating figure of happy Mercy, with the bright light from the Celestial City flashing upon him, and making his coat of mail shine like a great star of light, and with the cross-shaped handle of his great sword held up aloft before him, as symbol of Divine valor and Divine redemption.

When the curtain dropped I questioned if there was a dry eye to be found among the thickly-packed audience. "Ah!" said a voice beside me, "only they know how true, how beautiful this is, who themselves are making the pilgrimage and recognize each place of experience, of joy and of sorrow!" The voice came from a tender soul, herself just passed through the Valley of the Shadow — her face was wet with tears, but smiles lay beneath them.

A CURE FOR TRAMPS.

A SHORT TEMPERANCE DRAMA.

BY LIZZIE W. CHAMPNEY.

DRAMATIS PERSONÆ.

PROF. HARDHACKER; CHARLIE, *an artist;* PLUG UGLY, *from Baltimore;* JEW PEDLER; AUNT PERPETUA; POSY PINK; LACE PEDLER.

SCENE. *Interior of Kitchen. Posy Pink scouring a silver tankard (new bright tin quart cup).*

Posy Pink. "I never saw such a sight of old silver as Aunt Perpetua has; it's just a weariness of the flesh to keep it bright. There's that pepper-box that came over in the Mayflower, and this tankard that Paul Revere made; there is a story connected with it which I wish Aunt Perpetua would tell me. Oh! here she comes. If she looks good-natured I mean to ask her about it."

[*Enter* AUNT PERPETUA, *holding a bottle.*]

Aunt Perpetua. "Here, Posy Pink, I intend to open a bottle of currant wine to-day; it is Brother Hardhacker's birthday, and I mean to drink the poor soul's health, wherever he may be."

Posy Pink. "Tell me about Uncle Hardhacker, Aunt Perpetua, while I clean the lamps."

Aunt Perpetua. "Tramps! What's that you said about Tramps? How many have been here this morning?"

Posy Pink. "Oh, dear! how deaf you are, Aunty. I didn't say anything about tramps; to be sure they have been rather numerous. (*Loudly.*) Only five, Aunty."

Aunt Perpetua. "Twenty-five! We must get a dog; we must positively get a dog, or else a man. If Brother Hardhacker were only here, I should like to see a tramp show his face on the premises."

[*A loud knock.*]

Posy Pink. "Here's one now, Aunty; help me hide the silver (*thrusts the tankard under the table and turns a pail over it*).

[*Enter* LACE PEDLER *carrying a basket.*]

Lace Pedler. "Good mornin', mum. Would any of the ladies be afther wishin' to purchase some foine lace?—(*Opens basket and displays wares.*)

Foine Limerick point, mum; all made by hand. There's the work of a fortnight, mum, in a yard of it. It would make a lovely parroor for the young leddy, mum, give her quite the look of comin' from Paris; and if she's thinkin' of getting married, sure what would thrim a wedding dress more illegant intoirely."

Aunt Perpetua. " What does the creature say ? "

Lace Pedler. " Oh ! is it deaf the ould leddy is ? (*Screams.*) Would ye be afther wanting some lace for your Sunday cap, mum ? "

Aunt Perpetua. " She wants some catnip? Well, she does look kinder measly. Run up to the back garret Posy Pink ; pity not to let a poor creature have a sprig of catnip when she's sick." (*Exit Posy Pink.*)

Lace Pedler (*eyeing the bottle of wine*). " Sure it's powerful wake I feel " (*drops into a chair and faints. Aunt Perpetua rushes to her with the bottle*).

Aunt Perpetua. " The Bible says, ' Give strong drink to him that is ready to perish.' (*The woman comes out of her faint, seizes the bottle, and drinks greedily.*)

Lace Pedler. " May the saints presarve yees. Sure an I feel stronger now ; sure an it's Biddy O'Hollogan as will show her grathitude for the same. Good day to yees, mum." (*Exit.*)

Aunt Perpetua (*ruefully regarding the bottle*). " All that currant wine gone. Well, I must go down cellar and get another bottle." (*Exit.*)

[*Enter Posy Pink, with a bunch of fresh herbs.*]

Posy Pink. "I couldn't find anything but fennel, and spearmint, and sweet marjoram, and dill in the garret, so I ran down to the garden and picked some fresh catnip; but when I got to the door, the woman was by the gate making some sort of a mark on the stone outside. I took a look at it as soon as she was gone; it seemed to have been made with yellow chalk, an irregular triangle with the point downward. Now I wonder what that means?"

[*Enter* AUNT PERPETUA, *with second bottle.*]

Aunt Perpetua. "Set the table, Posy Pink, and we'll drink your Uncle Hardhacker's health."

[*Sits in great rocking chair and takes out knitting. Posy Pink busies herself setting the table. Replaces tankard.*]

Posy Pink. "Yes, Aunty, and please tell me while I do it, how Uncle Hardhacker came to go away."

Aunt Perpetua. "It was a long time ago, dear, a long time ago; before your own dear mother died and you came to live with your old Aunty. We lived up at the Corners then, Brother Hardhacker and I and Charlie."

Posy Pink. "Who was Charlie?"

Aunt Perpetua. Your cousin, my dear, Brother Hardhacker's only child, a dear boy but a trifle wild and wilful, but maybe if his mother had lived he would have been different. I tried to do a mother's duty by him but he got dissipated, and people began to call him Champagne Charlie. When his father heard that he came down on him dreadful; and Charlie, he had a good share of the Hardhacker spirit, and he answered back that if his father would give up his cider, he was willing to put his name on the same temperance pledge. Of course Brother Hardhacker would not stand such impudence as that, and he turned him out of doors, and I've never seen him from that day to this."

Posy Pink. "Poor fellow! and don't you know what became of him, Aunty?"

Aunt Perpetua. "No dear. But I pitied his father most; he went about just as usual for a year, but I could see his heart was broken. Then he took his hammer and chisel, he was Professor of Geology at the Academy, and started on a pedestrian tour for South America. He said he should keep straight on down through Mexico and Central America, and then he should follow the Andes straight down until he walked off into the ocean, for he didn't know as there was anything on earth that could turn him round again. Three years ago, he sent a box of specimens back to the Academy; and since then we haven't heard from him."

Posy Pink. "Poor man! and to think that one of the Hardhackers may be wandering about like any common tramp!"

Aunt Perpetua. " What's that about tramps? If there's another coming, lock the door, do."

Posy Pink. " No Aunty, but supper's already now but making the tea. If you will attend to that I'll run down to the post-office after the mail, and be back before supper."

[*She ties on her bonnet and exit at the right.* AUNT PERPETUA *takes up teapot and goes out at the left. Enter* PLUG UGLY, *at the right.*]

Plug Ugly. (*Lays down bundle and stick in chair, tiptoes to left and looks out.*) " Nobody at home but the old lady; table all set as if they were expecting me. Thank you, ma'am, since you insist, I will. (*Sits down and eats voraciously.*) We're a glorious band of brothers, we tramps. I never should have thought of finding an eye-opener in such a hard-shell Baptist-looking little cottage as this, if some wandering brother or sister before me, hadn't tipped me the signal on the stone by the gate. (*Empties the currant wine.*) Well, that tomb stone didn't lie, the spirit's as good as the epitaph. Here comes the old lady. I wonder if she made this wine — if she did, I must offer her my compliments."

[*Enter* AUNT PERPETUA.]

Aunt Perpetua. " My eyes, if there ain't a dirty tramp just a-helping himself! What's your name? What are you doing there?"

Plug Ugly. "I'm a-eating my dinner, ma'am; I don't believe I rightly know what my name is, but they call me a Plug Ugly from Baltimore."

Aunt Perpetua. "Did you say you didn't want any more? Well, I shouldn't think you would! You've eaten up a whole chicken pie, and drank a whole bottle of my precious currant wine."

Plug Ugly. "Yes, ma'am, and since I've finished the liquor, you can't surely have any need for this ere mug, so I'll just relieve you of it." (*Rises and takes tankard.*)

Aunt Perpetua. "No you won't, you dreadful man! Give me back my tankard! (*Screams.*) Murder! Thieves!"

[*Loud knocking at the door.*]

Plug Ugly. "Well, I didn't know you had neighbors so handy. (*Drops tankard.*) I'll just go this way, so's not to skeer 'em."

[*Exit at the left. Enter* POSY PINK, *at the right.*]

Aunt Perpetua. "Why, Posy Pink, was that you?"

Posy Pink. Yes, I saw him through the window, so I thumped away with a birch. I thought that would frighten him more than seeing me."

Aunt Perpetua. "Oh, dear! I wish I knew some cure for tramps. I shall have to look for a man or a dog. (*Sits at table.*) I don't see as he's left anything but the tankard, and we can't eat that. Did you get anything at the post-office, Posy Pink?"

Posy Pink. " Yes, ma'am, a letter from Paris."

Aunt Perpetua. (*Takes it.*) " Who could write to me from Paris." (*Reads.*) 'Dear Aunt Pet.' Why, nobody ever called me so but Charlie, and it's from Charlie, too. 'Dear Aunt Pet, I am coming home.' Well, that's good news."

Posy Pink. " Yes, indeed, he'll help keep off the tramps."

Aunt Perpetua. " Hush, child; let me read. 'Dear Aunt Pet, I'm coming home. I have tried to make reparation for my bad conduct. I came over here with the artist, Mr. Dupinceau; worked for him just as a servant, but he finally decided that I had some talent and has tried to make me an artist. I am coming back to paint your portrait and to set up a studio at the Corners. If I find I can't make my living that way, I am not above following the plow on the old farm, if you will give me the chance.—' The dear child, and he wants to paint my portrait too; think of that!

Posy Pink. " And he's an artist; how nice! Is that all, Aunty?"

Aunt Perpetua. " No, dear; there is some more, but these glasses are so blurry I can't read. Take it, child, and read it for me."

Posy Pink. (*Reads.*) "' I have some good news for you. I have heard from father. A gentleman who has recently come to Paris from Brazil, says that he has discovered a silver mine and would have made all our fortunes if he had not told the owner of the land all about it. Wasn't that just like father though? I wrote to him at once; have heard from him, and he too, is coming home. He said that he was willing now to give up his cider, and his only wish was to see our names on the same temperance pledge. So have one ready for us to sign. We ought to be with you in about two weeks from this time.'"

Aunt Perpetua. "And the letter is dated just a fortnight ago — we may expect them any moment. Let me see, I've got a pledge that I've saved for many years for this glad hour: (*Takes paper from drawer and reads.*)

"A pledge we make
No wine to take;
Nor brandy red
That turns the head;
No frenzy rum
That ruins home;
Nor brewer's beer
For that we fear;
And cider too
Will never do;—
So here we pledge perpetual hate
To all that can intoxicate."

Posy Pink. "Aunty, there's a foreign-looking man with blue spectacles and a long black beard, coming up the walk. He has a valise. I do believe —"

[*A loud knock is heard.* AUNT PERPETUA *rushes to the door.*]

Aunt Perpetua. "Yes, it is my long lost brother. (*Enters Jew Pedler.*) Oh, Hardhacker, Hardhacker, have you come home at last!"

Posy Pink. (*Bustles forward with arm chair.*) Sit right down, Uncle; how tired you must be! Did you walk all the way?"

Jew Pedler. "Vell, dot ish bleasant. No, I did not valk dot land across. I sailed dose seas ober mit a ferry-poat."

Aunt Perpetua. "Here is the pledge, Hardhacker, here is the pledge; put your name right down!"

Jew Pedler. "Vot ish dot paper?"

Posy Pink. "Why, Uncle, how funny you talk. I suppose you have caught the accent from the natives."

Aunt Perpetua. "It is the temperance pledge, Hardhacker."

Jew Pedler. "Temberance! I ish no temberance. You is no temberance neider. Vot says dot shtone by de gate? Dare ish some bery good vine in dish house, and one very fool vomans vot give it away."

Aunt Perpetua. "What did you say, Hardhacker?"

Posy Pink. " Oh Aunty, Aunty! it isn't Uncle at all. He's another dreadful tramp!"

Jew Pedler. "Tramp, I ish no tramp! I sells de ferry fine spectacles, but I no sells dem here. (*Takes his valise.*) You ish one stingy voman. You keeps de good currant wine, and you gife de poor travelling man noding but the temberance papers. I tells de breple about you." (*Leaves in a rage.*)

Aunt Perpetua. "I don't understand at all."

Posy Pink. (*Looking off.*) "O Aunty, he has stooped down and rubbed off that funny writing on the stone, and he's writing something else."

Aunt Perpetua. "I'm glad of it. I believe that pesky writing had something to do with the tramps. To think that I should have taken that dreadful man for poor dear Brother Hardhacker!"

Posy Pink. "Aunty, there's a ferocious looking scissors grinder coming up the lane."

Aunt Perpetua. "If I only had a dog or a man."

Posy Pink. "He looks desperate enough to murder us all. He is reading the writing on the stone. Why, he's going back again! What can be the reason."

Aunt Perpetua. "Go out and see what the pedler wrote."

Posy Pink. "I couldn't understand if I did; besides, there's a gipsy woman coming; let us wait and see what she does."

Aunt Perpetua. "She's read it and is going

away. (*Calls.*) I say, you woman, come here.

Woman (outside). No, no; I no want any Temperance."

Posy Pink. "That's it. We've found it at last; the cure for Tramps is the Temperance Pledge!"

Aunt Perpetua (falling into a chair). "Do you suppose that currant wine of mine was what brought them? Well, I never!"

Posy Pink. "There's another one looking at the inscription. It doesn't seem to frighten him; here he comes."

[*Enter the* PROFESSOR.]

Professor. "Good afternoon, madam. I have been examining a very curious formation at your gate. It apparently consists of a block of old red sandstone, but furrowed and striated in a most curious manner by lines of scaglia or chalk. I have examined these lines carefully, with my microscope, and find a few minute fossil organic remains. I am interested in ascertaining whether these striations are to be attributed to some geologic age, or whether they are the work of primeval man; say of the stone age, or are even analogous to the cuneiform found" —

Posy Pink. "Oh, Aunty! I'm sure this time it's a lunatic. It will be of no use to show him the pledge; do send him away."

Aunt Perpetua. "Leave the house instantly!

I have within that drawer a cure for tramps, never known to fail."

[*Exit* PROFESSOR, *at the right.* POSY PINK *hastily closes door. Enter* CHARLIE, *at the left: has artist's paint box, etc., strapped on shoulders.*]

Posy Pink "Goodness me, if here isn't an organ grinder. I suppose he came the back way and didn't see the writing on the stone."

Aunt Perpetua. "What do you mean by sneaking in at the back door, when I'm busy at the front? Never mind, I've got a cure for tramps here. Do you see this?" (*Thrusts the pledge in his face.*)

Charlie. "With the greatest of pleasure." (*Signs his name and presents the paper to Aunt Perpetua.*) "Why, Aunty, didn't you know me?"

Aunt Perpetua. "You don't say! It isn't Charlie?"

Charlie. "But it is."

[*All laugh.*]

Posy Pink. "And I thought you were an organ grinder!"

Charlie. "Oh, that's my artist's kit. Has father come yet, Aunty? I heard at the town that he had passed through?

Posy Pink. "I wonder now if that lunatic that was here last, and wanted to know about the big stone —"

Charlie. "Where?"

Posy Pink. " There by the gate, and there he is still."

Charlie. " Why that's father." (*Rushes to the door.*)

Aunt Perpetua. " What did he say ? "

[*Enter* CHARLIE *and* PROFESSOR, *hand in hand.*]

" My boys, both of my boys ! "

Professor. " Give me the pledge, sister." (*Signs his name.*) " You see I expected to find you at the Corners. I didn't know you had moved since I left, and seeing the inscription, put you entirely out of my head. The man who owned the land, was honest enough to give me a royalty on the silver mine, and I've come back to share it with you."

Aunt Perpetua. " What does he say about mine ? I'm sure all that's mine is his."

Posy Pink. " And we won't need to get a dog, now that we have two men in the house ! "

Charlie. " And better still the precious "

All. " Cure for Tramps."

Sunday Evening Exercises.

BY FANNIE M. STEELE.

NOTE.—In the following programmes the intention has been to develop a single truth by short readings and recitations, that as many as possible might take part, the interest upon such occasions being generally proportioned to the number of pupils engaged. The programmes are submitted as suggestive, and admit of considerable variation. Their chief use is that they may be adopted without the labor of searching and combining material, at least until the possibilities of each to locality are determined, when better ones can easily be substituted. The abundance of choice literature for children, continually dropping from the press, will enable those who give the subject attention to furnish fresh material constantly for similar occasions.

I.—COURAGE IN DOING RIGHT.

PROGRAMME.

1. MUSIC. Dare to do right.
2. SCHOOL. Recite in concert. Prov. 20: 11.
3. READING. Short story. A Great Admiral.
4. READING. The Biggest not the Bravest. Youth's Companion, Aug. 8, 1878.
5. RECITATION. Prov. 29: 23.
6. RECITATION. Prov. 10: 9.
7. RECITATION. What the quail says. Youth's Companion.
8. READING. Following the Crowd. Children's Sermons. *J. G. Merrill.*
9. MUSIC. O do not be discouraged for Jesus is your friend.
10. RECITATION. The Right must win. Hymns of Ages, 1st series, p. 39.

11. RECITATION. 1. Peter, 4 : 19.
12. READING. My friend, Col. Backus. St. Nich., May 1877.
13. RECITATION. 1 Peter 3 : 17.
14. MUSIC. Don't you go, Tommy ; or, Have courage, my boy, to say No.
15. RECITATION. Honest and True. Youth's Companion, Apr. 5th, 1877.
16. RECITATION. Prov. 28 : 6.
17. RECITATION. Prov. 12 : 22.
18. RECITATION. Doing God's Will. Hymns of Ages, 1st series, p. 45.
19. RECITATION. Prov. 5 : 21.
20. READING. Abraham Lincoln. Youth's Companion, Apr. 5, 1877.
21. RECITATION. For seven boys in succession. 1st boy, Rev. 2 : 7.
                       2d boy, Rev. 2 : 11.
                       3d boy, Rev. 2 : 17.
                       4th boy, Rev. 2 : 26—28.
                       5th boy, Rev. 3 : 5.
                       6th boy, Rev. 3 : 12.
                       7th boy, Rev. 3 : 21.
22. MUSIC. My soul be on thy guard.

SUNDAY EVENING EXERCISES.

TO TEACH COURAGE IN DOING RIGHT.

1. MUSIC. *Dare to do right.*

2. SCHOOL. *In concert.*

"Even a child is known by his doings, whether his work *be* pure, and whether *it be* right." — Prov. 22 : 11.

3. READING.

A GREAT ADMIRAL.

What boy has not read about the brave Admiral Farragut? The old hero of the seas has gone to his rest. But before he died (as the *Scholar's Companion* tells us) he thus spoke of his own career to a friend while sitting on the portico of a hotel at Long Branch:

"Would you like to know how I was enabled to serve my country? It was all owing to a resolution I had formed when I was ten years of age. My father was sent to New Orleans with the little navy we had, to look after the treason of Burr. I accompanied him as a cabin-boy. I had some qualities that I thought made a man of me. I could swear like an old salt, could drink a stiff glass of grog as if I had doubled Cape Horn, and could smoke like a locomotive. I was great at cards, and was fond of gambling in every shape. At the close of dinner one day my father turned everybody out of the cabin, locked the door, and said to me, 'David, what do you mean to be?' 'I mean to follow the sea!' 'Follow the sea! Yes; be a poor miserable, drunken sailor before the mast, kicked and cuffed about the world and die in some fever-hospital in some foreign clime.' 'No,' I said. 'I'll tread the quarter-deck and command as you do.' 'No, David; no boy ever trod the quarter-deck with such principles as you have and such habits as you exhibit. You'll have to change your whole course of life if you ever become a man.' My father left me and went on deck. I was stunned by the rebuke and overwhelmed with mortification. 'A poor, miserable, drunken sailor before the mast, kicked and cuffed about the world and to die in some fever-hospital! That's my fate, is it? I'll change my life, and change it at once! I will never utter another oath, never drink another drop of intoxicating liquors, never gamble.' And, as God is my witness, I have kept these three vows to this hour. Shortly after, I became a Christian; that act settled my temporal, as it settled my moral destiny."

4. READING. — *The Biggest not the Bravest.* From *Youth's Companion,* Aug. 4. 1878.

5. RECITATION. *In concert.*

"A man's pride shall bring him low: but honor shall uphold the humble in spirit." Prov. 29: 23.

6. RECITATION. *In concert.*

"Who can say, I have made my heart, I am pure from sin?" Prov. 10: 9.

7. RECITATION.

WHAT THE QUAIL SAYS.

Whistles the quail from the covert,
Whistles with all his might
High and shrill day after day;
Children, tell me, what does he say?
Gim — (the little one, bold and bright
Sure that he understands aright) —
"He says, 'Bob White! Bob White!'"

Calls the quail from the cornfield
Thick with its stubble set;
Misty rain-clouds floating by
Hide the blue of the August sky;
"What does he call now, loud and plain?"
Gold Locks — "That is a sign of rain!
He calls, 'More wet! more wet!'"

Pipes the quail from the fencetop
Perched there full in sight;
Quaint and trim, with quick bright eye,
Almost too round and plump to fly,
Whistling, calling, piping clear;
"What do *I* think he says? My dear,
He says 'Do right! do right!'"

8. READING. *From Children's Sermons. By Rev. J. G. Merrill.*

FOLLOWING THE CROWD.

"For the children of Israel walked in all the sins of Jeroboam which he did; they departed not from them."
—1 Kings 17: 22.

How easy it is to do wrong with the crowd? And first, children are apt to do what they see others doing. In the neighborhood where I live the boys are collecting postage stamps; they are trying to get one of each kind that has been made in all the world, and these stamps are as precious to them as money; they think about them the first thing in the morning, and the last thing at night; and I hear them talking about Germany and England, and all foreign countries which have stamps; and I like it; and the only reason I speak of it is to show how natural it is for one boy to do as the *others* do.

The same is true of girls, also. One week they are rolling hoops; the next are making earrings of violets; the next they are all doing something else.

But there is another thing to be seen in the life of children quite like the account in the text. Generally children follow one or two who are leaders. The children of Israel acted all alike, for they all did what they saw Jeroboam do.

Human nature is much like sheep nature in this thing. A farmer once told me that he was driving a flock of sheep from Illinois to Kansas, and came to a river which he must cross. The man who owned the ferry-boat asked too great a price to take the sheep over, so he took a little lamb that belonged to a mother sheep which was a leader among them all, and carried it across the river in a boat. Of course the lamb cried out, the mother heard it, and swam across, and the whole flock followed her. And I thought as he told me what he did, how often it is the case that children, like sheep, do what their leaders do; and there are always leaders among boys and girls. I could go to almost any of your school-teachers, and they could tell me which boy or girl was leader in the room to which they belonged. Some children are made to be leaders: most children to follow others.

But there is another thing to be learned from our text: that it is easy to follow a leader with a crowd into trouble and wrong. Jeroboam had done a very wicked thing; had made an idol to take the place of God, and the crowd of the people worshipped his idol. It is too bad that it is true, but it is a fact that it is much easier to get a crowd to do wrong than it is to do right, especially if you do as the crowd does. If a leader in school begins to whisper and be rude, do not the scholars catch that quicker than they do to take off their hats and be gentlemen because a leader does it? It is the other way with angels of course, but so long as you are boys and girls, you must remember that there is anger of doing wrong if you do as the crowd does; and if any of you are going to do what you see others do, I am afraid you will end in failure.

And this leads me to say, as the last lesson, and the one I want you to remember the best: If the crowd goes wrong, and follows a bad leader, dare to be alone. I do not find this in my text because all the people did as Jeroboam did. But this text is to be used as a caution, not as a guide. Just as if you were going along on the street some dark night, and should see here, just before you, several who had gotten into trouble because the water had washed away the road, you would be careful to keep out of that way, unless you should go there to keep others out; so this verse was intended to teach you and me that although all the people do wrong, it is no reason why you and I should.

When they catch apes in South America, a man goes under the trees where the apes are and washes his hands; then he takes bowls filled with pitch, instead of water, and places them about under the trees; down come the apes to wash their paws, and soon are all caught by the long hair on their paws, and carried off and sold. Now, would you think it wise because a hundred apes had been caught that way, for the one hundred and first to get caught in the same way? Perhaps an ape could not help it; but you are boys and girls, and if all whom you know do what is wrong and mean you should and *can* do right. God's book says: "Thou shalt not follow a multitude to do evil."

9. MUSIC. *O do not be discouraged, for Jesus is your friend.*

10. RECITATION. *From Hymns of Ages, p.* 34.

THE RIGHT MUST WIN.

Oh, it is hard to work for God,
To rise and take his part
Upon the battle-field of earth
And not sometimes lose heart!

He hides himself so wondrously
As though there were no God;
He is least seen when all the powers
Of ill are most abroad:

Or, he deserts us at the hour,
The fight is all but lost,
And *seems* to leave us to ourselves
Just when we need him most.

It is not so, but so it looks,
And we lose courage then,
And doubts will come if God hath kept
His promises to men.

Workman of God! O lose not heart
But learn what God is like,
And in the darkest battle-field
Thou shalt know where to strike.

O bless'd is he to whom is given
The instinct that can tell,

> That God is on the field, when He
> Is most invisible!
>
> And bless'd is he who can divine
> Where real right doth lie,
> And dares to take the side that seems
> Wrong to man's blindfold eye!
>
> For right is right, since God is God;
> And right the day must win:
> To doubt would be disloyalty,
> To falter would be sin! *Faber.*

11. RECITATION. *In concert.*

"Wherefore, let them that suffer according to the will of God commit the keeping of their souls *to him* in well-doing, as unto a faithful Creator. 1 Peter 4: 19.

12. READING. *From St. Nicholas, May, 1877. My friend, Colonel Backus: A talk with big boys, by J. G. Holland.*

<small>This is most excellent; we only omit giving it in full because of its length. St. Nicholas is, however, accessible to all and the piece should on no account be omitted from the programme.</small>

13. RECITATION. *In concert.*

"For it is better, if the will of God be so, that ye suffer for well doing, than for evil doing," 1 Peter 3: 17.

14. MUSIC. *Don't you go, Tommy; or, Have courage, my boy, to say No.*

15. RECITATION. *From Youth's Companion, Apl.* 2, '77.

HONEST AND TRUE.

Not many can stand in the sunlight,
'Neath skies ever arching and blue,
The children of fame and of fortune:
But all can be honest and true.

To inherit the kingdom of beauty,
May not be for me nor for you;
It is much to be born in the purple,
But 'tis more to be honest and true.

It is pleasant to stand with the highest
If only to share in their view;
To be friends with the best, and the wisest;
But 'tis more to be honest and true.

We may not be wise as a Solon,
We may not be rich as a Jew,
Or as grand as a king or a sultan:
But let us be honest and true.
      Clara B. Heath.

16. RECITATION. *In concert.*

"Better *is* the poor that walketh in his uprightness, than *he that is* perverse *in his* ways, though he *be* rich." Prov. 28: 6.

17. RECITATION. *In concert.*

"Lying lips are an abomination to the Lord: but they that deal truly *are* his delight." Prov. 12: 22.

18. RECITATION. *From Hymns of Ages*, *1st. series p. 45.*

DOING GOD'S WILL.

I have no cares, O, blessed will,
For all my cares are thine,
I live in triumph, Lord, for Thou
Hath made thy triumphs mine.

When obstacles and trials seem
Like prison-walls to be,
I do the little I can do
And leave the rest to Thee.

Man's weakness waiting upon God
Its end can never miss,
For men on earth no work can do
More angel-like than this.

He always wins who sides with God,
To him no chance is lost;
God's will is sweetest to him when
It triumphs at his cost.

Ill that he blesses is our good,
And unblest good is ill;
And all is right that *seems* most wrong
If it be His sweet will. *Faber*

19. RECITATION. *In concert.*
"For the ways of man *are* before the eyes of the Lord, and he pondereth all his goings." Prov. 5 : 21.

20. READING. *From Youth's Companion, Apr. 5, '77.*

ABRAHAM LINCOLN.

Abraham Lincoln has been recognized by all the world as peerless among the rulers of the time in which he lived and died. His beginnings were of the poorest, his early surroundings the humblest and the least hopeful. Generally when a lad born like Lincoln, in poverty and obscurity, makes his mark in the world, his success can be traced directly to the help of some one who invited him to his library to read, or to his office as a student, or to his home, encouraging his ambition, quickening his impulses and guiding his studies. But young Lincoln had no such aid as this. At his work with the axe and the plough, as a flat-boat man, as a clerk in a store, as an attorney, as a member of the State Legislature, as a congressman, he climbed upward step by step by his own native energy and integrity. As a lawyer no antagonist could shake the faith of juries in the uprightness of " Honest Abe Lincoln." In his outgoings and incomings among the people where he lived, no fraud, no extortion nor immorality, cast its shadow over his character. In political life no yielding to the prejudices of the masses, no stooping to conquer marred his record.

Early in his political life he was warned by an intimate friend that his party were not ready to stand by certain truths that he had uttered, and that he was endangering his own advancement. He replied: "I believe these sentiments are true to-day, and have been for six thousand years, and therefore I *will* speak them, if they not only jeopardize, but *sacrifice* every political prospect of my life. It was not long before his life, his character, his principles, and his frankness and fearlessness in teaching them became the subject of common talk, and everywhere the severest critics acknowledged that best of all things —

> "He lived himself the truth he taught,
> White-souled, clean-handed, pure of heart."

On his road to Washington to be inaugurated, he said at Independence Hall in Philadelphia: "It was the Declaration of Independence which gave hope that in due time the weight would be lifted from the shoulders of all men. If this country cannot be saved without giving up that principle, I was about to say, I would rather be assassinated here on the spot than to surrender it. I have said nothing but what I am willing to live by, and, if it be the pleasure of Almighty God, to die by."

In his freedom from passion and bitterness, in his acute sense of justice, in his courageous faith in the right, and his inextinguishable hatred of wrong, in his warm and heartfelt sympathy and mercy, in his coolness of judgment and unquestioned uprightness of intention, in his ability to lift himself for his country's sake above all thoughts of his own personal advancement — in all these marked traits of character, he has had no parallel since the days of Washington.

The lesson of Mr. Lincoln's life is, STAND BY THE RIGHT. In poverty or prosperity, in private or in public life, plant your feet upon the right. This is the secret of the wonderful career, the constantly increasing fame, the steady upward steps of him who, by his own energy and principle, rose from the humblest of cabins, and the obscurest of families, to the chief seat of honor among fifty millions of people. His was indeed:

> "A soul supreme, in each hard instance tried,
> Above all pain, all anger and all pride —
> The rage of power, the blast of public breath,
> The love of lucre, or the dread of death."
>
> *Colfax.*

21. RECITATION. *For seven boys in turn.*

1st. "To him that overcometh will I give to eat of the tree of life, which is in the midst of the paradise of God. Be thou faithful unto death, and I will give thee a crown of life. Rev. 2 : 7, 10.

2nd. He that overcometh shall not be hurt of the second death. Rev. 2 : 11.

3rd. To him that overcometh will I give to eat of the hidden manna, and will give him a white stone, and in the stone a new name written, which no man knoweth saving he that receiveth it. Rev. 2 : 17.

4th. And he that overcometh, and keepeth my works unto

the end, to him will I give power over the nations : Even as I received of my father. And I will give him the morning star. Rev, 2 : 26–28.

5th. He that overcometh, the same shall be clothed in white raiment; and I will not blot out his name out of the book of life, but I will confess his name before my Father, and before his angels. Rev. 3 : 5.

6th. Him that overcometh will I make a pillar in the temple of my God, and he shall go no more out : and I will write upon him the name of my God, and the name of the city of my God, *which is* new Jerusalem, which cometh down out of heaven from my God; and *I will write upon him* my new name. Rev. 3 : 12.

7th. To him that overcometh will I grant to sit with me in my throne, even as I also overcame, and am set down with my Father in his throne. Rev. 3 : 21.

22. MUSIC. *My soul be on thy guard.*

Sunday Evening Exercises.

II.—LOVE TO GOD.

1. Music. I think when I hear that sweet story of old.
2. Texts. In concert. Deut. 6:5; Matt. 19:19; Rom. 13:10.
   1 John 3:1; Jer. 31:3; Rom. 8:35;
   Rom. 8:38; Rom. 8;39; John 15:30.

Let the nine pupils who recite each a text in turn, carry to the platform letters of the sentence "God is Love," made of paste board and covered with red flannel, to be hung on pins driven in the wall in their proper places, upon a line slightly curved.

3. Recitation.

> "Love is my teacher, He can tell
>   The wonders that he learnt above,
> No other master knows so well,
>   'Tis Love alone can tell of Love.
>
> O, then of God if thou would'st learn,
>   His goodness, wisdom, glory, see;
> All human arts and knowledge spurn,
>   Let Love alone thy teacher be."

Madam Guyon.

4. Recitation. Says God,

> "Who comes toward me an inch through doubting dim,
> In blazing light, I do approach a yard toward him."

5. Text. In concert. Luke 15:20.
6. Music. I am so glad that our Father in Heaven.
7. Sermon. God's Love. Children's Sermons.   *J. G. Merrill.*

8. SENTENCE. By a pupil.

> "God's spirit falls on me, as dewdrops on a rose,
> If I but, like a rose, to Him my heart unclose."

Also, by a younger pupil:

> "Now, children, take your choice
>   Of the food your hearts shall eat;
> There are sourish thoughts, and brimstone thoughts,
>   And thoughts all good and sweet.
>
> "And whatever the heart feeds on,
>   Dear children, trust to me,
> Is precisely what this queer old world
>   Will seem to you to be."

9. SENTENCE. By another pupil.

> "Whatever thou lovest, man, that too become thou must —
> God, if thou lovest God; dust, if thou lovest dust."

10. READING. The Pet Lamb. National Sunday School Teacher, Feb., 1873.
11. MUSIC. Tell me the old, old story.
12. READING. Christ and the little ones. Whittier's Child Life, p. 16.
13. RECITATION. Hymn of St. Francis Xavier. Hymns of Ages, 1st series.
14. MUSIC. Dear Saviour, ever at thy side.

Sunday Evening Exercises.

III.—LOVE TO MEN.

1. MUSIC. Father of Mercies, send thy grace.
2. TEXTS. In concert, or succession. Matt. 22:37-40; 1 John, 4:21; 1 John 3:10; 1 John, 2:9, 10; 1 John, 3; 17; John 13:31.
3. RECITATION. Abou Ben Adhem. *Leigh Hunt.*
   Bryant's Library of Poetry and Song, p. 582.

4. RECITATION. *Whittier.*

   "Who counts his brother's welfare
      As sacred as his own,
   And loves, forgives, and pities,
      He serveth me alone."

   "I note each gracious purpose,
      Each kindly word and deed;
   Are ye not all my children?
      Shall not the Father heed?"

5. MUSIC. Who is my neighbor? Plymouth Col., 1051.
6. RECITATION. In School days. Whittier's Child Life, p. 175.
7. RECITATION. My Good for Nothing. Child Life, p. 9. *Hood.*
   or, Child and Mother. Child Life, p. 222.
8. TEXTS. In concert. Gal. 6:2; Heb. 13:1; Gal. 5:13.
9. MUSIC. Kind words can never die.
10. READING. The Loving Daughter. New Stories from an Old Book.
11. RECITATION. If I were a Sunbeam; or, Which loves Mother best?
12. Music, or Doxology.

NOTE. — If some of the numbers are not readily found, in their place may be put the following:

READING. The parable of St. Christopher. St. Nicholas, Jan., 1876; or the story of the Colored Soldier, who, when under fire, left the boat that was rounded on the bank to push it off, saying, "One of us must die for the others; it may as well be me;" or both; or the story about "Skates," in Pansy's Picture Book.

Sunday Evening Exercises.

IV.—LOVE OF GOD SHOWN IN NATURE.

1. MUSIC. The spacious firmament.
2. The following texts in order. By the school in concert, in alternation, or successively. Ps. 104:24; 33:6; 33:7; 74:16; 74:17; 74:19; 65:8; 65:9; 147:8; 104:10, 11, 12, 14; 145:16.
3. RECITATION. By young pupil.

   "This world is full of beauty,
      As other worlds above.
   And if we do our duty,
      It may be full of love."

4. SENTENCE. By one pupil.

   He prayeth well, who loveth well,
   Both bird, and man, and beast."

   By another:
   "He prayeth *best*, who loveth best
      All things both great and small;
   For the dear God who loveth us,
      He made and loveth all."

5. RECITATION.

   "There is no tree that rears its crest,
      No fern or flower that cleaves the sod,
   No bird that sings above its nest,
      But tries to speak the name of God,
   And dies when it has done its best."

6. MUSIC. Hymn. Not worlds on worlds in phalanx deep.
7. RECITATION. Do you ask what the birds say?   *Coleridge.*
   Bryant's Library of Poetry and Song, p. 45.
8. READING. Red Riding Hood.   St. Nicholas, May, 1877.   *Whittier.*

9. MUSIC. Hymn. Earth with her ten thousand flowers.
10. READING. Grace and her friends. *Lucy Larcom.*
    Whittier's ChildLife, p. 47.
11. RECITATION. Lady Moon. Dialogue for two children, a boy and a girl, small pupils. Child Life, p. 142. *Lord Houghton.*
12. SERMON. On the Weather. Children's Sermons. *J. G. Merrill.*
13. HYMN. The Lord my pasture shall prepare.

Sunday Evening Exercises.

V.—INFLUENCE OF LITTLE THINGS.

NOTE.— An evening may be well spent in considering the use of kind impulses and actions; the use of improving every-day opportunities; the certainty of unconscious influence; the chance of making an ordinary life of some consequence, even of power, and how God thinks of little things.

PROGRAMME.

PART I.

1. CHORUS.   "Scatter smiles, bright smiles,
   As you pass on your way."
2. SOLO AND CHORUS. Say: what are you going to do, brother? Gospel Hymns, No. 2.
3. RECITATION. What Tim did.
4. RECITATION. Somebody's mother. *Harper's Weekly.*
5. SOLO. Not a sparrow falleth. *T. L. Gilbert.*
6. RECITATION. In school days. *J. G. Whittier.*
7. RECITATION. Texts.
8. CHORUS. To the work, to the work! Gospel Hymns.

PART II.

1. RECITATION. Insect Cares.
2. CHORUS. By Infant class.
3. RECITATION. Newsboy's Debt.
4. RECITATION. By a five-year-old. Gran'ma Al'as Does.
5. RECITATION. The Unprofitable Servant.
6. SOLO. Ninety and Nine.
7. RECITATION. Smile when ere you can. Gospel Hymns, No. 2.
8. READING. By a teacher. Stop her, Pard, stop No. 29! From the Christian Union. *D. T. Wright.*
9. CHORUS. What shall the Harvest be?

If thought best, the recitations may be given from the seats occupied by the children, each speaker standing instead of ascending a platform.

1. Chorus. "*Scatter smiles,*" *etc.*

2. Solo and Chorus. *Say: what are you going to do, brother?*

3. Recitation.

WHAT TIM DID.

It surprised the shiners and news boys around the post-office the other day, to see Limpy Tim come among them in a quiet way, and to hear him say:

"Boys, I want to sell my kit. Here's two brushes, a hull box of blacking, a good stout box, and the outfit goes for twenty-five cents!"

"Goin' away, Tim?" asked one.

"Not 'zackly, boys; but I want a quarter the awfullest kind, just now."

"Goin' on a 'scursion?" asked another.

"Not to-day, but I *must* have a quarter," he answered."

One of the lads passed over the change and took the kit, and Tim walked straight to the counting-room of a daily paper, put down his money and said:

"I guess I can write if you will give me a pencil."

With slow moving fingers he wrote a death notice. It went into the paper almost as he wrote it.

He wrote: "Died. Little Ted of scarlet fever, aged three years, Funeral tomorrer, gone up to Heven, left won brother."

"Was it your brother?" asked the cashier.

Tim tried to brace up, but he couldn't. The big tears came up; his chin quivered, and he pointed to the notice on the counter and gasped — "I — I — had to sell my kit to do it, b — but he had his arms aroun' my neck, when he d — died!"

He hurried away home, but the news went to the boys, and they gathered in a group and talked.

Tim had not been home long before a barefooted boy left the kit on the door step, and in the box was a bunch of flowers which had been bought in the market with the pennies given by the crowd of ragged, but big-hearted boys.

4. RECITATION. *Somebody's mother.* *Harper's Weekly.*

5. SOLO. *Not a sparrow falleth.* *T. L. Gilbert.*

6. RECITATION. *In School Days.* *J. G. Whittier.*

7. RECITATION. *Texts.*

1st. "The conies are but a feeble folk, yet make they their houses in the rocks." Prov. 30: 26.

2nd. "The spider taketh hold with her hands, and is in kings' palaces." Prov. 30: 28.

3rd. "The locusts have no king, yet they go forth all of them by bands." Prov. 30: 27.

4th. "The ants *are* a people not strong, yet they prepare their meat in the summer. Go to the ant, thou sluggard."

5th. "The wolf also shall dwell with the lamb, and the leopard shall lie down with the kid; and the calf and young lion together; and a little child shall lead them." Isa. 11 : 6.

6th. "And Jesus called a little child unto him, and set him in the midst of them and said, Verily I say unto you, Except ye be converted and become as little children, ye shall not enter into the kingdom of heaven." Matt. 18 : 2, 3.

8. CHORUS. *To the work, to the work. Gospel Hymns.*

PART II.

1. RECITATION.

INSECT CARES.

Some poet characterizes as "insect cares" those trivial concerns that worry and torment poor careworn humanity, like flies and mosquitoes; and worse than these they haunt us in all seasons. They swarm about us in midwinter as vigorously as in fly time. And yet when one attempts to impale a specimen, they vanish from our grasp. We are worried by them, but can hardly tell how or why. And still they ply us with their tiny stings.

We resolve not to mind such trifles, and fall back on our dignity only to have it undermined by these little iconoclasts. Are we not too hasty in our judgments of trifles? We look back and discern some seeming nonentity, transmuted by experience into a momentous concern, and realize how:

> "The pebble in the streamlet scant
>   May turn the course of many a river;
> The dewdrop on the infant plant
>   May warp the giant oak forever."
>
> *Rev. W. E. Boise.*

2. CHORUS. *By Infant Class.*

3. RECITATION. *News-Boy's Debt.*

THE NEWS-BOY'S DEBT.

"Sir, if you please, my brother Jim —
    The one you gave the bill, you know —
He couldn't bring the money, sir,
    Because the back was hurted so.

"He didn't mean to keep the change;
    He got runned over up the street;
One wheel went right across his back
    And tother fore-wheel mashed his feet.

"They stopped the horses just in time,
    And then they took him up for dead,
And all that day and yesterday
    He wasn't rightly in his head.

"They took him to the hospital,
    One of the news-boys knew 'twas Jim,
And I went, too, because you see
    We two are brothers, I and him.

"He had that money in his hand,
    And never saw it any more;
Indeed, he didn't mean to steal!
    He never lost a cent before.

"He was afraid that you might think
    He *meant* to keep it any way,
This morning when they brought him to,
    He cried so, 'cause he couldn't pay.

"He made me bring his jacket here,
    It's torn and dirtied pretty bad;
But still 'twill do to sell for rags,
    And then, you know, it's all he had.

"When he gets well — it won't be long —
    If you will call the money lent,
He says he'll work his fingers off,
    But what he'll pay you every cent."

And then he cast a rueful glance
    At the soiled jacket, where it lay.
"No, no, my boy! Take back the coat.
    Your brother's badly hurt, you say?

"Where did they take him? just run out
    And hail a cab, then wait for me;
Why, I would give a thousand coats,
    And pounds, for such a boy as he!

A half-hour after this, we stood
  Together in the crowded wards,
And the nurse checked the hasty steps
  That fell so loudly on the boards.

I thought him smiling in his sleep,
  And scarce believed her when she said —
Smoothing away the tangled hair
  From brow and cheek — "the boy is dead."

Dead? dead so soon? how fair he looked
  One streak of sunshine on his hair —
Poor lad! well, it is warm in heaven,
  No need of 'change' and jackets there,

And something rising in my throat
  Made it so hard for me to speak,
I turned away, and left a tear
  Lying upon his sunburned cheek.

4. RECITATION. *By a five-year-old.*

GRAN'MA AL'AS DOES.

I wants to mend my wagon,
  And has to have some nails;
Jus' two, free, will be plenty,
  We're going to haul our rails;
The splendidest cob fences,
  We're makin' ever was!
I wis' you'd help us find em,
  Gran'ma al'as does.

My horse's name is Betsey,
    She jumped and broke her head;
I put her in a stable,
    And fed her milk and bread.
The stable's in the parlor,
    We didn't make no muss —
I wis' you'd let it stay there,
    Gran'ma al'as does.

I wants some bread and butter,
    I's hungry worstest kind;
And Teddie had better have some,
    Cause she wouldn't mind.
Put plenty sugar on it —
    I tell you what, I knows
It's *right* to put on sugar;
    Gran'ma al'as does.

            A. H. Poe, *in the " Bright Side."*

5. RECITATION. *The Unprofitable Servant.*

6. SOLO. *Ninety and Nine.*

7. RECITATION. *Smile whene'er you can.*

8. READING. *By a Teacher. " Stop her, Pard; stop No. 29." From the Christian Union, by D. T. Wright.*

Sunday Evening Exercises.

VI.— LESSONS FROM FLOWERS.

PROGRAMME.

1. MUSIC. The Lord is my Shepherd; or, When all thy mercies, O my God.
2. SCHOOL. Repeat in concert. Isa. 35 : 1, 2.
3. RECITATION. By an older boy, of Texts of Scripture, illustrated by living flowers, branches, vines, grass. To be found in Pansy's Picture Book, p. 173.
4. RECITATION. Oh, roses, roses, who shall sing? Mistress of the Manse, p. 165. *Dr. J. G. Holland.*
5. MUSIC, or Recitation. Not worlds on worlds in phalanx deep. Plymouth Coll., 1295, and in many other hymn books.
6. READING. Story of a French prisoner. Found in Hooker's Child's Book of Nature, in an early chapter.
7. RECITATION. Cornfields. Whittier's Child Life, p. 105. *Howitt.*
8. SCHOOL. In concert. Psa. 107:21.
9. USE OF FLOWERS. Bryant's Lib. of Poetry and Song, p. 370. *Howitt.*
10. MUSIC. What shall the harvest be? Gospel Hymns.
11. RECITATION. Discontent. St. Nicholas, Feb. 1876. *S. O. Jewett.*
12. MUSIC. Nothing but leaves. Gospel Hymns.
13. THE GOSPEL OF FLOWERS. National S. School Teacher, Sept. 1872.

In this last named exercise, eight little people recite in succession a descriptive verse, and then add a bouquet to the decoration of a cross.

Sunday Evening Exercises.

VII.—LITTLE DEEDS OF KINDNESS.

1. MUSIC. Little drops of water.
2. RECITATION.

> "Small service is true service while it lasts,
>   Of humblest friends, bright creature, scorn not one;
> The daisy, by the shadow that it casts,
>   Protects the lingering dewdrop from the sun."

3. RECITATION. The Angel's Ladder.   *M. F. Butts.*
   St. Nicholas, Mar. 1876. p. 303.
4. READING. Tongue of sandpaper or velvet.   *Rev. Parton Hood.*
   National S. School Teacher. Feb., 1873.
5. RECITATION.

> "It is not so much what you say,
>   As the manner in which you say it:
> It is not so much the language you use,
>   As the tone in which you convey it.
>
> "The words may be mild and fair,
>   And the tone may pierce like a dart;
> The words may be soft as the summer air,
>   And the tone may break the heart."

6. RECITATION.

> "Use gentle words, for who can tell
>   The blessings they impart?
> For oft they fall, as manna fell,
>   On some faint, weary heart.
>
> On lonely plains, by light-winged birds,
>   Rare seeds have oft been sown;
> And hope has sprung from gentle words,
>   Where only grief had grown."

7. RECITATION.
> "Speak we with the tongue or pen,
> To the sons of living men,
> Let our words be true and pure,
> Since their influence must endure."

8. RECITATION. Grass. St. Nicholas, May, 1877. *Edgar Fawcett.*
9. SENTENCE.
> "The least flower with a brimming cup,
> May share its dewdrop with another near."

10. MUSIC. Your Mission.
11. READING. The Little Nurse. Whittier's Child Life, p. 205.
12. RECITATION.
> "She doeth little kindnesses,
> Which most leave undone or despise;
> For nought that sets a heart at ease,
> And giveth happiness or peace,
> Is low esteemed in her eyes."

13. MUSIC. Scatter seeds of kindness.
14. READING. Buckle the throat latch. *Rev. John Todd.*
    National S. School Teacher, June, 1871.
15. RECITATION.
> "The works my calling doth propose,
> Let me not idly shun.
> For he whom idleness undoes
> Is more than twice undone."

16. MUSIC. Nothing but leaves.
17. RECITATION.
> "This thought I give you all to keep —
> Who soweth good will also reap,
> The year grows rich as it groweth old,
> And life's latest sands are its sands of gold.

18. MUSIC. What shall the harvest be? Gospel Hymns.
19. RECITATION. Mysteries. *Kate Cameron.*

> We are at best but broken reeds,
> Each fails the other in his needs.
> A single word to me would bring
> The vanished glory of life's spring;
> And thou, my friend, might'st speak that word,
> But ah! its sound is never heard,
> And I grope on, in doubt and pain,
> Beset by yearnings all in vain.
> Another waiteth for my smile
> Which might from weariness beguile;

How can I that slight boon withhold,
Worth more to thirsting heart than gold?
Oh! mystery of all and each!
We prize the bliss beyond our reach;
And often, by a cruel fate,
The longed-for blessing comes too late.

Yes! when some note discordant jars,
And thus life's sweetest music mars,
Each feels the sharp and sudden thrill,
Beyond the power of human will.
None can the mystic ties control,
That bind us closely soul to soul;
And none can break the magic chain,
Which vibrates between heart and brain.

No one on earth alone can live;
All must receive, and all must give;
And well for us, if naught but flowers
Are scattered by these hands of ours;
For oft the pathway that we tread
Is thickly strewn with thorns instead.
O, let us faithful vigils keep,
Wisely to sow, and gladly reap!

Sunday Evening Exercises.

VIII.—THE TEMPLE SERVICE.

BY LIZZIE W. CHAMPNEY.

PROGRAMME.

No. 1.

THE GOLDEN CANDLESTICKS.

This can be successfully presented by a class of seven girls, varying in age from twelve to sixteen. They should be aided by a director or teacher, and by a choir, or congregational singing. Two blackboards should be arranged facing the audience, on which, after the exercises have been opened by prayer and singing, two of the girls make large drawings — one a simple picture of the golden candlestick, and the other an outline map of the countries around the Mediterranean — Egypt, Palestine, Asia Minor, Greece and Italy. While the two girls are engaged in drawing, a third reads a composition giving the history of the candlesticks of the sanctuary, the history of the ornaments of the Temple, bringing in necessarily the various captivities — when they were carried away to Egypt, to Babylon, and finally to Rome. If a large photograph of the Arch of Titus can be procured, showing the candlestick carried in triumph, it will add to the effect to show and explain it after the reading of the composition. After a musical selection, another of the girls should, with a pointer, trace out on the map which No. 2 has drawn, the various countries to which the candlestick journeyed. Another may next give all the texts from the words of Christ in which the words candle, candlestick, and giving light occur. Another may jot down upon the map the seven cities referred to in the Revelation, as candlesticks.

The director should then call attention to the fact that wherever there is a candle there is a guardian star: wherever a church, "a watcher and holy one" set over it; and can close his remarks with the quotation:

> "Now the stars are lit in heaven,
>   We should light our lamps on earth;
> Every star a signal given
>   From the God of our new birth,
> Every lamp an answer faint,
>   Like the prayer of mortal saint."

After which the seven girls should take their positions on the platform for the final tableau. Each holds a candle a yard long, similar to the Roman processional candles. They can be very easily made by sawing off old broomsticks, inserting a small piece of candle at one end, and covering the stick smoothly with colored paper. Each candle should be of a different tint. Love, who stands in the center, holds the only one which is lighted.

LOVE,
Pink.

FAITH,   TRUTH,
White.   Blue.

HOPE,   COURAGE.
Green.   Red.

PATIENCE,   JOY,
Purple.   Yellow.

All sing (Tune, "Sheaf"):

> We are seven slender candles
>   In one golden candlestick,
> We have each received our orders :
>   Shine through the darkness thick.
> Though your light be faint and flickering,
>   Though the wind and rain combine
> To quench your taper's glimmer,
>   Shine steady, sisters, shine!
>
> We are seven shining candles —
>   Joy, Courage, perfect Truth,
> Love, Faith, and Hope, and Patience —
>   To guide the steps of youth.
> We have each received commandment
>   From the dear Lord above;
> To shine with clearest radiance,
>   You must light your lamps from Love.

At this point Faith and Truth turn so that they face each other, and, extending their candles until they form a pointed arch over the head of Love, they light their candles at hers, then wheel, facing Hope and Courage respectively, form arches with these, and, having lighted *their* candles, return to position facing the audience. Hope and Courage turn facing Patience and Joy, and light their candles in like manner. This has a very pretty effect. All then sing:

> Which candle shines the brightest
> Of all the sisters seven?

Joy replies:

> 'Tis Joy, whose glorious halo
> To the pure in heart is given.

Patience, at the other extremity of the line, answers:

> Nay, sisters, it is Patience,
> Throwing through tearful mist
> A light, subdued and tender,
> A ray of amethyst.

From this point on sing to "Shining Shore." Courage sings alone:

> O give the meed to Courage,
> The beacon flaming high,
> Whose flaring torch to battle leads,
> Redd'ning the earth and sky.
> The glorious band of martyrs,
> Who for the truth's sake bled,
> All bore the lamp of Courage,
> Its brave light flashing red.

HOPE.   The torch of Courage flickers;
               Without the light of Hope,
           Who with his earthly trials
               Would e'er have heart to cope?

TRUTH.   Ah! no, dear friends, though Hope be dead,
               We may at least be true,
           And faithfully my whole life long
               I'll hold my candle blue.

FAITH.   But when you cross the river,
               That cold, dark river, death,
           What lamp can gild its somber waves
               But the pure light of Faith?

LOVE.   What says the blessed Bible,
               Given by our God above?
           Each Christian grace, and even Faith,
               Is nothing without Love.

ALL.   Then let us shine together,
               That Christ may mark his own,
           And when we die, of each may say
               That while she lived she shone.

At the word "die" each raises her right hand, in which is concealed an extinguisher, and puts out her candle. The action should be graceful and simultaneous, and the effect will be very striking.

PROGRAMME.

No. 2.

THE ALTAR OF INCENSE.

This, if for an entire evening, may be arranged

in a similar manner to Programme No. 1, closing with the following tableau:

A young lady, dressed to represent an angel, stands upon an elevated platform, swaying a censer. If real incense can be burned, so much the better. A step or two below her stand five little girls, aged ten to fourteen, each holding a casket (fancy glove and handkerchief-boxes). Introducing the tableau, the superintendent or director repeats Revelation 8: 3, 4. The five girls sing:

> There stands a shining angel
>   Upon the heavenly strand,
> Swaying a golden censer
>   With gentle, tireless hand;
> And from the censer riseth
> A perfume sweet and faint —
> The prayer of every joyful
>   And each heart-broken saint.
> The incense in the censer
>   Is a perfume rich and rare;
> The deepest feelings of the heart
>   We offer God in prayer.
> We are spices for the incense,
>   Myrrh, aloes, spikenard good
> Frankincense very costly,
>   And odorous cassia bud.
> When you offer to the angels
>   Your incense, choose from these,
> If you with all sweet spices
>   The glorious king would please.

First Little Girl.

> When the Eastern monarch-sages
>   Their richest offerings brought,
> Their gardens, full of orient balm,
>   Full carefully they sought.
> They chose the costliest perfume
>   That glads the grateful sense,
> And laid before the Infant Christ,
>   With gold, their frankincense.
> Like theirs, oh! be thy offering
>   With heartiest thanks imbued,
> And prove by gift to others
>   Thy heartfelt gratitude.

(Extends the casket to the Angel, who appears to take some of its contents and place it in the censer.)

Second Little Girl.

> Ah! not alone by gifts of gold
>   And lordly frankincense
> Could we fulfil the Master's will
>   And perfume sweet dispense.
> There grows in Eastern gardens
>   By every cottage door
> A sweeter herb, prized by the rich
>   And by the lowly poor.
> It is the balmy cassia;
>   The lordly frankincense
> Without its blended perfume
>   Is odorless and dense.
> So gifts and thanks, though wafted
>   By the angel's hand above,
> Will not make pleasing incense
>   If all unmixed with Love.

(Lifts her casket to the Angel.)

THIRD LITTLE GIRL.

  Ah ! not alone with odors sweet
   We fill the censer bright ;
  The bitter herbs, with weeping plucked,
   We bring at dead of night —
  Myrrh, from the marble sepulchers
   Of those we've loved and lost,
  For prayer was made for sorrow
   And hearts all tempest-tossed.

(Lifts her casket to the Angel.)

FOURTH LITTLE GIRL.

  Though gall and wormwood be the herbs
   That grow beside the tomb,
  Repentance is the bitterest
   Of all the flowers that bloom.
  The heaviest of all sorrow —
   'Tis sorrowing for sin —
  We place as bitter aloes
   The censer's bowl within.

(Lifts her casket to the Angel.)

FIFTH LITTLE GIRL.

  But ah ! the bitter aloes
   Is never burned alone ;
  The angel places with it
   The sweetest spice e'er known—
  The perfume lavished on our Lord
   By Mary Magdalene —
  The spikenard's sacred fragrance,
   Joy for forgiven sin !

(Lifts her casket to the Angel.)

ALL.

  With fire from off the altar touched,
   The Christian's prayer should rise,

> A cloud of curling incense,
>   Seeking the lofty skies.

PROGRAMME.

No. 3.

THE ALTAR OF SACRIFICE.

Final tableau, arranged for five boys, who hold respectively:

1. Two rough pieces of wood, crossed and resting on the shoulders.
2. A cord.
3. A sword, or large bright knife.
4. A handkerchief, folded as a bandage.
5. A chafing-dish of coals or small lighted sticks.

The choir introduce the exercise by singing "Not all the blood of beasts," etc., adding these two verses:

> As Christ has died for us,
> So we ourselves would bring,
> Each yielding up himself to God,
> A whole burnt offering.

> They err who tell us that has passed
> The time of sacrifice;
> God calls us now to offer up
> Each darling fault and vice.

FIRST AND SECOND BOYS, *in concert*.

> We climb the mount like Isaac,
> Bearing the cord and wood.

FOURTH AND FIFTH BOYS.

    The fire, the cloth for binding,

THIRD BOY.

    The knife to shed our blood.

FIRST BOY.

    The wood, it speaks of Labor
    From the cedar to the fir;
    And Christ himself wrought upon wood,
    A lowly carpenter.

FIFTH BOY.

    The fire, it is the Spirit
    That quickens into zeal;
    As the wood is to the fire,
    So is labor 'neath its thrill,
    As the fire is without wood,
    So, earnest labor gone,
    E'en Inspiration's self is naught —
    Each falls when left alone.

SECOND BOY.

    The cord is Resignation:
    They bound e'en Thy dear Son;
    And meekly he submitted,
    Saying, " Thy will be done.'

FOURTH BOY.

    The bandage speaks of perfect Trust;

(Third and Fifth Boys blindfold No. 4.)

    Willing to nothing see,
    So I can hold my father's hand
    And know he leadeth me.

THIRD BOY.

    The final test of sacrifice,
    The sharp and dreadful knife,

> Bids that at call of our dear Lord
> We spare not limb nor life;
> That we give up at his command
> Each fault, though sweet and dear,
> "For even Christ pleased not himself,"
> While journeying 'mongst us here.

ALL, *in concert, very distinctly.*

> We bring the fire, the cord, the wood,
> The knife, the blinded eyes;
> And thus we yield ourselves to God,
> A whole burnt-sacrifice.

This exercise looks complicated; but on rehearsal will be found to be very simple.

Sunday Evening Exercises.

IX. — JESUS ONLY.

A large frame cross, covered with green paper and containing between thirty and forty augur-holes, stands on the platform. Nine nails, corresponding to the letters in JESUS ONLY, *are placed on the cross, equally distant from each other. Five little girls and four boys occupy the front pew, holding each a large letter to be hung on the cross.*

The Superintendent opens the exercises with prayer, and then explains that the object of the meeting is to consider some of the names and attributes of Christ. He calls upon the class before him to furnish one.

One of the girls rises and hangs upon the cross the letter J, *repeating the text, "Before Abraham was I am."*

The Superintendent then asks the question, "I am what?" and may give Mr. Moody's illustration of the blank check, "Christ proclaims himself just what we need; we may fill out the check with whatever we want. If we want rest, we can fill out the check with that word, and Christ replies, I am rest," and so on.

SINGING. *By the choir. Crusader's Hymn, "Fairest Lord Jesus."*

A little boy ascends the platform, and repeats the text:

"And they shall call his name Emmanuel, which being interpreted is, God with us."

Hangs the letter E upon the cross.

Choir, or congregation, sing, " *He leadeth me.*"

Second little girl recites :

" I am the Lord : and beside me is no Saviour." Isaiah 43 : 2.

" We have seen and do testify that the father sent the Son to be the Saviour of the world." John 4 : 14.

Hangs the letter S upon the cross.

SINGING. "*Jesus, lover of my soul ;*" *or,* "*When through the torn sail.*"

Second little boy recites :

" Unto us a child is born, unto us a son is given." Isaiah 9 : 6.

Hangs the letter U on the cross.

SINGING. " *While Shepherds watched their flocks by night.*"

Third little girl :

" And I saw, and bare record this is the Son of God." John 1 : 34.

Hangs the letter S on the cross.

SINGING. " *How beauteous are the marks divine,*" (*by A. C. Coxe*).

Third little boy :

" I am Alpha and Omega the first and the last." Rev. 1 : 2.

" The *last* enemy that shall be destroyed is death." 1 Cor. 15 : 26.

Hangs the letter O on the cross.

SINGING. *Dies Iræ, especially the last verse.*

Fourth little girl :

" Neither is there salvation in any other ; for there is *none* other *name* under heaven given among men whereby we must be saved." Acts 4 : 12.

Hangs the letter N on the cross.

SINGING. "*Jesus, the very thought of Thee.*"

Fourth little boy :

"Behold the *Lamb* of God which taketh away the sins of the world." John 1 : 29.

Hangs the letter L on the cross.

SINGING. "*O sacred head now wounded.*"

Fifth little girl :

(*Asks the question.*) "Are all the promises of the Bible fulfilled in Christ ? Will he fill out the sentence I am ?" (*Repeats the text.*) "For all the promises of God in him are *Yea.*" 2 Cor. 1 : 20.

Hangs the letter Y on the cross.

SINGING. "*How firm a foundation.*"

The Superintendent can lengthen the exercises by making remarks before or after the recitation of each text, and at the close should draw attention to the legend,

JESUS ONLY.

emblazoned on the cross.

After the class have hung all the letters, all the younger members of the Sunday-school should march up one aisle to the platform, carrying bouquets, and down the other aisle.

Two or more young ladies should receive the bouquets and rapidly place them in the holes in the cross. While this is being done the choir should sing, softly, "*Tell me the old, old story.*"

Sunday Evening Exercises.

X. — THE GOSPEL ARMOR.

PROGRAMME.

1. HYMN.
   "Stand up my soul, shake off thy fears,
   And gird the Gospel armor on."
2. RECITATION. Scripture.
3. HYMN.
   "Restraining prayer, we cease to fight,
   Prayer makes the Christian's armor bright;
   And Satan trembles when he sees
   The weakest saint upon his knees."
4. RECITATION. Selections from Sir Launfal. *Lowell.*
5. HYMN. The Son of God goes forth to war. Episcopal Hymnal.
6. RECITATION. Sir Galahad. *Tennyson.*
7. HYMN. Onward, Christian Soldiers. Episcopal Hymnal.
8. RECITATION. Heroes. *M. B. Smedley.*
9. HYMN. The Armor of Light. *Geo. T. Root.*
   or, Am I a soldier of the Cross ; (in the Prize.)
10. CLASS EXERCISE FOR TWELVE BOYS.
11. HYMNS. This life is a warfare ; and, Only an armor bearer.
12. RECITATION. The Battle of Life.
13. HYMN. Battle hymn of the Republic. (Tune : John Brown.)

DESCRIPTION OF PROGRAMME.

1, 3, 4, 5, 6, 7, 9, 11, 13 *need no explanation.*

2. RECITATION. *Scripture.* Ephesians 6: 11, 12, 13, 14, 15, 16, 17. Jeremiah 46: 3, 4. Psalms 91, 2. Last half of 4 and 5. Psalms 18, 2, 34, 39.

8. *"Heroes" may be found in "Touches of Nature." (Lippincott & Co.)*

10. CLASS EXERCISE FOR TWELVE BOYS. *Boys occupy the front seats in the hall or church. The first speaker rises in his seat and recites:*

THE INTRODUCTION.

" In the knightly times and olden,
    Before historic days,
There lived the good King Arthur,
    Sung in the Laureate's lays.
And he the goodliest fellowship
    Of noble knights did found;
And named them, as in hall they sat,
    Knights of the Table Round.
They pledged each other's honor,
    As we to-day will do,
To battle for the beautiful
    And all that's good and true;
To kindly lift the fallen,
    To shield the faint and weak,
And ever on the oppressor,
    A vengeance swift to wreak.
We've formed again the circle
    Of Arthur's Table Round;
Brave knights are we, though youthful —
    We wait the trumpet's sound."

Some one in the choir, or behind the scenes, sounds a charge upon the bugle. The boys rise and ascend the plat-

form in two lines, meeting, crossing, and halting in line. They sing as they go, Song A, to the tune of the Children's Marching Song, page 82, of The Sunny Side, published by Wm. A. Pond, 547 Broadway, N. Y.

SONG A.

Hear ye the bugle, march to its singing,
   Enter the ranks so bright and fair,
All together cheerily singing,
   For the grand review prepare.

Chorus.

Keep step ! Forward ! as we march along
Keep the step with happy song.
Answer the roll-call, each knightly name ;
   Never one dark, unworthy deed
Now or in the future put it to shame ;
   Answer the roll-call with speed.

The leader will then call the roll, giving only the name of the knight, which its bearer repeats, and adds his escutcheon and watchword.

ROLL CALL.

Sir Galahad, of the sword, without fear and without reproach. Watchword: Purity.

Sir Bedivere, of the shield. Watchword: Faith.

Sir Pelleas, of the breast-plate. Watchword: Righteousness,

Sir Lancelot, of the breast-plate. Watchword: Courtesy.

Sir Geraint, of the golden spurs. Watchword: Earnestness.

Sir Tristram, of the gauntlet. Watchword: Will.

Sir Gawain, of the velvet glove. Watchword: Gentleness.
Sir Bors, of the buckler. Watchword: Honesty.
Sir Percival, of the belt. Watchword: Truth.
Sir Morolt, of the battle-axe. Watchword: Temperance.
Sir Vanoc, of the sandals. Watchword: Peace.
King Arthur, of the helmet. Watchword: Salvation.

(*After the roll-call the choir sing*)

SONG B.

Arm ye, young soldiers, arm for the fight,
    The foe in his strength draweth near.
Quit you like men, and be strong for the right,
    Let the gospel's bright armor appear.

RECITATION. *Sir Galahad.*

Take the sword of the spirit, the word of our God,
    Which from age unto age standeth sure;
And which biddeth each knight, as a seraph of light,
    In heart and in word to be pure.

CHORUS. (*Sung by all the boys.*) Tune: "I know not the hour that my Lord will come."

Take the sword, the sword of the pure,
    Repeat.
And may every young knight, as a seraph of light,
    In heart and in word be all pure.

RECITATION. *Sir Bedivere.*

Take the shield of our faith, 'twill ward every blow
    The tempter surely will wield;
From the castle of doubt you can fight your way out,
    If you take the invincible shield.

CHORUS.
>Take the shield, the shield of the faith,
>>*Repeat.*
>For you never need yield if you take the brignt shield,
>>The invincible shield of our faith.

RECITATION. *Sir Pelleas.*
>Take the breastplate of righteousness, too,
>>Of kindness to keep the heart warm.
>If this be your dress, it will comfort and bless;
>>You'll be safe midst the arrows' fierce storm.

CHORUS.
>The breastplate bright of love and right,
>>*Repeat.*
>If once bound o'er the breast is a magical vest,
>>To turn every shaft in the fight.

RECITATION. *Sir Lancelot.*
>Take the lance that shows you a courteous knight,
>>True emblem of chivalry;
>The soldier of light should be gentle, polite,
>>A model of courtesy.

CHORUS.
>Take the lance so polished and bright,
>>*Repeat.*
>For no true knight may be without sweet courtesy,
>>The lance that's so polished and bright.

RECITATION. *Sir Geraint.*
>Take the spurs of a purpose so noble and high
>>That they'll urge on through dark to the light,
>For Hist'ry avers he must win the gold spurs
>>Who would wear the fair fame of a knight.

CHORUS.
>Take the spurs of a purpose strong,
>>*Repeat.*
>And each barrier steep you will lightly o'erleap
>>If an earnest heart urge you on.

RECITATION. *Sir Tristram and Sir Gawain.*
>Take the iron gauntlet of will
>>It will beat down your foes as they throng,
>But case it in love as a velvet glove —
>>Be gentle if you would be strong.

CHORUS.
>The iron hand in velvet glove,
>>*Repeat.*
>For a gauntlet of steel is a firm, manly will,
>>And kindness the velvet glove.

RECITATION. *Sir Bors and Sir Percival.*
>Take the buckler of honesty, metal of proof,
>>It will stand in temptation's fierce hour,
>Though trials assail it will surely prevail
>>And the truth is a girdle of power.

CHORUS.
>Take the buckler and belt so strong,
>>*Repeat.*
>And whatever you do, oh! be honest and true;
>>And you'll sing the conqueror's song.

RECITATION. *Sir Morolt and Sir Vanoc.*
>Take the battle-axe of temperance strong
>>And batter rum's strongholds with blow upon blow,
>Nor till Satan's wiles cease wear the sandals of peace,
>>Where lingers this dangerous foe.

CHORUS.
>Take the sandals and battle-axe too,
>>*Repeat.*
>Who deals blows in the fight, shall rest sweetly
>>at night,
>The sandals his strength will renew.

RECITATION.   *King Arthur.*
>Christ is our King, 'tis he bids us take
>>These weapons that suit every station.
>If this armor we bind, at length we shall find
>>The Helmet of our salvation.

CHORUS.
>And at the last may they sing of us
>>*Repeat,*
>The brave knights are all dust, and their good
>>swords are rust,
>Their souls are with the saints we trust.

Real armor should be piled picturesquely upon a table on the platform, around which the boys stand while reciting; or, if this cannot be obtained they may hold symbols made of card-board, and gold and silver paper. At the close of these recitations a young lady advances, bearing a white banner, with a crimson cross, and sings:

SONG C.
Tune: Star Spangled Banner.

I.

Receive this fair banner, each gallant young knight,
>Whom so proudly we hail in the morning's glad beaming.

Bear its cross proudly on through the perilous fight,
>Till o'er ramparts of Heaven its fair folds are streaming.

Through afflictions red glare, through temptation, despair,
Though dark be the night, may your flag be still there.

CHORUS.

    'Tis the cross-blazoned banner,
      O, long may it wave
    O'er souls that are true
      And o'er hearts that are brave.

II.

Oh! guard well your banner, ne'er trail it in dust,
  Nor too hard in its service find any exertion.
Keep your armor all bright, free from canker and rust
  May your roll call ne'er number a single desertion.
Then conquer you must, for your cause it is just,
  And this be your motto, In God is our Trust.

CHORUS.

    And the cross-blazoned banner,
      In triumph shall wave,
    O'er souls that are true,
      And o'er hearts that are brave.

No. 12 of the Programme can be found in Golden Leaves, from American Poets; a collection of poetry, published by Bunce & Huntington, New York.

Sunday Evening Exercises.

XI.—THE NEW JERUSALEM.

A little volume edited by William C. Prime, and entitled, "O Mother dear, Jerusalem," (published by Anson D. F. Randolph & Co, 770 Broadway, New York City), contains the original hymn of thirty-one verses, than which no other in the English language expresses better "the soul's breathing after her heavenly country."

This hymn, broken into several parts, and sung or read as a whole, would form the basis for a most beautiful exercise on Heaven, for the Sunday school. In the same volume may be found "The Celestial Country," a translation of the hymn, "Laus Patriæ Cœlestis," by Bernard de Clugny, of the twelfth century.

This hymn was one of Charlotte Cushman's favorites for private readings, and is full of fine rhetorical passages, while its quaint sweetness lends it an inexpressible charm.

An exercise on Paradise is given in the August, 1878, number of "Good Times," a magazine devoted to entertainments of this kind, and published by Mrs. M. B. C. Slade, Fall River, Mass. The exercise is by Mary E. Wilkins, and will be found on the ninth page.

Blumenthal's ballad, "Le Chemin du Paradis," furnishes material for an evening's entertainment of a similar nature, in the shape of a series of tableaux shown at intervals during the singing of the ballad, which is in itself very dramatic, and gives material for some touching pictures. The ballad is published in sheet form by Oliver Ditson & Co.

The twenty-first and twenty-second chapters of Revelation will furnish texts for responsive exercises or recitations.

Of hymns, "O City of our God," "As when the weary traveller gains," "Give me the wings of faith to rise," "There is a land of pure delight," "Oh, exiled Paradise," "There is a holy city," and others from the Plymouth Collection; "From all thy saints in warfare," Episcopal Hymnal, and "Beautiful Land of Rest," will give an abundant choice.

A very touching poem for recitation, appropriate in this connection, is "My ain Countrie."

MY AIN COUNTRIE.

"I am far frae my hame, an' I'm weary aftenwhiles,
For the lang'd for hame bringing, an' my Father's welcome smiles.
I'll ne'er be fu' content until my een do see
The gowden gates of Heaven, an' my ain countrie.

The earth is flecked wi' flowers, mony-tinted, fresh an' gay ;
The birdies warble blithely, for my Father made them sae ;
But these sichts, an' these soun's will as naething be to me,
When I hear the angels singing in my ain countrie.

I've his gude word of promise, that some gladsome day the King
To his ain royal palace, his banished hame will bring ;
Wi' een an' wi' heart running owre we shall see
The ' King in his beauty,' an' our ain countrie.

My sins hae been mony, an' my sorrows hae been sair ;
But there they'll never vex me, nor be remembered mair,
For his bluid has made me white, an' his hand shall dry my e'e,
When he brings me hame at last to my ain countrie.

Like a bairn to its mither, a wee birdie to its nest,
I wad fain be ganging noo until my Saviour's breast,
For he geithers in his bosom, witless, worthless lambs like me,
An' ' He carries them himsel,' to his ain countrie.

He is faithful that has promised, he'll surely come again,
He'll keep his tryst with me, at what hour I dinna ken ;
But he bids me still to wait, an' ready aye to be,
To gang at ony moment to my ain countrie.

So I'm watching aye, and singing o' my hame as I wait
For the soun'ing o' his footfa' this side the gowden gate.
God gie his grace to ilk ane wha listens noo to me,
That we may a' gang in gladness to our ain countrie."

And another, not so well known as it deserves, is,

YEARNINGS.

Our hearts cry out, Is it near or far,
The unseen world where the spirits are?
Our thoughts climb up by the starry way,
To the blissful realms of cloudless day;
That beautiful land, where free from sin,
Our loved and our lost have entered in.

How we miss them all! The children fair,
The saint-like men with silvery hair,
The maidens sweet, and the young men strong,
From our hearts and homes have tarried long;
In vain we watch, and in vain we wait,
They come not back thro' the pearly gate,

We know their hearts are still true and fond,
They *could* not change in the life beyond.
And we do not fear they will forget,
Having loved us once they love us yet.
Therefore we yearn, whether near or far,
To reach the home where our dear ones are.

Kate Cameron.

Sunday Evening Exercises.

XII.—THE DELECTABLE MOUNTAINS.

AN EXERCISE ON THE MOUNTAINS OF THE BIBLE.

PROGRAMME.

" The shepherds said moreover, We would that ye should stay here awhile, yet more to solace yourselves with the good of these Delectable Mountains."

John Bunyan.

1. ANTHEM. By choir. Let Mount Zion rejoice.
2. RECITATION OF SCRIPTURE. By classes from the Sunday-school.
3. SINGING. As when the weary traveller gains; and, How beautiful upon the Mountains.
4. READING. Selections from Ruskin.
5. RECITATION. Hymn of the Mountain Christian. *Mrs. Hemans.*
6. SINGING. Flee as a bird to the mountain; and Back to our Mountains. From Il Trovatore. *Verdi.*
7. SHORT RECITATIONS. Selected from The White Hills. *Thomas Starr King.*
8. SINGING. I will lift up mine eyes unto the hills.
9. EXERCISE. On Bible Mountains.
10. REMARKS. By Pastor.
11. SINGING. 'Tis by thy strength the mountains stand.
12. BENEDICTION.

EXPLANATION OF PROGRAMME.

1. ANTHEM. *By Choir. Let Mount Zion rejoice.*

Psalms — 121:1; 148:1 and 9; 95:4; 65:6, 11, 12; 72:3; 125:2.   Isaiah 44:23; 49:13; 52:7; 54:10; 55:12; Habakkuk 3:6; Deut. 33:13 and 15.

2. RECITATION. *Scripture. By classes from the Sunday-school.*

3. SINGING. *"As when the weary traveller gains,"* etc.

4. READING. *Selections from Ruskin.*

RUSKIN, in his Modern Painters, gives us many sublime word-paintings of the mountains, of which the following selection may serve as an example:

"The best image which the world can give of Paradise, is in the slope of the meadows, orchards, and cornfields on the sides of a great Alp, with its purple rocks and eternal snows above. Of the grandeur or expression of the hills I have not spoken; how far they are great, or strong, or terrible, I do not for the moment consider, because vastness, and strength, and terror, are not to all minds subjects of desired contemplation. It makes no difference to some men whether a natural object be large or small; whether it be strong or feeble. But loveliness of color, perfectness of form, endlessness of change, wonderfulness of structure, are precious to all undiseased human minds; and the superiority of the mountains, in all these things, to the lowland, is, I repeat, as measurable as the richness of a painted window matched with a white one; or the wealth of a museum compared with that of a simply furnished chamber. They seem to have been built for the human race, as at once their schools and their cathedrals, full of treasures of illuminated manuscript for the scholar, kindly in simple lessons to the worker, quiet in pale cloisters for the thinker, glorious in holiness for the worshipper. And of these great cathedrals of the earth, with their gates of rock, pavement of cloud, choirs of stream and stone, altars of snow and vaults of purple, traversed by the continual stars — of these it was written not long ago by one of the best of the poor human race for whom they were built : ' They are inhabited by the beasts.' "

5. RECITATION. *Hymn of the Mountain Christian.* *Mrs. Hemans.*

6. SINGING. *" Flee as a bird to the mountain ; "* and, *" Back to Our Mountains," from Il Trovatore. Verdi.*

7. SHORT RECITATIONS. *The White Hills. Thomas Starr King.*

8. SINGING. *I will lift up mine eyes unto the hills.*

9. *An exercise of mingled singing and recitation for seven girls. Any common metre tune may be chosen :*

THE MOUNTAINS OF THE BIBLE.

ALL SING:

  Mount Sinai with its thunder cloud
   Looms through the ages dim ;
  Mount Carmel and Mount Ararat,
   And sacred Gerezim.
  Of all the mounts of Palestine,
   In Bible hist'ry framed,
  What one is most delectable,
   For holiest memories framed ?

FIRST GIRL SINGS:

  And now of Nebo ven'rable,
   Our witness first shall be;
  For Moses climbed its sightly peak,
   The Promised Land to see.
  And higher yet, and still more high,
   For unto him was given
  The mountain-top of Nebo, for
   A stepping-stone to Heaven.

All recite in concert Deut. 34: 1, 5 and 6. First girl stepping a little forward, recites either Mount Nebo, by Ferdinand Freiligrath, or, The Burial of Moses, by C. F. Alexander, translated by J. Gostick. Both may be found in Longfellow's Poems of Places, Asia.

SECOND GIRL SINGS:

  A naked rock 'tis now, and gaunt;
   But once beside the sea,
  Green-mantled, towered Mount Lebanon,
   Its pride the cedar tree.
  Then there is Mount Moriah, where
   The Jewish temples stood;
  Costly with gems and metal work,
   And odorous cedar wood.

All recite 1 Kings 5: 2, 5, 6, 10. Second girl recites the following verses from Mrs. Howitt's poem:

CEDAR TREES.

  The power that formed the violet,
   The all-creating One,
  He made the stately cedar-trees
   That crowned Mount Lebanon.

And royal was the cedar,
  Above all other trees!
They chose of old its scented wood
  For kingly palaces.
In the temple of Jerusalem,
  That glorious temple old,
They only found the cedar-wood
  To match with carved gold.
But the glory of the cedar tree,
  Is as an old renown,
And few and dwindled grow they now
  Upon Mount Lebanon.
But dear they are to poet's heart,
  And dear to painter's eye;
And the beauty of the cedar tree
  On earth will never die!"

THIRD GIRL SINGS:

But ah! on Quarantania's brow,
  The blessed Saviour trod;
And there withstood the tempter's wiles,
  The spotless Son of God.

All recite Matt. 4: 8 to 11 inclusive. Third girl recites The Temptation, by Longfellow (in Poems of Places, Asia).

FOURTH GIRL SINGS:

We thank thee, Christ, for victory;
  But tenderer gratitude,
We offer at Tell Hattim's foot
  For each Beatitude.

All recite Matt. 5: 1.

Fourth girl recites Matt. 5: 2 to 12 inclusive.

Fifth Girl sings:

>   Tabor or Hermon, one of these
>   Transfiguration claims ;
>   We worship at the mountain's foot,
>   With Peter, John, and James.

All recite Luke 9 : 28 *and* 29.

Fifth girl recites

THE TRANSFIGURATION.

(Ancient Hymn.)

Bring, happy day, to light,
Things which dark-mantling night
  In envious silence hath so long been stealing ;
When on the mountain floor,
Before the three of yore,
  The Son of Man his glory was revealing.
And, through His flesh's shrouding shrine,
Illuminating ran the radiance divine.

The full irradiance flows,
To every limb it goes,
  With snowy light his fiery garments blending ;
Now awe-struck silence quakes,
And the live thunder speaks,
  From the bright cloud in majesty descending.
Then sounds the unutterable voice,
Proclaiming His dear Son, the everlasting choice,

With low-brow'd awe profound,
Be silent on the ground —
  The Lord of all is on His holy hill.
And now, with voice of fear,

Let angel hosts draw near,
  While all the listening world is still,
To sing the Spirit and the Word,
And Father, whose dread voice was in the thunder heard.

SIXTH GIRL SINGS:

Mount Olivet tells us of prayer,
  Of tears and agony,
Of strength vouchsafed for martyrdom,
  And angel ministry.

All recite Luke 22 : 39 to 43 inclusive.

Sixth girl recites The Olive Tree, by Mrs. Hemans.

SEVENTH GIRL SINGS:

But the mountain of all mountains,
  To Christian hearts must be,
That place with cruel murder dark,
  Blood-stained Mount Calvary.

All recite St. Luke 23 : 33.

Seventh girl recites the Stabat Mater, from Poems of Places, Asia.

ALL SING:

We know the road is sharp and steep,
  The mounts not always fair,
But every step doth upward lead,
  And Christ, our Lord, walked there.
Still stand the Mounts Delectable,
  Where Jesus loved to be,

> And ever over mountain tops,
> Dear Lord, we'll follow thee!

10. *Remarks by Pastor.*

11. *'Tis by thy strength the mountains stand.*

12. BENEDICTION.

If preferred, the singing may be given in every instance by all the girls, instead of by different individuals.

Sunday Evening Exercises.

XIII.—THREE-MINUTE SERMONS FOR CHILDREN.

BY REV. J. G. MERRILL.
DAVENPORT, IOWA.

(Reprinted by permission.)

1. THE CHILDREN'S CHURCH.
2. A GOOD NAME SPOILED.
3. LESSONS FROM A BONFIRE.
4. THE WEATHER.
5. RIGHT SIDE UP.
6. GIVING.
7. THE SNOW.
8. DEATH.

I.

THE CHILDREN'S CHURCH.

"But Jesus said: Suffer little children, and forbid them not to come unto me, for of such is the kingdom of heaven." — Matthew 19 : 14.

This is one of the texts which we have chosen to write upon our children's church, and as a good number of you are to join the children's church within a few days, I want, this morning, to tell you some things that your church means.

Three years ago there were about twenty boys and girls in the congregation who loved Jesus Christ, and whom I thought I would help by forming a children's church. So I got printed this sheet, which should tell what is meant by such a church. Let me read it:

CHILDREN'S CHURCH, DAVENPORT.

The foundation on which we build. John 3 : 16.
The promise given us. Matthew, 19 : 14.
Our Confession. I love Jesus.
Our Faith. I trust in Jesus as my own precious Saviour.
Our Repentance. I will try, by the help of Jesus, to give up everything sinful.
Our Hope. I want to be more like Jesus every day.
Our Worship. Daily prayer and reading the Bible. Loving everybody. Trying to be good.
Meetings in our Church, once a month.

Now, if you knew all that older people do about the truths and doctrines of religion, you would see that this paper has all in it that there is in the older people's belief — that is, all that is needed to make you good Christians. And some of you may say: "Why not have us children all join the real church, then?" I would be glad to have most of you do it; but I have seen that before men plant out trees where they are to stay until they die, they have them grow awhile in what is called a nursery, and when the little trees are large enough, and straight enough, and strong enough, to be dug up and placed on the lawn, they are established for life.

Now, nearly all who made up the children's church three years ago are in their father's and mother's church to-day; and, meanwhile, a large number of younger ones have come along, and they need to have the children's church started again.

Now, what help will it be to any of my young friends to join this little church?

First. You will have the same pastor that the other church has. If it is worth while for the older people to have a minister, it is certainly best that children should. We compare people to sheep, sometimes, and I think men and women are quite like sheep in many ways. If that is so, children are like lambs, and I guess a good farmer is more careful of his lambs than he is of the older sheep.

I have compared people to trees, and I have heard as the twig is bent, so is the tree inclined. If I should live to be pastor of this church twenty years more, some of you children would be my deacons and trustees — pillars in the church, as people call them — so, if I would have straight, strong pillars, I must keep you straight now. What a hard task it is to take crooked sticks and make fair timber of them; but if we can only have them straight to begin with, we can save a deal of trouble, and get better results.

My idea of what Christ meant when He said, "Suffer little children," etc., is that he wanted to have boy and girl Christians to make the best men and women Christians of. And this leads me to say, in the second place, that you have the same Saviour that the older church has.

I think one of the strangest notions that ever got agoing was that boys and girls all belonged to Satan. Why, a leading Christian man in this town told me that he did not want his boy to become a Christian until he was fourteen or fifteen years old. The Bible tells us that we belong either to Satan or to God, and I am glad that Jesus said, "Suffer *little* children to come unto me," and gave as a reason, "for of such is the kingdom of heaven." Jesus is even more tender and loving to the children's church than to the grown people's, and I don't wonder, for His heart is like that of many a man and woman who will watch, notice, and love little children because they are little; other and older people may be hungry, cold, and abused, before little children should suffer such things. It is bad enough for an old man to become lame and have to use crutches all his life through; but how much worse for a little boy to have his leg wither, and know that he can never walk upon it.

Then, in the third place, members of the children's church have the same kind of work to do that members of the large church do. Any one who belongs to either of the churches agrees to help others and obey God. We all of us will have to work hard to do it. And when a little boy brings a quart pail of water from the spring, or four sticks of wood from the pile, to save his mother steps, or because he would be a useful Christian boy, he has done just as good an act as the strong man with a pail full of water in each hand, or an armful of wood that would break a boy's back.

Then, lastly, children, your little church has the same hope that the greater church has. After a few years all of us, and after a few days some of us, are to go to a better land than this. No one can have a home there unless he has trusted in and loved Jesus, who is that land's king; and when you join your little church you say, and, I hope, feel, that you do trust in that Jesus who is at the head of all true churches — yours as much as the greatest the world has ever seen.

II.

A GOOD NAME SPOILED.

"Jeroboam, who made Israel to sin." 2. Kings 10:31.

Did you ever hear of any father or mother calling their boy Jeroboam? We know men by the names of Abraham, Isaac, Jacob, Jeremiah, David, and the like, and these are, some of them, no more pleasantly sounding names than is Jeroboam.

And when the little boy who had this name was named Jeroboam, it was because his parents wanted to give him a name that should signify to all who knew him how much they hoped from the child, for Jeroboam means one who increases his people. But so wicked was the life of this man that, instead of meaning one who increases his people, we always think of Jeroboam who made his people to sin.

How easy it is for us to spoil a good name. When we are babies father and mother hunt all about to find a name good enough for their little one. Mother says: "There was my father, the best man that ever lived; his name was Henry; I want the baby called Henry." Father says: "I would like to have him called Charles, for my classmate in college, who, I am sure is going to make his mark as a minister or lawyer." Or, if it be a little girl, how are all the names, that nice folks have, talked over until the very best is found.

But suppose that the parents like such a name as Frederick, or Frank, or Sarah, or Maud, and there should be among their friends or relatives a Frederick who was a miserable drunkard, or a Frank who had been put in jail, or a Sarah who was a great scold, or a Maud who would tell falsehoods, the baby would never be called by any of these pretty names.

Now, I suppose some of you do not like the names which you have, but one thing is very certain, that when you were named you were called by the best that father and mother, or some other good friend, could think of.

You were named for some dear relative or acquaintance, or for some great and good man or woman, or for some fancy name, which should show how hard your fathers and mothers tried to get a name good enough for you.

You may not have a name that sounds very sweetly, nor one that is very great, but you can, if you try, make the name that you have the best of all names. I have some friends whom I think a great deal of, and their names, such as Samuel, and William, and Martin, and Edward, all sound very pleasantly to me, although none of the names are in themselves very good. Then there are some names that I cannot bear, just because there are some mean men or women who have spoiled them for me.

Now, what I want of all my young friends, is that they shall be such boys and girls as to make their names the best and sweetest in all the neighborhood in which they live, so that the moment any one of your friends, by and by, shall hear another person called by the same name, they shall at once think of you with pleasure. And what is more, I want you to feel how dreadful it is to spoil a good name; to have it put on the church book when you are baptized that you are to be called after some dear friend, some honored acquaintance, and then to grow up and make the name the meanest and ugliest in all the town.

There are a few boys and girls who seem to be trying very hard to do this. They are like Jeroboam, who was to be a helper to his people, but really was the one who ruined them by making them to sin. I can see more plainly than you can, boys and girls, what a dreadful thing it is thus to disappoint your best friends and make yourselves a disgrace; and I hope that before it is too late you will turn square about and make yourselves worthy of all the love that gave you the names of your infancy. And one thing I want to have you all remember, that you do not need to have the long and ugly name of Jeroboam in order to deserve the dislike and disgust that everyone has towards it. Benedict Arnold was a nice name to call a boy before he was a traitor — it would be a dreadful name now. No man calls his child Cain, although it means the same as that sweet name, Theodore, God given. No one calls his boy Judas, and yet it means the praise of the Lord.

All of you have precious names, given by your dearest friends. Do not be like Jeroboam, who made a blessing into a curse.

III.

LESSONS FROM A BONFIRE.

"Many of them, also, which used curious arts, brought their books together and burned them before all men; and they counted the price of them, and found it fifty thousand pieces of silver." — Acts 19 : 19.

This was a great bonfire. It burned up nearly ten thousand dollars worth of books, and it was a good thing to do, for the books were bad. They were filled with rules by which those who owned the books could cheat other people; and although the men who brought them to be burned could have made fortune after fortune if they had kept and used their books, they would not do it, because they had become Christians, and learned how very wrong it was to cheat as they had been doing, and therefore they made up their minds to put the books where they would do nobody any more harm.

There are three lessons that I want to have you learn from this, and the first is: That those things which can only do harm should be destroyed. When a man is taken with the small-pox or yellow fever, and dies very suddenly in a fine suit of clothes, we should say a friend of his was crazy who should take the clothes and wear them because they cost a good deal and were nice. If a dog that cost fifty or a hundred dollars gets mad, he ought to be shot as soon as a gun can be found to shoot him. If a boy gives you a book that is written by wicked men, who want the boys and girls of America to be bad, like themselves, the very best thing that you can do with it is to burn it. Once in awhile there are books with filthy reading and pictures passed around at school, and no matter how much they cost, any clean boy or girl should, the very first thing, coax the scholar who has the books to burn them. Then there are other books that try to make people believe that there is no God, that the Bible is not true, that Christians are bad people, and when anyone gives you such a book, you may be very sure that the wisest thing you can do is to put it in the fire, where it cannot do you or anyone else harm.

Another lesson to be learned is, that we ought to care more for right than for money. When I go down town, and catch a word or two from the different people whom I meet or pass, I find that nearly all are talking about how to make money. We all have to have money to buy our food and clothes, and the other things that we need. And I suppose all of you children will have to spend many years of your lives in trying to get money. But there is one thing to learn at the beginning, and that is, that there is something better than money — it is to be right. I hope there is not a boy here who will ever grow up so anxious to get rich that he will be ready to sell rum or whisky, to keep a saloon; nor any other that will be ready to tell a lie so as to sell anything, as some men do who tell us that sugar is pure when they know there is sand in it, or plaster, or starch; that milk is clear when it is half water. When you grow older you will find that the world is full of men and women who care only to make money, nothing for right, and you will be tempted to do as they do, but I hope you will dare to do the right every time.

The last lesson to be learned is, that when we become Christians we should give up our bad practices. What if these men had said to themselves: "Now if I keep these books, and use them, I can make two or three thousand dollars every year, and then I can take the money and pay for Paul's journey, or send Timothy off as a missionary." Do you suppose Jesus would have been pleased? You know He would not. So you know that He is not pleased with any of you who think that you will hold on to your pet sins while you pretend to be Christians. Any of you girls who used to peep into your books so as to recite well, now that you are Christians, will leave the wicked habit. Any of you who used to love to tease your playmates when they had made mistakes or gotten into trouble, will be very careful not to hurt their feelings or wrong them in any way when you are Christ's.

In a word, I want to feel that all the boys and girls, young men and women, who are growing up here as Christians, are in earnest; that they hate the bad, love the right, and are willing to give up the best things they have rather than not to be Christ's. And you may be sure that you can hold on to everything that will make you truly happy, great, and good, while you hold on to Jesus.

IV.

THE WEATHER.

"Who can stay the bottles of heaven?" — Job 38: 37

In the Bible lands water was often very scarce, and hence very precious, and whenever it was necessary to save it to use on a long journey, or for any other reason, it was generally kept in bottles. These bottles, so-called, were made of the skins of animals, especially of the goat, and usually were, when filled, just the shape of the live animal with the head and feet cut off, and when the people wished to empty the skins they laid them on their sides and let the water run out.

It was this custom which led him who spoke the words of the text to ask, "Who can keep the water in the bottles of the heavens?" as often in poetry, like our text, such comparisons are made. Now, during the past week, it has seemed as though the bottles of heaven had been open nearly all the time, and I am afraid some of you children have grumbled about it, for children do not like rainy weather, and hence I have thought it a good plan to-day to find an answer to the question asked in our text, and then, perhaps, learn that it is not best to complain of the weather.

How does rain come? I will tell you one way, for there are many. When the wind blows from the southeast it comes from a warmer country than ours, and is often filled with moisture. As long as the wind is warm it can carry this moisture through the sky, and no one can see it at all, but if, in its journey north, it meets some colder air, and begins to get cold, it cannot hold the moisture as well, and so it forms clouds. Then, after a little, as the air grows still colder, the wind is less able to hold the moisture, the bottles are open, and down comes the rain.

Now, who made the moist wind come from the south? Was it not God? And He made it meet the cold wind, which squeezed the clouds as you would squeeze a wet sponge, and He made the rain to fall. When, therefore, we have stormy weather, we will remember —

First. God makes it rain. He knows when it is needed, and sends it to keep the ground wet enough to make the trees, plants, and flowers grow. So that one who complains of the weather is finding fault with God.

Second. We do not know when it ought to begin or to stop raining. Two years ago, if you had watched men digging post holes or cellars, you would have seen that the ground, three or four feet down, was as dry as ashes, and if you had gone out into the country you would have learned that the springs were dry, and there was very little water in the wells; and yet there was rain enough to make the corn grow, and the roads were very nice, and we were glad that it rained so little. But because there was no more rain the trees had nothing for their leaves and roots to drink, and so very many of them have died. Then, last year it rained a great deal, and everybody grumbled at the mud, and the clouds, and the storms, and all the while God was getting the ground ready to give us such a fruitful season this year as we have not had for a long time. And now, if this fall it rains again, remember that God knows better than you and I do how much the trees need to drink, and how much rain it will take to keep the springs full and keep the wells from drying up.

Third. We should remember that, if the rain comes when we are not ready for it, our little plans are of very little account. You don't like to put on your rubbers and old clothes to go to school; you wish it would not rain while school keeps. Surely, you would not want it to rain Saturday, nor all vacation; and your father, if he keeps store, don't want it to rain Saturday, either, for that is the best day for people to come in from the country to trade. Then I come in and say: " I think it is bad to have it rain Sundays, for there are so many men and women who seem to feel that a Sunday rain is the wettest of all rains, and that it will wash them away if they go out in it." So all the time that it can rain and suit everybody is nights, and then, how muddy the roads would be every day; that would displease everybody, and by the time you had everybody suited before the rain should come, it would not come at all.

Suppose there should be a vote taken: the minister votes against Sunday, the wash-woman Monday, the hay-makers Tuesday, a picnic Wednesday, those who want to go to prayer meeting Thursday, the temperance celebration Friday, the merchant Saturday. I rather think, children, that we had better let the rain bottles alone, and when God sees fit to have the rain come feel that He knows best, that it is better to have His great plans carried out than our little ones; and more than all, we should not allow a little mud, or the trouble of drying clothes, or an uncomfortable feeling in here when it is cloudy or stormy, to lead us to find fault with Him who is so kind as to send His rain on the unthankful as well as the thankful.

V.

RIGHT SIDE UP.

"These that have turned the world upside down are come hither also." — Acts 17 : 9.

It was an easy thing to have a mob in old times. There were always big boys loafing about, or lewd fellows of the baser sort, as Luke calls them, who were ready for mischief, and when they begun a disturbance no man could tell where it would end. Some of these men seized hold of the man Jason, in Thessalonica, because he had let a travelling minister stop at his house, and had taken him, with some others, to the city officers, saying, "that the men who turned the world upside down had come;" and what they charged was true, for, in the first place, the world is wrong side up. I mean by this that if we let things go along of themselves the bad gets the better of the good. Let a piece of land lie still and it will grow up to weeds. If you do not take great care of it, a machine becomes rusty and useless. I have never seen a boy or girl who did not grow worse and worse unless they kept watching themselves very closely. It is so much more easy to go down hill than to climb up, to say yes than no, when we want to do wrong. The world is wrong side up.

Then, second, there are a great many who are trying to keep the wrong side up, like these roughs of Thessalonia. There are boys, and girls too, who seem to like nothing better than to be doing that which they ought not, disobeying father and mother, bothering brother and sister, getting into mischief everywhere; and then, when they grow up, if anybody tries to save them, saying that they want to be let alone. There is a young man in this city. I have seen him come out of saloons now and then; he has a most beautiful wife, and how dark the future is before her, because he is a slave to drink! A minister thought he would try and save him; spoke to him kindly. The young man looked up and said: "Well, sir, how long have you been in Davenport?" "Three years," answered the minister. "I have been here twice as long as you; if you will attend to your business, I will attend to mine," said the young man. He wanted to have the world stay wrong side up, just as all the other wicked men do who are not ready to give up their sins.

But I notice, in the third place, that God wants to have the world put upside down. Of course He does, for He wants to see things as they should be, and to be right everything should be right side up.

You would think it very foolish to try and bring a basket of apples home from the grocery, handle downward; to fasten horses to a carriage that had tipped over without righting it.

God knows what it is to have things as they should be, and when He sees them wrong, wants them made right; and when He sees any of you thinking that it is smarter to be unkind than kind, rough than gentle, impure than pure, untrue than true, to stay away from Sunday-school and church than to go regularly to them, He knows that you are wrong side up, and wants to make you right.

And one thing more: you all should belong to the company of those who are putting the upside down. This is what all good people are trying to do. Your parents keep talking to you, trying with all their power to keep under all that is bad and bring the good to the top; your teacher is putting ignorance and laziness down, and learning and studiousness up; the church is working all the time to help all overcome the evil and make strong the right. So I want you to join the company of those who are turning the world upside down. Commence with yourself, and instead of doing that which is easier, work away at yourself until you have put at the bottom all that is mean or ugly, and in any way wrong, and put at the top all that is beautiful, and true, and good. Then, when you have done this, you can help others to right themselves.

Once in a while there is a tornado that goes across our prairies and tips over everything, and he is the most useful and best man who goes at once to work and sets up everything on his own farm, and also helps his neighbors who need his help.

The whole world is full of boys and girls who need you to help them to be right side up; and I can tell you that when you get through life, if you have worked hard to keep straight yourself, and helped others to keep straight, nothing you could have done could have made you happier than to know that you belonged to the number who are trying to turn the world upside down.

The poor world has turned its face away from the sun, and it is very, very dark in the shadow. Let us all work with a will to turn it back towards the sun, and in turning it upside down get it right side up.

VI.

GIVING.

"Thanks be unto God for His unspeakable gift."—2 Cor. 9: 15.

I have heard of a minister who, every morning, used to go to his outside door, and looking up toward the sky, say, "Thank you." Perhaps he felt as Paul when he wrote: "He that spared not His own Son, but delivered Him up for us all, how shall He not with Him also freely give us all things?" And so, every day the sunshine or the rain, the wind or the calm, was just the best thing for that day, and reminded him always of that Saviour through whom all good gifts come, and who is Himself the unspeakable gift.

You have all had a great many things given you, and sometimes when I visit your homes you show me what has been given you and tell me all about it, and I like to have you. But there are some of you who have received a gift that is unspeakable, that is, it is so great that no words can describe it.

But you have all heard that actions speak louder than words, and in the chapter of which my text is the last verse, Paul has told of a kind of actions that do tell whether people are Christians — have received the unspeakable gift. It is Christian giving.

There are some poor people in a far-off city whom the people to whom Paul wrote had promised to help; they had promised a great deal, and Paul says that they must not only give it, but give it cheerfully, and if they do they will not only make the poor thankful, but will in that way express their thanks to God for His great gift.

I have seen a little girl have a present of a large orange: she likes oranges very much; she eats this very eagerly, for she has not had any for a long time; but before eating it she cuts out and lays aside a portion for some poor child who does not have any oranges. And I am very sure that were I the one who gave that little girl the orange, I should know that she was thankful, not merely because she said "thank you," but because she desired herself to make another as happy as I had tried to make her; and don't you think I would be right in so thinking?

In old times God made a rule that all the people should give a tenth and more to show their thankfulness, and there are some now-a-days who do this. I spent a Sunday, once, in a rich man's house. He was making a great deal of money. Did he live in a very large, nice house? No, he had a neat, comfortable home. Did he have a handsome carriage and pair of bay horses? No, he had a plain carriage, and the horse was so homely and ugly-looking that when I rode out with his son to see the asylum where insane people are kept, one of the crazy women knew enough to see how ugly it was, but did not know enough to keep from laughing about it, and making fun, so loud that we all heard her. Did he have costly things to eat and wear? No, he lived and dressed very plainly. And why was all this? He wanted to show God how thankful he was for His unspeakable gift, and so he gave away all that he could earn, and it was thousands of dollars a year, to buy food and clothes for the hungry and naked, and to furnish the gospel to those who had never heard it.

Now, I suppose that the reason why we do not do more to make others happy, and to make them good, is because we do not feel thankful for what

God has given us. I am told that little boys and girls in heathen lands, when they become Christians, give a great deal to those that need. They know what an awful thing it is to live in a land without Christ, what an unspeakable gift it is to have Jesus. And I hope that you will all learn, first of all, what a precious thing it is to have Jesus as your own Saviour, and then show Him how thankful you are by denying yourselves to help others who need your help.

There are many things besides money that you can give, although I think you all ought to learn early to earn, save, and give your little moneys. You can give a kind word to a playmate who never hears kind words at home; you can give a helping hand to mother who is tired, or your brother who is small; you can give sunshine to all who see you, and if you do these things because you are Christians, and want to do what you can to please Christ, you are, by your deeds, thanking God for his unspeakable gift.

VII.

THE SNOW.

"Hast thou entered into the treasures of the snow?"
—Job. 38 : 22.

Children feel that snow is sent for their special benefit, and how they clap their hands at the first snow-flakes in the late fall! This winter has been a remarkable one for children, because there has been so much snow, and I have thought that the best subject that I could choose for your sermon would be the snow, and what the Bible tells about it.

Job says: "If I wash myself with snow-water, and make my hands never so clean, yet mine own clothes should abhor me." The water in the country where Job lived was much of it hard, and would not clean things as soft water and melted snow can. I have seen boys and girls living in like countries; it seemed as though they never had clean faces, much less clean hands; and it was a mercy when the rain or snow came, making soft water. But there are some things that the softest water cannot wash clean — the stains of sin, the stains upon our souls; and any of you who have said unkind, untruthful, unclean words, have such stains upon your souls, and there is nothing on earth that can wash them out. I know that there are a great many people who say that children are pure and good, that they have no marks of sin upon them. God does not think so. He is so pure that the least sin looks black to Him. When the sun came out last Thursday morning, after the great storm, and the world was spotless, how dingy the white houses and fences looked. Paint that we called white before, became smoky and dirty. Just so, children who think they are good, and kind, and pure, and loving, can learn by putting themselves alongside of the spotless Jesus that they are stained, needing to be cleansed.

But there is another snow text that should go with the one that I have just read; you will find it in Isaiah. It is a verse that your fathers and mothers like to hear, a most precious verse; " Come, now, and let us reason together, saith the Lord; though your sins be as scarlet they shall be white as snow." This is a promise from the mouth of God, and although there is nothing in the world that can wash out the stain of any sin, God has found a way to wash out the stains of the worst sins. And there are some of you, children, who know what this means; you feel sure that God has cleansed you from all sin. You all love to sing the precious hymn from the Gospel Songs:

> "What! lay my sins on Jesus,
> God's well beloved Son!
> No! 'tis a truth most precious
> That God e'en that has done."

And how the chorus does ring out:

> "Hallelujah! Jesus saves me,
> He makes me white as snow."

And there is nothing more delightful than to feel that God will help us keep ourselves pure as snow, and I trust that every day we shall keep this snow-white life as pure and clean as it can be. You are not to do this by sitting still and doing nothing, but by all the time trying to do right, good, pure, true deeds.

By and by you will learn in school that white light, like the snow, contains in it all the colors of the rainbow; that a ray of white light is made up of blue, red, yellow, and the like. So I think that the white robes which God gives us, white as snow, are kept white by uniting all the beautiful colors — there is the blue, which is the color of the modest violet, telling us to be humble, the red of the rose, by which others are made glad, the yellow of the cowslip, of use in the meadow, telling us how to be helpful, and so on, until putting together prayer, kind words, thoughtful acts, trust in Christ, all these beautiful virtues, we can, with God's help, keep from stain the robe, white as snow, given us by our Father in heaven, through Jesus Christ, His Son.

VIII.

DEATH.

"She is not dead, but sleepeth."—Luke 8: 52.

This was spoken of a little girl twelve years old. Her friends all supposed that she was dead. They were right; she was soon to be buried. Jesus came, and, knowing that she was dead, said, in the words of your text, "She is not dead, but sleepeth." What did He mean? He wanted to have the friends know that He thought that they had a wrong idea of death, and wrong feelings in regard to it; and in the sense in which they spoke and thought of death, the little girl was not dead.

Now, there have been a large number of deaths during the last few weeks, and I can see that many of the people in town are thinking wrongly of death, and therefore I want to say a few words to you about it, for I am quite sure that Jesus had the right idea, and so long as it is true that half of the graves in Oakdale are children's graves, I am very anxious to have you think and feel as you should concerning death.

It is a blessed thing to go to sleep, when we are tired out and can drop to sleep in an instant. Sometimes we wish we could have more time to play, but when the hour of sleep comes, how sweetly it takes us in its arms, and nothing is more beautiful than a sleeping child. And it was only a few days ago that I saw a little child who had been suffering day after day, die, and only in a few moments such a sweet smile came upon her lips, and I could not help saying, " How sweetly she sleeps."

The next thing for you to remember is, that those who go to sleep wake up. When you have been to school six hours, and have helped mother at home, and have played very hard all the spare moments, you begin to find it very hard to hold up your head, and nothing seems bright and pleasant; but in the morning, when the sun looks in at the window, and says, " My little man, or little woman, it is time to get up," how bright the world looks; how strong and happy you feel; how very different from the way in which you felt the night before. So when any of us are put to sleep by Jesus, we can know that there is a morning coming, and when that has come we shall be so strong, and beautiful, and happy, that the night of our sleep will seem to have been very short. But I hear some little child say, " I do not want to go to sleep in the ground; I do not want to be put in a coffin;" and you need not. Once in a while my little girl says, " Papa, I don't want to go to bed up stairs;" she does not want to be alone, so her mother allows her to make her bed upon the lounge in the bright sitting-room. At length she falls asleep; then, when I am through with my studies, I carry her to her bed, and she knows nothing of the dark night nor the lonely room. In the same way no child of you will ever know anything about the grave or coffin, if you have to be buried in them. You fall asleep at home, and when you wake, if you are Christ's, you awake in a better home.

But another thing, we all grow when we are asleep. The reason why some children do not grow more is because they do not have sleep enough. A few months ago a farmer's boy put a kernel of corn in the ground; you could pinch it between your little fingers, or hold a hundred kernels in your hand; but when the corn slept it grew, and to-day it has become a tall stalk, with full ears and long rows of kernels. So, if a little child's body is taken to the cemetery and left sleeping, it will not be very long, as God counts time, before it will come forth in heaven a most beautiful body, worthy to live in the beautiful land.

And once again: do you not sometimes dream when you are asleep? What does this mean? That your mind is awake, waiting for your refreshed body in the morning. So when you put the body to sleep in the grave, it is not the soul sleeping; that has gone to be with Jesus whom he loved, and as you all know that the soul is the most precious thing you have, you should remember, when you put the body away, it is like laying aside the rough soil that holds a jewel, until the Master can fashion it, and place it in a beautiful casket. All we have to do when death comes, is to say, "Now I lay me down to sleep, I pray Thee, Lord, my soul to keep."

BEAUTY AND THE BEAST;

OR,

Handsome Is That Handsome Does.

A LITTLE PLAY, IN THREE SCENES.

TO BE ACTED BY CHILDREN.

By SUSAN HALE.

CHARACTERS.

BEAUTY.
1st SISTER.
2nd SISTER.

MERCHANT.
BEAST.
TWO VOICES BEHIND THE SCENES.

BEAUTY. *This must be played by a little girl, as a little girl, with a short dress and long braids, in the first scene, and with the manners of a spoiled child. In the second scene she wears a grown-up dress, but must manage it awkwardly, as if she were wearing it for the first time. Her dress in the third scene is the same, with a bonnet and parasol.*

TWO PROUD SISTERS. *These two characters are much alike; they must be played as two disagreeable young ladies, with grown-up long dresses, and a great many airs. These parts should, however, be quietly acted, and without any pushing or rudeness.*

MERCHANT. *This part is the most difficult one; and if some condescending grown person of nineteen or even thirty will represent it, the piece will go off all the better. It should seem to be a fussy old gentleman, dressed for travelling, with a shawl or large colored handkerchief round his throat and a great-coat and umbrella. The same costume will do for the last scene.*

BEAST. *The only difficulty with this part is that it is a very warm as well as an ardent one. The Beast must be dressed like a gentleman of the nineteenth century underneath, but must wear over this a fur coat, if possible, or a coat lined with fur, the lining turned outward; he must* have fur gloves, and a beast's head, either obtained from a toy-shop on purpose or manufactured ingeniously at home. In the days when bonnets were bonnets, and had crowns, a felt or beaver bonnet put on " hind-side before," with a red tongue hanging out, was effective. But those simple days are over and ingenuity has given way to extravagance, sometimes to the loss of the audience; for the freshness and originality which necessity taught to invention, were often more amusing than the realistic accuracy which can be produced from a "furnishing establishment."

In the garden scene, the disguise of the Beast must be firmly fastened on, but in the last scene it must be loosely arranged so that it can be suddenly thrown off and reveal the Prince.

And now one word to the little actors and actresses before they begin to learn their parts. The great secret of good acting is unconsciousness, that is, you must forget yourself and your own way, and try and make yourself feel like the character you are representing. Beauty must not be wondering how she looks, or whether people will praise her, but must try and behave just like a little girl whose papa gives her to a beast. And the Beast must act as he thinks a good kind beast would be likely to do.

Another thing is to help along the scene by watching all the time, to be sure you are in the right places, not in order to show yourself off, but to give the scene the effect of a real conversation going on. It is not the vain and conceited boys and girls who dress themselves up and seize the best parts who make in the end the best actors: but those who try to do any part that is given them so well as to improve the general effect of the whole. If you are only a sheep in a farm scene, and baa in the right place, you will add more to the pleasure of the audience than if you talk and call down their attention upon yourself, in the wrong one.

SCENE I. — *Merchant's house. Any parlor will do, with very little change of furniture. Proud sister, before a looking glass trying on a dress. This can be an old party dress covered with flounces and flowers, put on over the other dress.*

Beauty, sitting on the floor, playing with a doll, blocks, toys, etc., scattered about her:

1st *Sister.* "Can't you pinch it up a little in the neck? It don't look right."

2d *Sister.* "Your neck is so long, no dress can come within a mile of it."

1st *Sister.* "I have a great mind to take out the sleeves entirely. That would make it more stylish."

2d *Sister.* "What! after spending money on all that lace to put on them?"

1st *Sister.* "Hitch it up a little more behind."

Beauty. "You are having a great deal of trouble with that dress. I should think you would be sorry Aunt Maria gave it to you."

2d *Sister.* "If she had given it to me, I could have worn it just as it was."

1st *Sister.* "Shut up, Beauty, and attend to your dolls. It was my turn to have whatever came from Aunt Maria."

2d Sister. "Well, fix it yourself, for I'm tired of standing up,"

[*Throws herself down on a sofa, and takes up a newspaper. 1st Sister goes on pulling at the dress and fussing over it at the looking glass.*]

2d Sister. "Oh dear! I wonder when father will come home. (*Reads.*) 'Steamers arrived.' Who knows whether he'll come in a Cunard or a White Star?"

1st Sister. "He may come overland."

Beauty. "I think he said he should come by the Air-line."

2d Sister. "Well, I hope he will come soon, for I'm dying for my piano."

Beauty. "Oh, sister! did you ask for a piano?"

2d Sister. "Yes, I did, of course, why not? he said for us to choose just what we liked best. I told him a Steinway Grand, but I shan't object if it is only an upright."

1st Sister. "Yes, and Beauty asked for *only a rose!* So affected; as if we should not put in for exactly what we wanted. For my part, the only trouble was to think what, and I've written him seventeen times to change my mind."

Beauty. "Why, what did you ask for, sister?"

1st Sister. "Oh! first I thought a saddle-horse, and then I thought what a fool to have a horse and not any habit, so then I said a riding habit, from Worth."

Beauty. ⎫ "But you can't have but one
2d Sister. ⎭ thing!!"

1st Sister. "I know it, so I took them both back and said finally, a Saratoga trunk, full of clothes from Paris."

2d Sister. "Oh! how mean! that's ever so many more than one thing!"

1st Sister. "No, it's not. In Paris now they have them all ready-made and packed."

2d Sister. "I wonder you did not ask for a whole elephant."

1st Sister. "I dare say it's no harder to get than a *rose!* 'Only a rose!'"

1st ⎫
2d ⎭ *Sisters (repeating).* ⎫ "Only a rose!"
⎭ "Only a rose!"

Beauty (almost crying). "I don't care! a rose was just what I wanted. I've just learned how to make rose-cakes and do them up in a paper, and you put brown sugar in them, and bury them in the ground, or put them under the bed-post, which is better, because the ants don't get at them; but what's the use, if I had not any rose, and I knew papa would get one for me, even if it was winter, in some menagerie."

1st Sister. "You mean Conservatory. The child is almost a fool."

2d Sister. "Well, don't nag her; it saves bother to hear her want nothing but a rose."

[*Noise heard without, galloping like horses, cracking of whips, cries of Whoa! Whoa! All rush to the window.*]

All (*at once*). "It's papa, he's come home. It's papa!"

Beauty. "In an express cart!"

1st Sister. "With my trunk!"

2d Sister. "And piano behind!"

All (*at once*). "Two carts!"

Beauty. "Dear papa! I'll go and meet him and show him my woolly dog."

[*Takes toy from floor, hastily, and goes out. The sisters continue looking out of the window.*]

1st Sister. "Oh, my! There's my trunk! See the men lifting it out."

2d Sister. "Oh, what a bother they are having! That's more than a Saratoga. It's a Saratogera."

1st Sister. "Oh, pshaw! Don't pun — hullo, papa!"

[*She turns round slowly and extends hand. Enter* MERCHANT; BEAUTY *behind him, feeling in his pockets.*]

1st Sister (*indifferently*). "How'do, papa! Had a nice time?"

2d Sister (*equally cool*). "Got back, papa dear?" (*Turns her cheek to be kissed.*)

[MERCHANT *takes off his hat and wipes his forehead with a large bandana handkerchief. He stands in the middle of the stage with umbrella and hat in his hand.*]

Merchant. "Oh, my children!"

[*Beauty places chair for him in the middle and kneels by his side. He sits. Sisters group behind, standing.*]

Beauty. "Did you have a good journey, papa?"
Sisters (*together*). "Did you bring our things?"

[*Tremendous thumping outside.*]

2d Sister (*aside to 1st Sister*). "It's the piano!"
1st Sister (*aside to 2d Sister*). "No, it's my trunk."
Merchant. "Yes, my love; but oh, my children!"

[*He wraps his head in his handkerchief and weeps audibly. Hat and umbrella fall. Beauty picks them up.*]

Beauty. "Did you forget about the rose? no matter, dear papa"—
Merchant (*springing up*). "Oh, the rose! I was sitting on it, it is in my pocket."
Voice at the door. "Where shall we put the pianner?"
2d voice at the door. "Is the trunk to go further up?"
Merchant. "Oh, yes! oh! I had forgotten; my daughters, there are your gifts, — but, oh! my children, my children! (*Sits down again on pocket, overcome by grief.*)
1st Sister (*aside*). "Why don't he give some directions to the men?"

2d Sister. " Why don't he present us with the things, and then we could thank him and be done with it! "

1st and 2d Sisters. " Well, papa ! Are those our things ? "

Beauty. " Speak, papa. Don't take on so ! "

Merchant. " Yes, my daughters, there is the piano, and there is the trunk. I hear them coming up-stairs. Take them, they are yours; and here is the rose."

[*Draws out rose from his pocket, pinned up in a good deal of cotton-wool. It may be a large full-blown artificial one.*]

Beauty. " Oh, papa, it is a lovely rose ! "

Merchant. " But oh, my children ! (*Again overcome by grief.*)

1st Sister. " Come along, sister."

2d Sister. " Oh, bother, we can't wait ! " (*Exeunt.*)

Beauty. " Papa, what is the matter; are you hungry ? Can't I get you anything ? "

Merchant. " Oh, no, my dear ! I have had my meals very regular. It is not that, but oh, my children ! (*Handkerchief again.*)

Beauty. " Brace up, papa ! Sisters have gone to look at their things.

Thumping again outside and Sisters speaking, saying, " *in here,*" " *up-stairs,*" *etc.*

Merchant. " All that is well, but why, why,

my child, did you come to meet me? Alas! alas!"

[*He must continually interrupt himself to weep; but I shall not write it down any more.*]

Beauty. "Begin at the beginning, papa; I know it will make you feel better."

Merchant. "Very true, my dear. My business, which I went for, prospered very well. I succeeded in exchanging my government bonds for railroad stock, and in watering my Calumet and Hecla, although " —

Beauty. "Yes, papa, but I don't mind so very much about that."

Merchant. "Oh, no! Oh, no! Very well, my dear; well, I telegraphed before I left home for your sisters' things, and they have been down at my store waiting ever since, for I thought it would be better for us all to arrive together; but the rose, the rose; alas, my children " —

Beauty. "Oh, *why* did I ask for a rose?"

[*Enter* PROUD SISTERS.]

1st Sister. "Yes, why indeed! just to be affected."

2d Sister. "Don't interrupt him, he is just getting to the point."

Merchant. "Yes, my daughters, and it is very sharp, indeed."

Two Sisters. "Very good, papa, now go on."

Merchant. "The only place of any importance

at which I stopped, for I took a through train, was the Desert of Sahara. The hotels are very good there now; they have almost every thing brought by Simoom, which also takes the place of the telegraph; but I didn't see any thing in the way of a rose. Oh, my children! My idea of course was to look for an oasis, but the nearest I came to it was a Carmelite nun I saw in the street."

Two Sisters. "Oh, a sister! Very good, papa, now go on."

Merchant. "Till one day I read an advertisement in the local paper of Promenade Gardens. I hastened to the spot. It was Sunday, and therefore shut, but I scrambled through a hole in the board fence, and found myself in the enclosure. Just the place. It was full of Marshal Neils, Bon Sileries, Jacqueminots, tea, moss, musk, tube, and prim and other roses. It was in fact an *embarras de choix.*"

1st Sister (aside). "That's French."

2d Sister (aside). "Result of travel."

Merchant. "Finally I selected this one, (*takes it from Beauty*) which, being artificial, I thought more likely to keep. It came off hard, on account of the wire, and I was obliged to use my patent knife with screw-driver attached before I got it off the branch (*gives rose back*). As I succeeded, I heard a low *growl* behind me!—oh, my children!"

All. "Oh, don't stop, papa!"

Merchant. " And turning round, I beheld the — Proprietor of the Gardens ! "

All. " Oh, papa ! "

Merchant. " And oh, my children ! What do you think he was ? — A BEAST ! "

[*All shriek.*]

1st Sister. " What kind of a Beast, papa? there are Beasts and Beasts."

2d Sister. " Don't interrupt ! it's such a bother. Go on, papa ! "

Merchant. " Well, my children, he was the very worst kind of a Beast. I have seen Beasts in the Zoological Gardens — but I won't describe him; you'll see him soon enough ! "

All. " See him ! "

Merchant. Yes, and I must be brief. Suffice it to say that he was very wroth at my taking the rose ; said it was a particular one that he was saving for seed. In vain I showed him that it was double, and wouldn't have any. All contradiction seemed to irritate him farther. At last he said I might keep it, on one condition. Oh, my children " —

All. " Go on, go on, papa ! "

Merchant. "That, in addition to thirty-five cents, the regular price for a Jacqueminot, I should *give him* the first thing I met on my return to my own house. (*Speaking rapidly, as if in a hurry to get through.*) Of course I thought it would be the dog from next door who always *is* on our front steps — never occurred to me it would be anything else, and a good chance to get rid of him. So I said, all right, and hastened to catch my train. Now, as it is just time for the next from Sahara (*looking at his watch*) he may be here any minute, and — oh, my children " —

All. " Well, well, papa."

Merchant. " Don't you see? don't you understand? The first thing I saw was

BEAUTY!!"

[*All shriek. Violent ringing at the door-bell. Growls, and a thumping sound on the stairs. Enter at back the* BEAST.

TABLEAU.

PROUD SISTERS.   BEAST.
(*hands and eyes uplifted*).   MERCHANT (*kneeling to Beast*).
     BEAUTY (*in a swoon on the floor*).

[*Curtain falls.*]

Scene II.— *The Garden of the Beast. This can be easily represented by moving back all the natural furniture of the room, and introducing a few pots with plants in them. If none are at hand, let all the scenery be the work of the imagination.*

Enter Beauty, gathering roses. She is now dressed in a long, trailing skirt which she manages awkwardly, and her hair is put up on the top of her head:

Beauty. "Now I can pick all the roses I like. I have already a rose-cake under every bed-post. What a kind Beast! He says he only spoke so fiercely to papa, in order to get some little girl to come and live with him. It seems little girls always run to meet their papas first. His voice is rather gruff, to be sure, but I'm going to get him to try Brown's Bronchial Troches. Oh, here he comes.

Beast (with a very growling voice). "Good morning, my dear. Did you sleep well?"

Beauty. "Oh, yes, splendidly. And when I got up I found all these good clothes to put on. I have always been longing to wear them long, but sisters would not let me."

Beast. "You are still a child, but a lovely one." (*Smiles and looks languishing.*)

Beauty. "Oh! how you do show your teeth! but they are very white. You never eat children with them, I suppose?"

Beast. "What do you take me for! I am a vegetarian. No, Beauty dear, I only want some society in my garden, and if you will be happy here, it is all I ask."

[*He crouches down before her. She takes a low seat, and scratches his head, pats and pets him. He growls melodiously.*]

Beauty. "Do you know, I think Beasts are nicer than people, that is than sisters."

Beast. "Ah! those sisters! they are cross to you, are they? I should like to tear them limb from limb." (*Growing fierce.*)

Beauty. "Oh, no! don't! you know you are a vegetarian."

Beast. "True. Well, no matter. They can't come here to scold you, and you can do just as you please all the day long. Did you like your breakfast?"

Beauty. "Oh, yes, broiled children and no oatmeal."

Beast. "By the way, there are always peanuts in the pockets of all your dresses."

Beauty. "Are there really? What a dear Beast."

Beast. "Tell me, Beauty, do you think you can be happy in my garden here?"

Beauty. "Yes, indeed, perfectly happy."

Beast. "Is every wish of your heart gratified?"

Beauty (after reflection). "Yes, all but just one."

Beast. "What is that?"

Beauty. "I only wish sisters could see my good clothes."

Beast (growls). "What do you care for those hateful girls?"

Beauty. "Besides, there's papa. I know he misses me."

Beast. "Well, well, sometime you shall go home to see them. But not to-day. You don't want to go to-day?"

Beauty. "Oh, no, I have not explored the Garden yet."

Beast. "No, you have not seen the croquet ground, nor the monkeys, nor the swing."

Beauty. "Oh! how lovely — let's go and see everything."

Beast. "Look here, my dear, as the grounds are very large, extending, in short, from the Mediterranean Sea across the Equator, you may sometime get lost, and not find your way back here to the Rose-Garden."

Beauty. "Oh, dear me! I'm so sorry I have neglected my geography. I never got as far as Africa before. But it takes so long to get through the United States!"

Beast (scratching his head). "That's it. You never study the geography of a place until you have been there, and then you know it without studying. But as I was saying (*taking ring from one of his large ears*), that is where I keep things,—this ring you can wear always, and whenever you want me you have only to turn it round and wish for me, and I shall come."

Beauty. "Would it not be nice if you could do that to make some people go away?"

Beast. "Yes, but that is harder. Moreover, whenever you turn your ring you can wish yourself to any place on the time-table—to your father's for instance."

Beauty. "What, without any travelling?"

Beast. "Yes, as we came you know. Don't you remember? we did not come in a palace car?"

Beauty. "To be sure; how odd." (*Puts on ring.*)

Beast. "But be careful about turning it, for you might get there without meaning to."

Beauty. "Yes, and I want to time it when papa is at home."

Beast. "Very well, but now, Beauty (*growing tender, and putting out a paw*), I want to ask you something. If you are happy here, with visits home now and then, couldn't you live here with me?"

Beauty. "Oh, yes! I thought I had got to."

Beast. "Yes, but I mean—oh, Beauty! (*falling on his knees*), can you, can't you love me? Can't you marry me?"

[*Stamps her foot. Beast rolls over on his back in great grief and kicking.*]

Beauty (*starting up*). "What! marry you! Marry a Beast! Never! never! never!!" Take me away! Take me away! Take me home! (*Suddenly remembers to turn the ring, which she must do very conspicuously.*) Oh my ring! how lucky."

[*Curtain falls quickly.*]

Scene III. — *Merchant's house. Same as Scene 1st. If there is a piano in the room, 2d Sister may be drumming on it; but this is not important. 1st Sister is trying on a shawl at the glass.*

[*Enter* Merchant, *hat, muffler and umbrella as before.*]

Merchant (*cheerfully*). "Well, girls, here is a telegram from your sister — that is — from — (*Reads.*) 'Arrived safely. Beauty in good spirits.'
'BEAST.'
That's encouraging, that's encouraging — but oh, my children!" (*Weeps.*)

1st Sister. "Come, pa, don't take on so."

2d Sister. "What's the use making such a bother."

Merchant. "But here are her little toys; here is her doll!" (*Exit.*)

1st Sister. "It can't be so very bad; a Beast that sends telegrams must be different from the ordinary tiger of the jungle."

2d Sister. "Oh yes, and Beauty is fond of animals."

Merchant. "Yes, yes, my daughters, very true. I have been thinking of it all night. That place where he lives was not like the Zoological Gardens. There was no smell of the animals."

1st Sister. "While he was here, you know, he stood upon his hind legs all the time."

2d Sister. "And I did not dare to ask him to sit down."

Merchant. "His visit was brief, very brief. And he took Beauty away. Oh, my children!" (*Weeps.*)

1st Sister. "There you are, at it again?"

2d Sister. "We can't keep consoling you, papa."

Merchant. "There was certainly something uncommon about him. A *je ne sais quoi*."

2 Sisters (*aside*). "French again!"

Merchant. "I had all the time, did not you my daughters? the feeling one has in associating with persons of distinction. I seemed almost to see a decoration in his button-hole on the left breast."

1st Sister. "How absurd, papa, beasts don't have button-holes."

2d Sister. "No, their skins are all *whole*."

Merchant. "Well, well, we must hope for the best. I must go to my office."

[*Wipes eyes, puts away handkerchief, buttons up coat, and takes umbrella. In turning to go out, he kicks the woolly dog. Takes it up and weeps.* "Oh my children!" *Finally, Exit.*]

1st Sister. "What a fuss he makes over these things! Let us throw them out of the window."

2d Sister. "Good idea, and not be bothered with them. Besides, it is something to do. I am tired of my piano. I wish I had said a hand-organ with monkey attachment."

1st Sister. "My dear, the attachment of one Beast is enough for the family."

2d Sister. "Don't pun."

1st Sister. "It is a bad habit. As you say, there is nothing to do, for I have tried on all the clothes in my trunk, so that's played out."

[*They throw the playthings out of the window till none are left.*]

1st Sister (*at the window*). "Oh, do look here! See what is coming up the street! It is a barge! 'The Ocean Queen!'"

2d Sister. "It's stopping here!"

1st Sister. "It's Beauty!"

2d / 1st *Sisters.* } " Back again ! "

[*They run back to the glass and piano, or sofa. Enter* BEAUTY *with stylish little bonnet and parasol.*]

Beauty. " Sisters ! I've come home ! "

2 Sisters. " Oh, so you have ! "

Beauty (*kissing them*). " Aren't you glad to see me ? "

1st Sister. " Oh, yes, only it don't seem long since you left."

2d Sister. " Papa has only just got a telegram to say you arrived."

Beauty (*aside*). " Dear Beast ! how thoughtful of him to send it ! "

1st Sister. " How do you like this shawl, sister ? "

2d Sister. " Oh, well enough. What sort of a place is it, Beauty, where the Beast puts up ? "

1st Sister. " Kind of Barnum's circus, I suppose ? "

2d Sister. " Of course you live in a tent ? "

Beauty. " No, it's *content*."

1st Sister. " When your Beast came in yesterday I was frightened to death. But he was quite meek. I suppose he never was in a house before."

Beauty. " House ! Well no, to be sure, I suppose he never was in a common house like this ; for he lives in a palace."

2d Sister. "I suppose you mean a cage, with bars in front of it."

Beauty. "No, it is strictly temperance. If you'd only let me I would tell you about it."

1st Sister. "My dear, little children should be seen and not heard. Keep your Beast to yourself, only don't talk about him."

2d Sister. "It's very well to tell her to keep her Beast, but her Beast did not keep her long."

Beauty. "Where's papa, don't he miss me?" (*Half crying.*)

1st Sister. "Gone down town of course."

2d Sister. "Now, don't bother, Beauty, but get something to do.

Beauty (*sighs, and looks about her*). "Well where are my playthings? I found my doll on the doorstep, and her nose is broken."

1st & *2d Sisters.* "We threw them all out of the window."

Beauty (*crying*) — "How could you! but — (*smiling again*). I forgot! I came back chiefly to show you my long dress."

[*Shows off her train, and turns round and round.*]

1st Sister (*inspecting her*). "Mm! Old Arab fashions, I suppose; that's as far as they've got in Sahara."

2d Sister (*from the sofa*). "Everything is worn short here now."

1st Sister. "Let's see your hair. Turned up.

Hm! (*Takes off Beauty's bonnet and tries it on herself.*) "Unbecoming thing!" (*Tosses it down.*)

Beauty (*bursting into tears*). "I'm sorry I came! You hateful things. I wish, I almost wish I'd said I would marry the Beast."

[*Comes hastily forward and very distinctly turns her ring round. Tremendous ringing at the door-bell, and bumping sound on the stairs. Sisters scream. Enter* BEAST. BEAUTY *springs forward with joy and embraces his nose with both hands.*]

Beauty. "Oh! I'm so glad."

Beast (*kneels before her*). "Beauty, did you, didn't you say you would almost —— "

Beauty. "Yes, yes, Beast, if you will only take me away again I *will* MARRY YOU!"

2 Sisters. "Marry a Beast!!"

Beast (*suddenly flings away all his fur, pulls off his head, and kneels as a young man in dress suit*). "I am a Prince!"

1st Sister. "What! what."

2d Sister. "Oh, my!"

[*They stand back right and left.*]

[*Enter* MERCHANT. *He extends his arms over Beauty and the Beast who are kneeling.*]

Merchant. "Oh, my children!"

[*Curtain falls.*]

LIVING PICTURES; Or, TABLEAUX.

BY FANNIE M. STEELE.

NOTE. — Living pictures, or tableaux, of the size of easel pictures, are to be shown as if hanging on an ordinary wall, in an ordinary frame.

These may be arranged with charming effect, and may be shown in a small public hall, or a large parlor with very simple appliances. Of course all the beauty depends upon the judicious use of color, and upon a sufficient but still a rather mysterious lighting. In the first place, a gilt, or walnut and gilt, picture frame must be hung in a common doorway, or between two sliding doors closed to the size of the frame, while the space above and below is covered with material of some dark color. The whole wall, or the doors which represent the wall, should also be covered with the same dark color. The picture frame must be hung just so high that by standing on the floor the head of an adult will be in the centre of the frame. Now fasten a wire across the audience room three or four inches in front of your frame. This will hold the curtain, which should be suspended from it with rings. The curtain should be of thick material. Behind the picture frame you will need a firm, high screen made of two uprights of scantling, with a cross-piece on top, and another half way down to strengthen it, and feet to widen the base. This screen should be nine feet high, at least; so high, at all events, that when seated in the front row of seats and looking through the frame, an observer will not be able to see the ceiling beyond. This screen is to hold the materials which form the background of the picture. When the figure is posed, the screen is to be pushed as close to the figure and the picture-frame as possible, to avoid the appearance of depth to the picture; that is, to make the living figure appear as if it were a painting on a flat surface.

We will say that the opening of the frame is thirty inches by twenty-four. Thirty-six by thirty would be better. That may be too large for some of the figures you would like to represent. An inner mat, as it is called, made of building paper with light strips of wood across each end, will be useful. Two screw eyes at the upper corners, corresponding with two screw-hooks in the frame proper, will allow the mats to be easily adjusted. These mats may be covered with gilt paper, the outer rim corresponding with the inner rim of the frame; that is, thirty by twenty-four inches, or thirty-six by thirty, the inner opening being either an oval or a square with rounded corners. This arrangement changes the size and varies the shape of the pictures.

As to the frame itself, if nothing better is at hand, one may be made of pine and covered with brown muslin and gilt paper, imitating a walnut and gilt picture frame. This will be sufficiently good, as the light is to fall only on the picture in the opening, and the audience room will be dark.

Now for the lighting, which is the most important of all. It is best to have a magic lantern so placed in the back of the room that a square of light shall fall upon the opening in the picture frame. An engine head-light will answer a good purpose if its light is bounded by a square opening, so that it throws a square light instead of a circular one. Also a fair arrangement would be two or three bull's-eye lanterns, placed in a close group on a firm, high stand near the frame, a little to the left in front, these so adjusted that their light will fall upon the opening in the picture frame. If the last means of lighting is used, it will be necessary to supplement it by the use of a bracket kerosene lamp, with reflector, so hung that its light will fall upon the person posed in the picture frame, the light falling through the space between the frame and the screen which is to form the background. Of course this lamp and reflector must hang in the room beyond the picture frame. The light must not be *too* intense, as *some* shadows are needed upon the face for beauty. Lights from both sides at once, throw cross shadows which are ruinous to good looks or artistic effect. Light from above is good if it can be screened from the view of the audience, who are to sit in the dark.

THE MANAGERS. First, a chief, who shall stand outside the frame in the audience room, pose the models for the pictures, decide about the colors, ring the bell for music, as well as draw the curtain, enveloping herself in its folds as it slides back.

Second. Head of the dressing-room, who shall, at the beginning of the evening, take care that the costumes are complete, each group of articles laid by itself, and ticketed according to the numbers of the programme, 1, 2, 3, etc. It should be her business to see, also, that the models for at least three pictures ahead should stand dressed and waiting : this to avoid the tiresome delays that occur between tableaux.

Third. Manager of the background shades, who shall remove one background and supply the next expeditiously. A step-ladder or some firm boxes will be needed for this purpose.

Fourth. A musician, who should have her notes placed in the order required on the piano, which should stand behind scenes.

Each officer should have a programme, relating only to her own peculiar duties, fastened up at her post of duty. She should understand her business thoroughly, and never turn aside from it. Then there will be no need of the noise of questions, nor the delay of confusion.

DIRECTIONS.— When the picture is posed satisfactorily by the chief, she is to ring a bell for silence in the audience ; a second bell for the music, which plays a strain or two till all are in the mood of its sentiment, then another bell, and the chief will herself draw the curtain, while the music continues till the curtain is closed for the last time. Then each officer rushes to her own work, and the next picture is soon ready for exhibition.

In the first evening's entertainment here given, the names of the artists may be announced, if the original pictures are closely copied. For instance: "The Duchess of Devonshire," by Gainsborough, the portrait lately stolen; or, "Cherubs," by Sir Joshua Reynolds; or, "Betty," by Nichols; or, "Italian Girl," by Fortuny, etc.

LIVING PICTURES.

PROGRAMME.

PART I.

OPENING MUSIC: A piano solo.

Tableaux.	*Music.*
1. EGYPTIAN GIRL.	Strauss Waltz.
2. MAUDE MULLER.	Last Smile, by Wollerhaupt.
3. BLESSED ARE THEY THAT MOURN.	A melody, by Rubinstein.
4. DUCHESS OF DEVONSHIRE.	La Gazelle, by Hoffman.
5. EVA AND TOPSY.	Shoo-fly.
6. WHAT THE DAISY LIVED TO SEE.	We met by chance.
7. CHERUBS.	I want to be an Angel; or, Les Deux Anges.

PART II.

OPENING MUSIC: Monastery Bells.

Tableaux.	*Music.*
1. A NUN.	Avé Maria.
2. BETTY, THE MILKMAID.	Comin' through the rye.
3. ORIENTAL GIRL.	Traumerei.
4. MARGUERITE.	Airs from Faust.
5. MIGNON.	How can I leave thee.
6. SPANISH LADY.	La Manola.
7. ITALIAN GIRL.	Il Bacio.
8. THE RESCUE.	The Erl King.

DESCRIPTION.

Costumes, Positions and Backgrounds.

1. EGYPTIAN GIRL.

Represented by a brunette with sparkling black eyes, dressed in a cream-colored embroidered robe, bordered with deep maroon velvet, arms bare, several pairs of armlets and bangles upon them, black Spanish lace veil over hair which must be dressed very high to support it, ear rings, coin necklace, coins on band across forehead. The jewels may be made of gilt paper.

Pose. She stands with body in profile, facing left, left hand on hip, elbow straight forward. Right hand drawing veil half across her face.

Background. A Persian rug or its imitation, or a gay striped pink and green bit of drapery. Use the mat with rounded corners for this picture.

It is only necessary to costume the figures to the waistline or a few inches below it. If it is impossible to copy the descriptions given, which were once actually carried out with great success, try to adhere to the colors, varying, if necessary, the detail.

2. MAUD MULLER.

She may be a sun-burned girl with expressive dark eyes.

Dress. A pale calico waist of no particular color, sleeves rolled up. Faded red silk handkerchief tied about the neck loosely, and a torn, wide, sunburned, straw hat.

Pose. She leans forward on a fence, chin buried in right palm, a longing look upon her face as if the Judge were disappearing in the distance, "It might have been" in her eyes. The wood-cut in one of the early volumes of *The Aldine* may be consulted.

Background. Pale blue sky. Something made to simulate a fence and a rake handle leaning against it, at her left.

3. Blessed are they that mourn.

Composed of two figures, the first an angel who should be a golden haired girl with wings attached to her shoulders, and her dress or drapery cream colored. Second, a brunette, pale and thin, prominent nose. She should be draped in dove color. medium tint, over head and arms like sleeves with a fold of white cambric underneath, next the face.

Pose. Angel with wings spread forward, hands expressing support, eyes uplifted, expression prayerful. This figure stands behind. The mourner kneels in an attitude of grief, hands clasped. She should seem entirely unconscious of the presence of the angel although her head touches the angel's breast, or the head may fall forward on the clasped hands. A French picture, L'Intercesseur, is a good model.

Background. Maroon color. Mat, oval. A pedestal table will be needed to support the mourner's hands. The wings may be white muslin stretched upon a wire frame with a few touches of India ink wash to represent feathers.

4. Duchess of Devonshire.

A bewitching, pretty girl in a blue silk waist (Marie Louise blue), with square neck and elbow sleeves, white illusion lace drawn over shoulders in a point, fastened with pink flowers in front. An extremely wide brimmed hat of black velvet turned up at one side with nodding plumes. A farmer's straw hat lined with velveteen will answer the purpose. Hair powered and curled and fastened irregularly.

Pose. She stands facing the left, head turned toward audience. Copy Gainsborough's portrait. Do not spoil this by a dark blue dress which will not light up.

Background. Fawn color. Mat with rounded corners.

5. Eva and Topsy.

Eva in white, with long yellow curls. Topsy in burlap and wig, one coral earring in her ear. It would be far better, of course, if there was no need of wig and burnt cork.

Pose. Eva holds up her finger while chiding Topsy for stealing Rosa's earring. Topsy grinning turns her ear to show Eva the wonderful ornament.

Background. A light fawn color. No mat.

6. WHAT THE DAISY LIVED TO SEE.

First figure is a young man with a straw hat having a blue band, ordinary suit of clothes. Second, a young girl in blue dress, white Swiss muslin basque with black velvet sash, hat fallen off, croquet mallet under her arm.

Pose. The young man stands in profile, with croquet mallet over his shoulders, looking down delightfully at the young girl who puts a daisy in his button hole, while she looks shyly but lovingly up to his face.

Background. Dark green. No mat.

7. CHERUBS.

Background. A frame corresponding with the opening of the picture frame, covered with gray cambric on which is fastened clouds of white tarleton. This hung in the frame like a mat. Before the clouds are fastened on, make three openings in this background by cross cuts like this figure X one of which should be above — and two underneath. Three little heads are to be pushed through these openings and a pair of little wings fastened at the side of each opening.

The children must be supported at the right height by boxes; the upper head looks down and should be covered with light curls; one of the lower cherubs looks up, the other straight forward. The wings may be made of white wiggin and feathers drawn upon them. They should be fastened to the background with pins.

Or, in place of the last, the Sistine Cherubs may be represented by two pretty negro children in the attitude of the famous cherubs, and with little black wings fastened to their shoulders.

Background. A flannel blanket with two green festoon-like curtains draped across the upper corners.

This is very amusing, as the black eyes never fail to be very expressive. Since the light is directly in the face of the models, and the audience sit in the dark, it is impossible for them to recognize friends in the company, therefore, it is easy for them to hold any expression, not being confused.

PART II.

1. THE NUN.

May be a mild-faced blonde with large, liquid eyes. First pin a band of white muslin across the forehead concealing all hair. Then take three yards of white cambric, using it wrong side out, and pin it round the face, pinning it under the chin; let it hang smoothly to her hips, then bring it back over her wrists and pin for flowing sleeves. A black shawl is then laid over the head and in the same way over the wrists. This is a simple way to represent a nun's dress.

Pose. Hands are lifted in prayer, with a crucifix clasped in them, and a rosary hanging from them. The head thrown back, eyes tearfully uplifted.

Background. Fawn color. Mat, oval.

2. BETTY.

A rosy, plump girl in light calico, with a thin white kerchief tied above a pointed-necked dress, wide straw hat caught up at one side with poppies and daisies, short sleeves or rather sleeves rolled up.

Pose. Body to the left, milk pail under right arm filled with field flowers, while she seems to be singing on the way.

Background. Pale blue as of sky.

4. ORIENTAL BEAUTY.

A dark, sallow, black-eyed girl in a light brocade dress, red sash tied once straight about the waist, crossed behind and brought forward and tied again in front two or three inches below the waist. Red and yellow crape turban. Let her have a large, gay fan of oriental design. She is to appear seated among cushions of gay colors. Two chairs, so placed that they do not prevent the screen being drawn up close to the figure, should have a narrow board on which the model is to be posed with her feet lying toward the left, as if raising herself on her left elbow.

Background. Olive brown. No mat.

4. MARGUERITE.

A sweet-faced, light-haired girl, with two braids hanging down; in a white square-necked dress with chemisette tied with drawing string. The sleeves should be tight sleeves, with a pointed cuff of the same falling over the hand and puffs at the elbow.

Pose. She faces the left and holds a daisy, as if she were saying, "He loves me, he loves me not."

Background. Dark green. Oval mat.

5. MIGNON.

A young girl with fluffy, black hair combed back loosely only confined by a narrow band of red. A dark blue waist, low round neck with chemisette, and light blue apron across her lap.

Pose. Seated with elbows on knee, an expression of homesickness, longing for Italy.

Background. A very light cold gray.

6. A SPANISH LADY.

A pretty, regular-featured girl, a brunette, with red satin waist, black veil draped over high comb, little water curls at the ear, a rose at one side of hair in the veil. Fan and jewels.

Pose. She seems to have just passed through a curtain which she still holds in one hand and looks forward as if from a balcony, her fan spread in the other hand.

Background. Green, with fawn color draped across it like a curtain, drawn at one side in a festoon.

7. Italian Contadina.

A dark girl, in brown peasant waist, gay Roman apron, round-necked chemisette, white sleeves to the elbow, gold beads, a red Italian head-dress made of flannel, folded about six inches wide and laid on the top of the head and allowed to hang to shoulders behind; a similar fold of white cloth is underneath of the same width. Red coral bells for ears and coral bracelets. The hair should be divided in half behind and braided, then each braid brought forward around and above the ears and fastened again behind, underneath head-dress.

Pose. As if leaning against a wall, hands folded behind head.

Background. Stone color.

8. The Rescue.

First figure is a fireman in wide hard leather hat and red shirt with dingy face, descending a ladder with a little, curly-headed child tucked awkwardly under his arm. The child in a night-gown. Both figures expressive of fear and danger. The ladder must be firmly fixed close as possible to the frame. No drapery on background screen, but a few blackened boards leaning carelessly as if fallen by chance. Red fire on a tin plate should be burned at the back of the screen, the illumination and smoke being very effective.

Singing may be introduced between the parts of the programme.

With this as an example many similar entertainments will no doubt be suggested. One, showing the prominent characters of the Old Testament, would be very effective and make a lasting impression.

A BIRD CONCERT.

NOTE. — So called because birds are to furnish much of the music, and because the solos, recitations and dialogues are all concerning birds, or bear their names.

The stage and concert hall should be made very beautiful and forest-like by decorations consisting of small trees, boughs and flowers, wreaths of evergreen, of oak leaves and arbor-vitæ. As many canary birds, in their cages, as can be obtained for the occasion, twenty or thirty perhaps, should be hung at the front of the stage and at regular distances down the hall. The cages of some, at least, should be covered, and the hall darkened until time for curtain to rise. Then turn on the gas, uncover the birds, and you have the opening chorus of the evening, a delightful flutter of song, which will continue fitfully during the evening but will always prove a harmonious accompaniment, especially to a vocal solo.

The stage should represent a grove or garden. This effect can be produced by small trees and potted plants, a large rock, green drugget or carpet on the floor, etc. Stuffed birds of all varieties should be placed here and there amid the green.

Upon the sides of the stage near the foot-lights, place the larger fowls such as ducks, swans, pelicans, an eagle overhead.

The piano may represent a bank of vines and flowers as it stands across the left-hand corner of the stage, so that the pianist is seen from the audience in profile. The pianist and soloist should enter hand in hand, salute the audience, and take their positions gracefully. In case of a piano solo, some one will enter with the pianist, draw out the stool, and stand at the right to turn the leaves of the music. On rising to leave, the face of the pianist should be kept toward the audience as long as possible.

PROGRAMME.

PART I.

1. PIANO SOLO. Birdie Darling. *Schmidt*
    or, The Prisoner and Swallow. *Croiser.*
2. CHORUS. Go, Birdie, tell Winnie I'm waiting; or, Don't you see me coming?
    G. F. Root.
3. DECLAMATION IN COSTUME. Jimmy Butler, and The Owl.
4. SOLO AND CHORUS. Come, Birdie, come; *White.*
    or, Robin Redbreast. *J. M. Hubbard.*
5. SOLO. Lover and the Bird. *Guelielmo.*
6. TWO TABLEAUX. The Babes in the Wood.

PART II.

1. PIANO SOLO. Wild Bird's Song; *Warnelink.*
    or, If I were a bird I'd fly to thee. *Henselt.*
2. PART SONG. The Sky-lark; *Barnabee.*
    or, Quartette: The night-birds whisper soft and low. *White.*
3. SOLO. Bird of Beauty; *M. R. Scott.*
    or, The Nightingale's trill. *Ganz.*
4. SOLO. The Bird that came in Spring; *Benedict.*
    or, Messenger Swallow. *Balfe.*
5. Which bird would you rather be? From *The Jimmy Johns* (a little book by Mrs. Diaz).

DESCRIPTION OF PROGRAMME.

PART I.

1. Gives a selection of solos, both rather ambitious pieces; suitable for one of the older girls of the Sunday-school.

2. The first is a pretty chorus for little girls from eight to eleven. The second a very simple solo and chorus for the same.

3. A good declamation for a boy of sixteen. He should have ragged clothes, a stick and a bundle, and a dilapidated silk hat, which he holds in his hand and then puts on the floor of the stage. This may be found in Howard's Recitations, a collection of comic sermons and pathetic pieces published by Happy Hours Company, No. 1 Chambers Street, New York.

4. The first is a solo and chorus for girls of ten, the second a simple solo.

5. Is a solo for an older pupil or teacher, the second for a cultivated voice.

6. The first tableau is a forest scene. Two little boys of four and six, or six and seven, are seen hugging close together in fright, while the stage is dark, and a fitful magnesium light and the roll of a gong imitate a storm. In the second tab-

leau the children apparently lie dead, with their heads upon boughs, while stuffed robins are arranged to run down wires and cross the stage with leaves in their mouths. The following verses are read behind the curtain, one before each tableau :

>Poets tell a simple story
>>Of two babes who long ago
>Wandered through a forest hoary
>>Where the meek-eyed violets blow.
>There the night came down and found them
>>Far from home with weary feet,
>Spread her stormy mantle round them
>>And then laid them down to sleep.

>Soon God's angels, winged reapers,
>>In the storm and in the cold,
>Sought the little tired sleepers,
>>Bore them to their Father's fold.
>Then the robins, sweet-voiced mourners,
>>Softly spread a leafy shroud,
>Woven by the autumn sunbeams,
>>Tinted like a twilight cloud.

Part II.

1. The first is not a difficult number, and the second is a selection for a good pianist.

2. Is a somewhat difficult piece for a double quartette, and and the second is suitable for large pupils.

3. Is an old song, but one rarely well sung. The warble should be fluent and sweet, and instead of it may be sung the nightingale's trill, a solo for a cultivated voice.

4. Offers a choice of songs for an older pupil.

5. Is an interesting, sprightly dialogue for little folks from five to twelve, very easy to learn as each child has but few

sentences to commit. The children should be gracefully posed and drilled by teachers. The part of each child should be written out, with the sense of what was said by the last speaker for a clue, these separate parts taken home by the children to commit to memory. If the children enter into it with spirit, as they doubtless will, the effect is very pleasing. It has been successfully repeated in the same town and to full houses; and, what is of more importance, the children are entertained and benefited by learning to have happy times in innocent ways.

WHICH BIRD WOULD YOU RATHER BE?

(Reprinted by permission.)

A DIALOGUE.

SPEAKERS.

MARY.	EDITH.	EVA.	FRED.
DOLLY.	CAROLINE.	MINNIE.	ARTHUR.
DORA.	HETTIE.	JOE.	JOHNNY.
		GUSSIE.	

MARY, CAROLINE, DOLLY *and* DORA *are the largest, among the girls:* MINNIE *and* EVA *the smallest.* FRED *and* JOE *are the largest boys;* JOHNNY *is the smallest.*

SCENE. *At recess, or waiting for school to begin. Mary and Hettie are sitting together with Mary's arm around Hettie. Johnnie stands whittling. Gussie is seated with open book in hand. Dolly occasionally swings her hat by one string. Caroline sits with slate before her. Fred leans back in his chair and sharpens a lead-pencil. Arthur stands winding a ball, unravelling a stocking. Minnie sits on a low stool playing with a few flowers. The children should be arranged in such a way that there shall be no stiffness in the general effect. They may move about a very little and gesticulate. Two figures should stand in the middle of the stage at the back, several be seated toward front of the stage, turning slightly to right and left. Confused noise of talking behind the curtain.*

[*Curtain rises.*]

Mary (as if continuing conversation). "Now, I should rather be a robin. He sings so pretty a song! Everybody likes to hear a robin sing. I don't believe even a boy would shoot a robin."

Johnny. "'Course he wouldn't!"

Minnie. "Robin red-breast covered up the two little childuns when they got lost in the woods."

Caroline. "And they don't do like other birds, live here all summer and have a good time, and then fly off and leave us. They stay by."

Gussie. "How do you know that?"

Caroline. "Oh, I've heard they stay in swamps and barns, waiting for the spring. Don't you remember? (*Sings.*)

The north wind doth blow, and we shall have snow,
And what will the robin do then, poor thing?
He will sit in the barn, and keep himself warm,
And hide his head under his wing, poor thing."

[*Others join in the song, one or two at a time, until all are singing.*]

Mary. "Yes, he comes close up to our back door and eats the crumbs, and perches on the apple-tree boughs. Mamma says, 'it seems as if he were one of the family.'"

Dolly. "Now I should a great deal rather be a swallow and fly away. Then I would fly down South, where the oranges grow, and figs, and sugar-cane, and see all the wonderful sights. And I'd go to the beautiful, sunny islands over the seas."

Johnny. "You'd get tired, may be, and drop down into the water."

Joe. "No, he'd light on the topmasts of ships, that's the way they do."

Dolly. "'Twould be a great deal better than living in a barn all winter."

Dora. "Oh, this morning I saw the prettiest bird I ever saw in all my life. Oh, if he wasn't pretty! Father said it was a Baltimore oriole. Part of him was black and part of him red as fire. Oh, he *was* a beauty! If ever I am a bird I'll be an oriole."

Arthur. " Uncle Daniel calls him the hang-fire bird."

Fred. " That's because his nest hangs down from the bough like a bag."

Caroline. " Don't you know what that's for? Where they came from, down in the torrid zone, they build their nests that way so the monkeys and serpents can't get their eggs."

Arthur. " I've got a hang-bird's egg!"

Edith. " Do they have red eggs?"

Fred. " No, black and white. My father calls him the golden robin."

Caroline. " I tell you what I'd be — a mocking bird—and I tell you why—because a mocking bird can sing every time he hears. It does vex me so when I hear a pretty tune and can't sing it! Sometimes I can remember one line and then I can't rest till I get the whole. Mother says I ought to have been born a mocking bird."

Fred. " Of course, Caroline would want to *carol.*"

[*Groans and cries of " O, Fred" by the others.*]

Caroline. " Mother says he can whistle to the dog, and chirp like a chicken, or scream like a hawk, and can imitate any kind of sound, filing or planing, or anything."

Mary. " And he can sing sweeter than a nightingale."

Arthur. "I'd be a lark, for he goes up highest."

Fred. "He has a low enough place to start from."

Caroline. "I know it, 'way down on the ground 'mongst the grass."

Dolly. "No matter what a low place he starts from so long as he gets up high at last! Don't you know Lincoln?"

Joe. "I know what I'd be — some kind of a water-fowl, then I could go to sea."

Johnny. "You better be a coot."

Fred. "Or, one of Mother Carey's chickens."

Joe. "No; I'd be that great, strong bird (I forget his name) that flies and flies over the great ocean and never stops to rest, through storms and darkness right overhead. *He* doesn't have to take in sail or cut away the masts. I'd be an albatross. Guss, what do you think about it?"

Guss. "Well, I think I'd be an ostrich, then I can run and fly both together."

Arthur. "And you wouldn't be afraid to eat things."

Guss. "No, that's so. They swallow down leather, stones, old iron, and nothing ever hurts them."

Dolly. "I heard of one swallowing a lady's parasol once."

Johnny. "But they'd pull out your feathers."

Guss. "No matter, the girls have to have them for their hats."

Johnny. " I know what I'd be. I'd be an owl, then I could sit up late at night."

Hettie. " You'd be scared of the dark."

Johnny. " 'Twouldn't be dark if I was an owl."

Mary " Can't you play enough daytimes ? "

Johnny. " Oh, daytimes isn't good for anything. They have all the fun after we're gone to bed. I and Charlie "—

Fred. " ' Twont do for little boys to hear every thing that goes on."

Guss. " You little fellows are apt to make a noise and disturb us."

Hettie. " Mother says if I weren't a chatterbox I could stay up later. *I'd* choose to be a parrot, for parrots can talk just when they want to, and have blue wings and green wings, and red and yellow and all colors."

Edith. " I'd rather be a canary bird, because they have sponge cake and sugar plums every day."

Hettie. " Oh, I wouldn't be a canary bird, shut up in a cage ! "

Dora. " I'd rather live on dry sticks."

Minnie. " My mamma's got a canary bird, and he sings, and he's yellow."

Hettie. " Parrots are the prettiest."

Mary. " Why doesn't somebody be a flamingo ? He is flame-colored."

Arthur. " I should think some of you girls would want to be a peacock."

Fred. *I* know who seems like a peacock — Nannie Watkins — I saw her stepping off the other day just as proud — about seventeen flounces and yellow kids and yellow boots and curls and streamers — (*first looking at his dress, then at his hands, then at his boots*) this way (*imitates*).

Dolly. " Well, if some girls are peacocks, some boys are hawks. I saw that great Joshua Lowe come pouncing down on a flock of little boys yesterday and do every thing he could think of to 'em, just to show he could master them."

Mary. " And if you want a crow-fighter take Andy Barrows; he's always picking a quarrel."

Dora. " I know it, I've heard him. ' Come on,' he says, ' come on, I'll fight yer.' " (*Imitates.*)

Caroline. " I think as a general thing girls behave better than boys. What do you think, little Minnie? You don't say much."

Minnie (*looking up from her flowers*). " I'd be a humming bird."

Edith. " She thinks we are talking about birds."

Caroline. " And what would you be a humming bird for?"

Minnie. " 'Cause they're so pretty and cunning."

Hettie. " So they are, Minnie."

Minnie. " And they keep within the flowers all the time, and eat honey."

Edith. " My brother found a humming bird's nest; oh, inside it was just as soft as wool! And little bits of white eggs, just like little bits of white beans."

Dora (*looking at Eva and taking her hand*). "Now here's a little girl sitting still all this time, and not saying a word."

Caroline. "I know it. Isn't she a dear little girl?" (*Stroking her hair.*)

Mary. "She ought to be a dove, she is so gentle and still."

Dolly. "You dear little pigeon-dove, what would *you* be?"

Eva (*looking up*). "I'd be a sparrow."

Mary. "You would? And what would you be a sparrow for?"

Eva. "'Cause my mamma says, not a sparrow falls to the ground."

[*Girls look at each other.*]

Dolly (*softly*). "Isn't she cunning?"

Mary and Dora. "I think she is just as cunning as can be."

Joe. "Fred has not said what he'd be yet."

Fred. "Eagle. He's the grandest of all. He can fly in the face of the sun."

Johnny. "Eagles can beat every other bird."

Joe. "Of course, Fred would't be anything short of an eagle."

Fred. "No, nor anything short of the American eagle."

All the boys. " Three cheers for the American eagle." (*Rising.*)

All together. " Hurrah, hurrah, hurrah! "

[*Curtain falls; or, if there be no curtain, a boy rushes in to say that the organ-man is coming and they all rush out.*]

ANOTHER BIRD CONCERT.

This concert could be given in the afternoon. In that case there would be a better chance for its spirited performance, especially for the smaller children.

In some localities music and recitation might be successfully undertaken when tableaux would be impracticable. The following list might be available:

"The bird let loose in Eastern skies." A duet.	*Shaw.*
"Sing, birdie, sing." A solo.	*Ganz.*
"Who's at my window?" A solo.	*Osborne.*
[The last two for trained voices.]	
"Fly forth, oh gentle dove," and, "The Swallow." Solos.	*Pinsuti.*
"Oh Swallow, happy swallow." A duet.	*Kucken.*
"Flee as a bird to your mountain."	
"One morning, oh, so early." A solo.	*Gatty.*
(This composition is a Bird Concert in itself; the words by *Jean Ingelow*.)	
"Sing, sweet bird."	*Ganz.*
"Beautiful bird, sing on."	*Howe.*
"Like a lark." A duet.	*Franz Abt.*

Many of the above are to be found in "Gems of English Song."

For suitable recitations the first three verses of a "A Bird's-eye View" might be used as a dialogue. It may be found in Whittier's Child Life.

"Sing on, blithe bird." To be found in Child Life.	*Motherwell.*
"To a Waterfowl."	*W. C. Bryant.*
"Who stole the Bird's nest?" might be divided among six little people.	
	L. Maria Child.

"The little Maiden and the little Birds" may be used as a dialogue. "The Brown Thrush," by *Lucy Larcom*, and "Robert of Lincoln," by *Bryant*, are also exceedingly appropriate. All these are to be found in that admirable collection of children's classics by *Whittier*. The readers of St. Nicholas, Wide Awake, The Youth's Companion, and other periodicals for children, will find many other available articles published since Child Life was issued in 1875.

A PORTRAIT OF A FELLOW-CITIZEN;

Or, THE ARTIST AND THE CRITICS.

ANNOUNCEMENT.

"A portrait of a fellow-citizen will now be unveiled for the first time. A few of our art critics have been asked to express their opinions about it."

The portrait is represented by a young man with decided features, who sits in profile behind a frame, while a background of plain dark-brown muslin is hung behind his head as close up to the frame as possible. The wrong side of glazed cambric must be used, but woolen is better, reflecting no light.

The artist stands with palette, maul stick, and brushes in his hand —has a velvet coat, smoking cap, etc. He receives the criticisms with suave politeness, is Frenchy in accent and shrug of shoulders, would wish to suit his friends exactly, etc.

The critics do not remember the subject as having so prominent a forehead, are sure the nose is a little too long —" Ah, yes, that is better." "We think the chin should recede a little more." " The portrait is rather young looking, has not the lines of character in it which mark our much esteemed fellow-citizen, etc., etc."

The artist is much obliged for the kind criticism, and very willingly makes the necessary changes. His palette is arranged beforehand, with brown paint exactly matching the background, with flesh tint, and with a soft brownish gray, to deepen the lines of the face, The changes are made upon the face of the person sitting. Brown paint is used where the line altered touches the background, with flesh tint where it does not. In a few moments all trace of the original is gone, and the effect is ludicrous in the extreme.

The artist is very grateful and begs to present to the audience the finished portrait of their distinguished friend Mr. ——, announcing the name of the subject. Of course the original of the portrait is perfectly still all this time preserving a stolid expression.

The critics express themselves delighted, think their advice has been of great value, and declare the portrait is more life-like than before.

This instructive lesson in the value of art criticism is appropriately added to an entertainment of tableaux through a picture frame. If the Songs of Seven is illustrated in this way, the unveiling of a portrait will make an entertaining close to the entertainment.

MOTHER GOOSE ENTERTAINMENT.

(COMBINED FROM MRS. WHITNEY AND OTHERS.)

Before the curtain rises some skilful piano-player behind the scenes should give a medley of Mother Goose airs from Mother Goose Melodies by Elliot, The Baby's Opera, or Mrs. Partington's Edition, choosing only those which are set to the original rhymes. Later productions may be very pretty, but are out of place in an entertainment belonging strictly to Mother Goose.

When the curtain is raised it discloses the old lady herself, dressed in a short red skirt, with high colored, large figured over-dress looped up all around, a long pointed bodice, short flowing sleeves, striped stockings, low pointed slippers with high heels, a white cap with a broad frill, over this a black hat running to a point about a foot high, with a large buckle in front, and a small round black cape over one shoulder. She carries a cane and wears glasses, indeed, as nearly like the pictures of her as may be. She comes hobbling in, and approaching the front of the stage recites:

> You'd scarce expect one of my age
> To speak in public on the stage;

But I'm the children's much loved poet
And hope all future years will show it.
I trust, dear friends, you welcome me
The jolly friend of infancy;
Rocking your cradle times without number
My "Lullaby, Baby" soothed you to slumber,
"Patty cake, patty cake," taught you to frolic,
And "High-diddle-diddle" charmed away colic.
The little pet with chubby feet
Rosy and dimpled, soft and sweet,
The wasted child of want and woe —
All loved my music long ago.
And just as fresh and new to-day
Is little Boy Blue asleep in the hay,
Or Jacky Horner, or Johnny Tucker,
Like any boy who wants his supper.

  Not only the little toddlers
   Perched high on papa's knee
  Bound for a ride to London town
   On childish journeys go;
    For we all go up, up, up,
     And all go down, down, down-y,
    And all go backward and forward,
     And all go round, round, round-y.

  Still do we search for sunbeams
   And learn the rattle's trick;
  The great, big watch of Father Time
   How we love to hear it tick!

  So pat-a-cake for our Tommy,
   And pat-a-cake for ourself —
  For that alone we labor and strive
   And hoard up our golden pelf.

This little pig goes to market,
   This little pig stays at home,
And we all cry, " Wee," for our mammy
   Wherever we chance to roam.

We seek our bed with Sleepy-head,
   We stay awhile with Slow,
And fill the pot with Greedy, glad
   To sup before we go.

When Jack and Jill go up the hill
   To fetch their pail of water;
As sure as Jack comes tumbling down
   Poor Jill comes tumbling after.

Mistress Marys are still contrary,
   Marjorie Daws still sell;
Mother Hubbards ransack their cupboards,
   For bones for their ne'er-do-well.

" What do you want ? " " A pot of beer ? "
   Alack the bitter wrong!
That grenadier an army hath
   Of many a million strong!

Our wise men into brambles stroll,
   Do jump with might and main;
And those who go to sea in bowls
   Rarely come back again.

And don't some hearts, deploring
   The things that gnaw and harrow,
Let fall the wheelbarrow, wife and all
   When lanes are rough and narrow?

Ah yes! The old rhymes suit us
    As well as ever they did;
For the jist of our lives, from first to last,
    Is under their jingle hid;
        As we all go up, up, up,
            As we all go down, down, down-y,
        As we all go backward and forward,
            As we go round, round, round-y.

Some men may strive for grander thought,
    But six times out of every seven
My old philosophy hath taught
    All they can master, this side heaven.

They use my quills and leave me out,
    Forgetting that I wear the wings;
Or, that a Goose has been about
    When every little gosling sings,

And generations, yet to come,
Will bless my name, in happy homes;
And wise and prudent ones to nursery use
Devote the lyrics of old Mother Goose.

I'll prove the nursery poet still,
Cackling forever with the same good will,
Giving good counsel in a foolish way
And solemn warning in the guise of play.

Though always with you in the ancient song;
My stay from Dreamland must not be long
So then before my parting leave I take
Look on these pictures for my sake.

With a gesture of warning she goes on:

Hark, hark!
The dogs do bark;
The beggars are coming to town
Some in rags,
Some in tags,
And some in velvet gown.

Music strikes up, playing the Gypsy Chorus from Bohemian Girl; it continues while a group of eight or ten persons dressed in rags and tattered finery pass across the stage, entering at one side and leaving at the other to reappear in the same way, or the procession doubles upon itself passing round Mother Goose. They should walk in a lounging manner and without hurry, and hold out their hands to the audience as if begging. When they have passed out finally, and the music has ceased, MOTHER GOOSE *reads slowly and distinctly*:

Coming, coming always!
 Crowding into earth,
Seizing on this human life —
 Beggars from the birth.

Beggars, beggars, all of us!
 Expectants from our youth,
With hands outstretched and asking alms
 Of Hope, and Love, and Truth.

Coming, coming always!
 And the bluff Apostle waits
As the throng pours upward from the earth,
 To Heaven's eternal gate.

But a ghostly beggar knocketh
 In self-complacent trim,
And Peter riseth up to see —
 Especially to him.

"Good morrow, saint, I'm going in
    To take a stroll you know—
Not that I *want* for anything
    But just to see the show,"

"Hold," thundereth St. Peter,
    "Be pleased to pause a bit!
For seats celestial, let me say,
    Your garments are not fit.

"Whatever may be thought on earth
    We've other rules in Heaven,
And only poverty *confessed*
    Finds free admittance given."

The curtain drops long enough to have two boys take their places on the stage, MOTHER GOOSE *sitting a little one side of the middle, either in front of the boys or quite behind them. One boy has a toy gun which he discharges at the proper time; the other boy must be provided with two wigs, one made of flesh-colored material with a fringe for hair around the lower part. This should cover completely the natural hair and should be fastened securely by strings around the ears. The other to be shot off, must be so arranged by threads to his arms that when the arms are thrown up in fright the wig will be pulled off, leaving him apparently bald. He must appear afraid, and when the music comes to Pop, the gun must flash, bullets fall on the floor, the wig drop off, and the boys retreat backward in great terror. The music should play Pop goes the Weasel, from the time the curtain drops upon* MOTHER GOOSE'S *reading. When the curtain rises again* MOTHER GOOSE *repeats.*

There was a little man, and he had a little gun,
   And the bullets were made of lead, lead, lead.
He shot John Sprigg through the middle of his wig,
   And knocked it right off his head, head, head.

The curtain drops long enough to have the boys leave, and rising again upon MOTHER GOOSE *sitting a little at one side. In the middle of the stage sits a young girl apparently in deep thought:* MOTHER GOOSE *repeats:*

Bonnie lass, bonnie lass, will you be mine?
   You shall neither wash dishes, nor serve the wine;
But sit on a cushion and sew up a seam,
   And you shall have stawberries, and sugar, and cream.

The music should play Blue Eyed Mary, or Bonnie Doon, or the air and accompaniment of Franz Abt's song, Embarrassment. It will stop playing after two minutes when MOTHER GOOSE *begins to read, the Bonnie Lass sitting quietly:*

Bonnie lassie sat with her golden curls,
   And her eyes like the violets blue,
Wondering if all her lover had said
   In the future would prove itself true.

She thought of her Jamie, far o'er the blue sea,
   So royal, so loving, so brave;
Of the cot he had promised, when perils were o'er,
   And the promise she solemnly gave

To be his evermore; then she drove from her mind
   The past with its visions of bliss
And said to herself, "This is wiser by far —
   What life could be better than this?

"No cares to annoy, no duties to vex,
  Life will be but a beautiful dream;
Nothing from morning till night to do
  But sew, and eat berries and cream."

The bonnie lass went to her lover's home
  Singing like bird to her nest:
No dishes to wash, no serving of wine:
  Was ever a bride so blest?

Here the curtain falls, and when it rises again MOTHER GOOSE *is seated as usual.* BONNIE LASS *is sitting in a gloomy, despairing attitude, on a low seat, with hair in disorder and dress shabby, a plate of berries and cream on the floor or table beside her.* MOTHER GOOSE *resumes:*

But when the new dresses had all been worn out
  And she wearied of berries and cream,
She fretted, and wished she had something to do;
  Poor bonnie lass, woke from her dream.

"Oh, had I but married the man that I loved
  And toiled for my daily bread —
I should happier be at the end of my life
  And wiser in heart and head.

"For I see, when too late, that in duties well done —
  In service to other lives given,
Is the blessing that makes us forever the heirs,
  Of a heritage lasting as Heaven."

The curtain falls long enough to have BONNIE LASS *retire, and the necessary preparations for the next tableau are made expeditiously as possible. A mother is to* sit beside a cradle rocking it, with a baby, or the semblance of a baby, in it. This picture ought to be as charming as any of the old Madonnas. It may easily be if not spoiled by over-dressing. *The curtain rises, and* MOTHER GOOSE *repeats:*

>Rockaby, baby,
> Your cradle is green;
>Father's a nobleman;
> Mother's a queen;
>And Betty's a lady
> And wears a gold ring;
>And Johnny's a drummer,
> And drums for the king.

Music starts up and continues playing Greenville, the mother rocking and sewing, the curtain falling after a few minutes. As absolute stillness is not required in these tableaux, the curtain may remain up a longer time than usual. When it drops, everything must be removed again except MOTHER GOOSE, *who reads:*

>O golden gift of childhood!
> That with its kingly touch
>Transforms to more than royalty
> The thing it loveth much!
>
>Though he be the humblest craftsman,
> No silk nor ermine piled
>Could make the father seem a whit
> More noble to the child.
>
>And the mother — ah, what queenlier crown
> Could rest upon her brow
>Than the fair and gentle dignity
> It weareth to him now?

E'en the gilded ring that Michael
　　For a penny farthing bought,
Is the seal of Betty's ladyhood
　　To his untutored thought;

And the darling drum about his neck,
　　His very newest toy,
A bondsman unto Majesty
　　Hath straightway made the boy!

O golden gift of childhood!
　　If the talisman might last,
How the dull Present still should gleam
　　With the glory of the Past.

The curtain falls. Music plays, " God Save the Queen." As soon as possible there is put upon the stage a large shoe, made of pasteboard, at least four feet long. It should stand a little to the left of the middle of the stage, the toe toward the audience, nearer the left of the stage than the heel. The heel should be high enough to allow a little fellow to lie under it. The shoe is to be filled with little children. They may be taken from the audience upon the moment, and be trusted to be uneasy enough to give a good effect. The curtain rises and MOTHER GOOSE *announces:*

　　　　There was an old woman
　　　　　　Who lived in a shoe,
　　　　She had so many children
　　　　　　She didn't know what to do.

　　　　To some she gave broth,
　　　　　　And to some she gave bread,
　　　　And some she whipped soundly
　　　　　　And sent them to bed.

One of the children in the shoe should be dressed as an old woman with a whip at her side, a bowl and enormous spoon in her hand, with which she undertakes to feed them all. She is soon obliged to lay down the spoon, ply the whip and settle one little fellow to sleep under the heel of the shoe. That accomplished, and having dropped her spoon and given a few pieces of bread, she tries to make another little boy drink from the bowl. He refuses and escapes from her, tumbling over the side, and stands at a little distance toward the right — the very image of sturdy rebellion — taking off his coat, rolling up his sleeves and squaring himself for a fight. All this in pantomime, the music playing except while MOTHER GOOSE speaks. The curtain falls. Music strikes up Yankee Doodle. Another shoe like the first is put upon the stage, the toe pointing toward the right. A rope is fastened to each, ready to be joined like a finishing string of a pair of shoes, each half of the rope to be concealed at first. The curtain rises and shows the rebellious boy standing in the second shoe. One by one other children come on the stage and join him till the second shoe is as full as the first. All eagerly looking to know what is going to take place, the little fellow, who is supposed to be asleep, crawls half out to see. Those in the last shoe keep up a constant hurrahing. Finally one boy leaves each shoe and taking in his hand the rope helps join them together in the middle. If the boy leaving the second shoe should be named Field, and be well known to the audience, all the better. If not, let his back be labelled Cyrus W. Field, and as he helps tie the knot let him stand with his back toward the audience. Both sides hurrah and throw up their hands in delight. The curtain drops, music still playing Yankee Doodle. Every thing is removed.

Curtain rises. Music stops, and MOTHER GOOSE *reads slowly and distinctly:*

>Do you find out the likeness?
>   A portly old Dame —
>The mother of millions,
>   Brittania by name;
>And, howe'er it may strike you
>   In reading the song
>Not stinted in space
>   For bestowing the throng:
>Since the Sun can himself
>   Hardly manage to go
>In a day and a night
>   From the heel to the toe.
>Yet — though justly of all
>   Her fine family proud
>'Tis no light undertaking
>   To rule such a crowd;
>Not to mention the trouble
>   Of seeing them fed,
>And with justice dispensing
>   The broth and the bread.
>Some will seize upon one —
>   Some are left with the other —
>And so the whole household
>   Gets into a pother.
>But the rigid old Dame
>   Has a summary way
>Of her own, when she finds
>   There is mischief to pay.
>She just takes up her rod
>   As she lays down her spoon
>And makes their rebellious backs
>   Tingle right soon.

Then she bids them, while yet
    The sore smarting they feel,
To lie down, and go sleep
    Quick, under her heel.
Only once was she 'posed,
    When the little boy Sam
Who had always before
    Been as meek as a lamb,
Refused to take tea
    As his mother had bid,
And returned saucy answers
    Because he was chid.
Not content even then,
    He cut loose from the throne
And set about making
    A shoe of his own,
Which succeeded so well
    And was filled up so fast,
That the world in amazement
    Confessed, at the last —
Looking on at the work
    With a gasp and a stare,
That it was hard to tell which
    Would be best of the pair.
Side by side are they standing
    'Together to-day;
Side by side may they keep
    Their strong foothold for aye;
And beneath the broad sea,
    Whose blue depths intervene,
May the finishing string
    Lie unbroken between.

Curtain falls to prepare for My Pretty Maid, a pantomime, in which the characters are a pretty milkmaid in the dress of the last century, short waist, short sleeves, neckerchief, dress tucked up at one side showing petticoat and buckled slippers. A milk-pail in one hand, a milking stool under the other arm. A young man in top boots, knee breeches, swallow-tail coat, ruffled shirt, white cravat and powdered hair. Milkmaid enters upon one side, young man from the other; he intercepts her and a singer from behind the scenes in clear distinct tones sings the ballet as it is rendered in Baby's Opera, or from the published song of Where are you going, my pretty maid? At every line the actors conform their motions to the sentiment sung. For instance:

"Where are you going, my pretty Maid?"

[*Young man bows and extends his hand as if asking a question.*]

"I'm going a milking, sir," she said.

[*Milkmaid points to her pail, and bows slightly.*]

Her motions should be slow to occupy all the time used by the singer to repeat the answer.

"Shall I go with you, my pretty Maid?"

[*Young man is more entreating in manner.*]

"Yes, if you please, kind sir," she says.

[*Milkmaid assents with pleasure.*]

"What is your fortune, my Pretty Maid?"

[*Young man with eagerness.*]

"My face is my fortune, sir," she said.

[*Milkmaid, with dignity, taking a pail of water and stool in one hand and touching her face with the other.*]

"Then, I cannot marry you, my Pretty Maid."

[*Young man turns away.*]

"Nobody asked you, sir," she said.

[*She answers saucily and turns away with indifference.*]

There should be more indifference than scorn imitated. It should not be overacted. The colors chosen for the dresses should be becoming and then harmonious. The young man's dress should be in grave colors. For the shape of the garments, the picture in the Baby's Opera will be a good model. MOTHER GOOSE *remains on the stage. When the curtain rises after the* Pretty Maid *has left, it discloses a quartette of male voices, who sing:*

>There was a man in our town
>   And he was wondrous wise,
>He jumped into a bramble bush
>   And scratched out both his eyes.
>
>And when he found his eyes were out,
>   With all his might and main
>He jumped into a bramble bush
>   And scratched them in again.

After the singers have left the stage MOTHER GOOSE *reads:*

>Old Dr. Hahnnemann read the tale
>   (And he was wondrous wise)
>Of the man who in the bramble bush
>   Had scratched out both his eyes.
>And the fancy tickled mightily
>   His misty German brain,

That by jumping in another bush
   He got them back again.

So he called it homo-hop-athy
   And soon it came about
That a curious crowd about the thorns
   Was hopping in and out.
Yet, disguise it by the longest name
   They may, it is no use
For all the world knew the discovery
   Was made by Mother Goose.

Then stepping forward she recites:

There once was a woman
   And what do you think?
She lived upon nothing
   But victuals and drink.
Victuals and drink
   Were the chief of her diet,
And yet this poor woman
   Scarce ever was quiet.

Music plays Money Musk or Vive l'amour, and a little woman enters with knitting and chair. She fidgets continually, sitting for a few moments and wandering about, peeping into everything. Presently she goes off and MOTHER GOOSE *reads:*

And were you so foolish
   As really to think
That all she could want
   Was her victuals and drink?
And that while she was furnished
   With that sort of diet,
Her feeling and fancy
   Would starve and be quiet?

O many a woman
  Goes starving, I wean,
Who lives in a palace,
  And fares like a queen,
Till the famishing heart,
  And the feverish brain
Have spelled out to life's end,
  The long lesson of pain.

Still there are men and women
  Would force you to think
They *choose* to live only
  On victuals and drink.

O restless and craving
  Unsatisfied hearts,
Whence never the vulture
  Of hunger departs!
How long on the husks
  Of your life will ye feed?
Ignoring the same
  And its famishing need.

Curtain falls. MOTHER GOOSE *arranges herself in the middle at the back of the stage. On one side, and toward the front, sits a little girl on a cushion, eating from a bowl. At the other side, not so far forward, sits a pair of lovers in blissful ignorance of others, the girl nearest the edge of the stage. Curtain rises.* MOTHER GOOSE *repeats:*

  Little Miss Muffet
  Sat on a tuffet
  Eating curds and whey,
  There came a black spider
  And sat down beside her
  And frightened Miss Muffet away.

Music strikes up Shoo-fly. An enormous spider, as big as one's head, is slowly let down by a fine thread till it drops beside Miss Muffet who, seeing it, jumps up, drops bowl and spoon and runs away. Then directly enters an old woman (the one who could not keep quiet will do) with a chair and sits down before the lovers who suddenly become aware of her presence. The girl slips away and presently her lover follows her. After a moment the old lady picks up the spider by its thread and goes out. Music stops and MOTHER GOOSE *reads:*

>Of all mortal blisses,
>From comfits to kisses,
>There's sure to be something by way of alloy;
>Each new expectation
>Brings fresh aggravation,
>And a doubtful amalgam's the best of our joy.

>You may sit on your tuffet
>Yes — cushion and stuff it;
>And provide what you please, if you don't like whey;
>And before you can eat it,
>There'll be — I repeat it —
>Some sort of black spider to come in the way.

Curtain drops, and in the middle of the back of the stage are placed two high-backed elaborately carved chairs in which sit a King and Queen side by side with a small table before them according to the old custom of kings and queens. On a table, covered with a scant cloth that does not hide the grandeur of cotton flannel ermine and gilt paper finery, stands a pie filled with stuffed blackbirds, or their imitation in black cloth, well wired. If there is a large circular dish-cover available the birds may be fas-

tened with hairpins upon the top of the crust and covered. If not, a cover of paste is made and baked and carefully laid over. The curtain rises. A singer behind the scenes sings the ballad from the Baby's Opera or Elliott's Mother Goose Melodies; as the music ceases a servant enters, walks in front of the table, removes the cover or cuts the pastry, and immediately retires. As soon as the cover is removed the sound of the warbling of birds is to be imitated by the blowing of quill-whistle in water. The king and queen start up in surprise, and the curtain drops. Every thing is removed quickly and the curtain rises. MOTHER GOOSE, *sitting in one of the high-backed chairs, reads:*

> It doesn't take a conqueror to see
> What sort of curious pastry this might be;
> A flock of flying rumors, caught alive
> And housed, like swarming bees, within a hive.
> And so a dish of dainty gossip making
> Smooth, covered over with a show of secrecy,
> That one but takes the pleasant pains of breaking,
> And out the wide-mouthed knaves pop eagerly.
>
> Black birds, indeed! Each separate scandal
> Is truly black as soot of a candle.
> But mark the sequel! When the laugh is over,
> The crust once broken, you may seek in vain
> To catch the birds, or coax them in again;
> When, therefore, as not seldom it may be
> Even in the soberest community
> Strong revelations sometimes get about,
> Like a mysterious cholera breaking out —
> When daily papers then with many a hint
> That daubs them darker even than their print,
> Conclude without a reasonable doubt
> If you could sift the thing, or trace it out,

You'd find *some one* had sown a pocketfull of rye
Or, been regaling on a blackbird pie!

MOTHER GOOSE *rises and repeats:*

As Tommy Snooks and Bessie Brooks
  Were walking out one Sunday,
Says Tommy Snooks to Bessie Brooks
  To-morrow will be Monday.

Music plays: Walking down Broadway; or, Sparking Sunday Night. A boy and girl enters arm-and-arm, apparently in close conversation. They saunter back and forth, and go out. They may be dressed in old-time fashion or in the costume of to-day, if it is a simple one. They go out and the music ceases. MOTHER GOOSE *reads:*

No doubt you are smiling at such a remark,
And thinking poor Snooks but a pitiful spark;
'Tis a pity indeed in that moment of leisure,
To dampen poor Bessie's hardly-earned pleasure
Suggesting that close on the beautiful Sunday
Must come all the common-place horrors of Monday.

That he to his toiling, and she to her tub
Must turn, and take up with another week's rub;
Yet a truth for us all, since the shade of the real
Follow fast on the track of each sunny ideal.
Now and then we may pause on Life's pleasant oases
But between, lie the desert's grim, desolate spaces,
And our feet with all patience must travel them still.
Reaching forward to blessing, through bearing of ill.
Yet for Snooks and his Bessie — for me and for you,
Comes a Saturday night when the wages are due;
And we'll say to each other right joyfully one day
To-morrow — the endless to-morrow is Sunday.

In farewell:

> One parting word and I am gone;
> If I've prevailed to make you see
> These things as they appear to me
> Then I have proved this Goose a Swan —
>
>   Good night.

"Sweet by and by" *might be played while the audience disperse.*

SONGS OF SEVEN.

NOTE.—There can hardly be a choicer entertainment for the Sunday-school, nor for the social circle than the illustration of *Jean Ingelow's* Songs of Seven. It contains artistic pictures, good reading, fine music, and choice poetry. There are seven poems illustrating different ages in woman's life, from childhood to old age. Because the characters to be represented are few it is admirably suited for tableaux. An artist introduces nothing into his pictures to withdraw attention from the principal figures or the lesson taught or sentiment expressed, therefore it is important that those who personate the characters should utterly forget their own personality and conform dress and attitude to the illustration of the poem. The determination of each actor to look her prettiest is the bane of tableaux. Everyone taking part should cheerfully submit herself to the one who has the management, to be dressed, and sacrificed if necessary, to the beauty of the picture as a whole. There are several editions of the poem whose illustrations will be good guides. The stage may represent a garden in Seven times One. The school-girl may sit beside a table strewn with books, slate, etc., and forget herself in a reverie in Seven times Two. Instead of leaning out of a window to listen for the steps of her lover, she may be listening, and he looking in at open window, in Seven times Three. Of course a mother surrounded by little children may be made an indoor scene in Seven times Four. Widowhood, in Seven Times Five, may be expressed by a posture of abandoned grief, with clasped hands and bowed head upon a table, with closed Bible. Seven times Six affords a fine contrast in color between lustreless black and the sheen of white satin. Seven times Seven may be the widow finding her greatest comfort in religion. She sits before her table, with its open Bible, as though she were absorbed in its teachings, and raising her head and eyes with a look of prayer and resignation. Let but few colors be introduced in each picture — no jewelry. Let the folds and forms of the dresses be the simplest possible—an utter absence of flounces—for so only can artistic tableaux be presented. There must be a striking impression, and a few prominent forms and tints produce it, in the short interval while the curtain is raised. Elaborate, or even moderate detail is destructive to the general effect.

Before the curtain rises, each poem should be read by some one who stands behind the scenes, and when all is ready the reader should repeat the verse that more particularly describes the tableaux; then the music should begin and continue while the picture is displayed.

MUSIC TO ACCOMPANY SONGS OF SEVEN.

1. Opening Overture. Figaro. — *Mozart.*
2. La Source. — *Dwight.*
3. "Like a dream." From Martha.
4. O Summer Night.
5. Air du Roi. — *Louis XIII.*
6. Funeral March. — *Beethoven.*
7. Father, lead me. — *Butterfield.*
8. Les Deux Anges. — *Blumenthal.*
9. Chorus. God is the refuge of his people. From Cantata of Esther.

AN IDYL.

NOTE.—A Series of Idyls is an entertainment which may be made more enjoyable than the ordinary programme of tableaux, because so many are not required to fill up an evening's amusement, the disadvantage attending tableaux always being that they require a great deal of effort for a short-lived pleasure. In this series of pictures short bits of poetry are distinctly read by some good reader behind the scenes, preparing the audience for the sentiment of the picture. Detailed descriptions of the management of the tableaux would occupy too much space. In most neighborhoods the artistic taste and mechanical ingenuity can be readily supplied, always remembering that few objects, simple forms, few and harmonious colors, no elaboration, and very little detail, are the prime elements of success.

PROGRAMME.

1. PIANO SOLO.
2. MOTHER'S LOVE. *Burridge.*
   May be found in Bryant's Library of Poetry and Song, p. 11.
3. MUSIC. Piano accompaniment to Wagner's Slumber Song.
4. SOLO. Mother, Home, and Heaven. *Eliza Sproat Turner.*
5. A LITTLE GOOSE. Whittier's Child Life, p. 188.
6. MUSIC. Lulu is our darling pride.
7. SOLO. Only a baby small.
8. THE SMACK IN SCHOOL. Lib. of Poetry and Song, p. 25. *J. W. Palmer.*
9. MUSIC. Rory O'Moore.
10. SOLO. Comin' thro' the Rye.
11. THE GRAY SWAN. Child Life, p. 233. *Alice Carey.*
12. MUSIC. I'm afloat.
13. SOLO.—Home again, from a foreign shore.
14. Wilkins and his Dinah. (Pantomime). Our Young Folks, July, 1871.
15. THE AFTERNOON NAP. Child Life, p. 171. *Eastman.*
16. MUSIC. Old house at home.
17. SOLO. My old woman and I.
18. JENNIE KISSED ME. *Leigh Hunt.*
    Library of Poetry and Song, p. 25.
19. MUSIC. Kiss waltz *Il Bacio.*
20. SOLO. Bright things can never die.
21. MARY HAD A LITTLE LAMB. In pantomime, with singing. Wide Awake, April, 1878.
22. Lively march to close.

Music is suggested to accompany the showing of the tableaux, and when happily chosen adds very much to the pleasure of the occasion. It is instrumental, of course. To an audience of little people, the necessary pauses required for scene-shifting are often wearisome. Songs are suggested to fill the interval. More difficult music may be substituted of course.

Babes in the Wood.

A BURLESQUE PANTOMIME.

CHARACTERS.

Covetous Uncle. Two Infants.
Two Ruffians. Three Robins.

Note.—Two tender orphans, the heirs to a large fortune, are left to the care of a covetous uncle, who is overcome by the temptation to secure the money for himself. He hires two ruffians to carry the children to the woods and there murder them. The ruffians take the children to the forest. Becoming enraged at each other they commence to fight, the children stray away and are never found. Being exhausted, they lie down to die, and the sweet-voiced robins cover them with leaves.

Costumes. The Uncle appears in dressing-gown and slippers. The Ruffians are two very short men, or half-grown boys in high boots up to their hips, slouched hats, knives and pistols in belt, and swords in hands, heavy mustaches marked with burnt cork, and if possible a smile painted on their faces. The Babes should be personated by two of the largest, tallest young men to be found. If six feet high, so much the better. The first Babe has on a pink calico apron, buttoned behind; a very wide straw hat, and a stick of red and white candy a foot and a half long. The second Babe is dressed in frock, apron, pantalettes, a round ruffled collar and false braids. She holds a hat by the string.

Scene First. A sitting room in Uncle's house, Uncle discovered at the table with back to children, counting over a bag of gold. The Babes sit on the floor playing with a doll, and soon play "horsey." By and by the Ruffians appear. They seem to talk earnestly with the Uncle, who points to the clock, apparently directing them to seize the children when the clock shall strike. Clock strikes, the timid children are seized, they embrace each other, sob, and are led off.

Scene Second. Trees set in boxes covered with green cambric stand at back of stage. Leaves on the ground.

Enter Ruffians with Babes. The Ruffians engage in angry looks, nods, gesticulations, and forget the children. Soon they come to blows, fence with their swords and in their passion crowd each other off the stage behind. The Babes being alone become frightened, begin to cry and howl, then comfort each other sucking the candy from the same stick. Then wandering back and forth they cry again, and finally drop asleep on a bank from weariness.

Scene Third. Babes discovered dead (faces are powdered) and after a pause the Robins appear, hop about, look at the children, hop to the side of the stage where a cabbage leaf is fastened in their bills; and then back to lay them over children.

These Robins are the most amusing of creatures when well dressed and personated, and never fail to elicit great applause. Boys are dressed in gray and red muslin. First in the dressing a pasteboard bill is fastened to the head by several strings. The bill has a slit in it to hold a cabbage leaf — and the mouth has a whistle with which to warble, a child's pillow is fastened about the neck to form the full breast of the bird; a square of red cambric with one corner turned down is fastened close under the chin around the neck. The cambric should be three-quarters of a yard square. The corner opposite the one that is turned in at the neck is brought down over the breast and fastened between the legs on the pantaloons. Then the head and body are to be fitted with a dark brown or black cambric cover, with arm holes, over which, the arms being doubled up, the wings are to be sewed as well as possible. They are made also of muslin, into one side is sewn a long whalebone, and the rest of the wing made of deep folds of muslin running lengthwise of the wing, the folds laid deeply and pressed in with a hot iron, lying of course very close at the arm-hole and drooping more or less toward the end, where they slope off toward the upper whalebone; this must be securely fastened away from back to give the appearance of the body. The tail may be made of the same muslin folds into which pasteboard is fastened, or it may be made of a feather duster securely fastened with wire around the boy's wrist; eyes may be made of a circle of black cloth fastened upon a circle of white that is a little larger. The dark muslin cover of the head must come down over the roots of the bill and cover the mouth aud the upper edge of the Robin's red breast. Over the mouth the muslin must be slit in short frequent openings to allow air for breathing. Twelve yards of dark colored muslin and three yards of red cambric will dress three robins.

The effect will be greatly enhanced if waltz music is played all through the pantomime, all the characters, except the Robins, moving with a gliding step in time to the music. These few hints may be further elaborated, and as an evening pantomime it is very laughable.

OTHER GOOD THINGS.

There are some excellent publications, not so well known as they deserve, to which we would refer those having in charge church or society entertainments. Pre-eminent among these are the little dramas of Mrs. Abby Morton Diaz, "William Henry," and others, which can be obtained of the publishers, Messrs. Houghton & Osgood. Mr. G. B. Bartlett, the veteran of the amateur stage, has published a little book (through Osgood & Co.) which will be found very useful in holiday merry-makings. It contains the best Mrs. Jarley that we know of. D. Lothrop & Co. publish a very choice collection of Mr. Bartlett's amusements. J. C. Johnson (Oliver Ditson & Co.) gives a series of attractive Juvenile Oratorios, among which are the "Festival of the Rose," and the "Children of Jerusalem." The same publishers give collections of Old Folks' Concert Tunes, of Christmas and Easter Carols, The Flower Queen, and other capital Cantatas by George F. Root, with chorus books, part songs, hymnals, etc., without number and generally of great merit. They are also especially to be commended for endeavoring to make the music of the best masters, of Mendelssohn, Mozart, Schubert, Bach, Handel, Haydn, Beethoven, Rossini, Blumenthal, Von Weber, Abt and others, available and familiar.

Mrs. M. B. Slade, of Fall River, Mass., publishes a little journal (monthly) called *Good Times*, devoted to Sunday-school Concerts of a very simple description with no attempt at theatrical effect, but with a lesson in every line.

If some one with a ready pen would compose a new dialogue for "Punch and Judy," an entertainment of this kind might be very amusing for Children's Christmas parties. The apparatus, as sold in the toy-shops, is quite expensive; but a little ingenuity will construct it very readily at home. George Sand tells of her Marionette, or Theatre of Puppets, and of the complicated performances they went through under skilful manipulation. The plays which she herself composed for them must have been a great treat to the listeners, who were often distinguished people, while noted musicians frequently assisted in the orchestra.

Miss Helen Potter has been giving for some time past capital personations or imitations of well-known lecturers and actors. Any one with a genius for mimicry and extended opportunities for hearing the best speakers, might entertain a company in the same manner.

Some of Miss Potter's roles are:

The Sleep Walking Scene, from Macbeth; *a la* Mrs. Scott Siddons.
For Your Own Sakes; *a la* Anna Dickinson.
Girls; *a la* Olive Logan.
Temperance; *a la* John B. Gough.
Katharine of Arragon, and Meg Merillies; *a la* Miss Cushman.
Queen Elizabeth; *a la* Mme. Ristori.
Equal Rights; *a la* E. Cady Stanton.
Cassius to Brutus; *a la* Lawrence Barrett.
On Trial for Voting; *a la* Susan B. Anthony.
Lecture to Women; *a la* Sojourner Truth.

"An Evening with the Poets," in which all the exercises tableaux, recitations, songs, etc,, are taken from the poets, forms an entertainment very easy to arrange, and, with persons of taste on the committee, certain of being delightful.

"A Carnival of Authors," provides for a fancy-dress party

for a whole town, to be held in a large hall. A Queen of Carnival should be chosen, and a Grand Chamberlain, or Master of Ceremonies, whose business it is to introduce everyone present to the Queen.

"A Dickens Evening," where every one present enacts a character from the great caricaturist, gives opportunity for a charming fancy-dress party of less ponderous proportions than the "Carnival of Authors."

"A Waverly Evening," or "Shakspearian Evening," may be managed in the same way.

"The decoration of churches and churchyards with evergreens and flowers," says Bishop Coxe, "and such customs as those of 'The Rush-bearing' and 'Posy Sunday' which are still extant in England, though wholly voluntary and not ordained by the Church, are with unprejudiced persons, a beautiful illustration of the faculty by which she invests every good gift of God with sacred associations."

The holy George Herbert speaks as follows in his country parson: "The country parson takes order that the church be swept and kept clean — and at great festivals strewed and stuck with boughs, and perfumed with incense."

So Worsdworth describes the village children's morning:

"By rustic music led,
Through the still churchyard, each with garland gay,
But carried scepter-like, o'ertops the head
Of the proud bearer."

ACCESSORIES, DECORATIONS, SCENERY, &c.

["SHAPES" or "FORMS," to be covered with Greens, Gilt, &c., can be obtained by addressing
MESSRS. J. & R. LAMB, 59 Carmine Street, New York.]

However fine the performance on the platform, if given in a public hall whose glistening white walls rise in chalky Dover Cliffs on either side, reflecting a glare of light, the audience will find it difficult to feel *at home*, and even the prettiest chapel wears an added charm in a garniture of evergreen; while what lady of taste will throw open her parlors to an amateur entertainment, without robbing her garden, or consulting her florist for the decorations?

Especially at Christmas-time, when we miss out-door greenery, do we insist on evergreen, wreath and garland, motto and festoon, with "Star in the East," high on the wall that faces toward Jerusalem.

Six-pointed Star.

Star of Bethlehem.

Star of Bethlehem in Circle.

Six-pointed Star in Circle.

> "The last leaf has departed
>   From off the old oak tree,
> But there is a wreath of mistletoe
>   Where the green leaf used to be.
> The holly's scarlet berries,
>   Amid the leaves appear;
> It is an elfin armory,
>   With banner and with spear.
> Christmas is coming my brother dear,
>   And Christmas comes, my brother, but once
>   a year."

Mrs. Landon's homesick longing for England, from Sasson in the Deccan, breathes the same thought:

> "It is merry there at Christmas —
>   We have no Christmas here;
> 'Tis a weary thing, a summer
>   That lasts throughout the year.
>
> I remember how the banners
>   Hung round our ancient hall,
> Bound with wreaths of shining holly,
>   Brave winter's coronal.
>
> And above each rusty helmet
>   Waved a new and cheering plume,
> A branch of crimson berries,
>   And the latest rose in bloom;
>
> And the white and pearly mistletoe
>   Hung half concealed o'erhead —
> I remember one sweet maiden
>   Whose cheek it dyed with red!"

Evergreen is the most appropriate material for Christmas decorations. In the West the cedar is almost the only available evergreen, and no better could be wished for sewing on pasteboard mottoes and ornamental forms. In the East we have hemlock, pine, laurel, etc., for large festoons and for finer work ground, feather and bouquet pine, pressed ferns, varnished autumn leaves, grasses, immortelles, myrrh, box, which, with festoons of smilax from the florist's, artificial flowers sparingly and judiciously used when the distance is sufficiently great, and hot-house flowers as many as can be obtained, furnishes material to make a bower of beauty of the most unattractive surroundings.

Where money is not so great a consideration, the patent body or foundation sold by Mr. J. R. Lamb (see advertisement) will be found of great advantage in making the different designs. All used in the illustration of this article are furnished by him, and can be easily executed on his flexible foundation. If the finances of the society will not allow of the purchase, a little ingenuity must be made to take its place; cord must serve for the festoons and the other designs may be bent in wire or cut from cardboard. After the Star of Bethlehem, the design most indispensable for Christmas

Greek Cross.   Cross-Crosslet.   Cross of Jerusalem.

time, as referring directly to Christ, is the cross. Indeed for all other seasons it is the most appropriate and the one which takes the lead in all church decorations. We give some of the different forms. These may be combined at will with more intricate designs, for instance, with the monogram of

Cross of Iona.

Trefoil Roman Cross.

our Lord, the letters I. H. S. as in the pattern given further on for cutting from velvet paper. After the cross the crown.

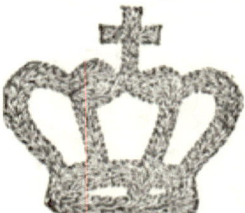
Round Crown.

Eastern Crown. Flat for the Wall.

For borders, etc., we may use the Greek key pattern, always effective, though so well known. Trefoils and quatrefoils, and trefoils with triangles, come in well to fill up any vacant

Triangle and Trefoil form.

Whole Triangle and Trefoil combined.

spaces. The anchor is a beautiful form and may be used in combination with the cross or alone.

Anchors.

Faith and Hope.

For Christmas mottoes each letter should be cut from stiff paper or cardboard and the evergreen sewed on neatly, sprig lapping over sprig. Old English alphabets are better than German text, as being more legible, though when the mottoes or text are very familiar, the more ornamental German text may be used.

CAROL.

For a fragrant crown,
When the Lord comes down,
   Of the deathless green we braid,
Over the altar bright,
Where the tissues white
   Like winter snow is laid;
And we think it meet
Our Lord to greet
   As the wise men did of old,
With the spiceries
Of incense trees,
   And hearts like the hoarded gold.
And so we shake
The snowy flake
   From cedar and myrtle fair
And the boughs that nod
On the hills of God
     We raise to his glory there.

For oh! we fling
Each fragrant thing
   In the paths of the newly wed;
And when we weep,
Put flowers to sleep
   On the breast of the early dead;

  And the altar's lawn
  At morning's dawn
   We deck at Eastertide;
  And the font's fair brim
  So tells of Him
   Who liveth though he died!
  Of flowers he spake,
  And for His sake
   Whose text was the lilies' bloom,
  We search abroad
  For the flowers of God,
   To give Him their sweet perfume.

From Christian Ballads by Bishop A. C. Coxe.

FERNS AND AUTUMN LEAVES.

No church adornment can be more beautiful than graceful arches and festoons of feathery-woven ferns entwined with autumn leaves.

The method of utilizing them is easy and inexpensive. Secure a few square yards of paper the tint of the church wall, so as to be invisible. Decide on the size and position upon the wall of the arches of ferns, then cut accordingly narrow curved bands of the tinted paper — not over three inches wide except the middle which may widen to six inches — and on them *pin* the ferns and autumn leaves. Two pins are sufficient to fasten a fern. The stems of the ferns should project upward, otherwise the ferns may curl. In the centre of the arch have a large bunch of ferns and autumn leaves, then let the arch taper off to a point at the ends. For the sake of variety have some of the arches inverted, ends pointing upward, festoon fashion. The weight of these even when finished is so slight that three or four very fine tacks, with heads scarcely larger than that of a pin, are sufficient to hold them on the wall.

Wall-pockets may be made of splinters of black walnut (sold in market in bunches) woven together like basket-work fastened with bright wools. These may be filled with gay grasses, ferns, autumn leaves and immortelles.

There are so many ways of fern arrangement that description seems difficult. Special occasions require specific directions. Much must be left to the taste and the inventive inspiration of the hour. But we will suppose the occasion to be a Missionary concert.

An idol or other heathern symbol may be set on a bracket for a centre piece. Above it on an arch of the tinted paper, about a yard in length, paste the gold letters L I G H T. Just above the letters have simulated rays of light, and just below them, near the idol's head, the small letters FOR. Beneath the idol may be the word Africa; far to the left, Peru, far to the right, India ; each surmounted by an arch of ferns. Now, over the whole throw a very long arch of ferns and autumn leaves. At each end, as if upholding it, may be placed a wall-pocket holding an autumn bouquet. The effect of the entire wall, thus decorated, is beautiful.

It will be readily seen that this decoration is just as well adapted to other occasions as to this by simply changing the centre-piece and the mottoes to suit the subject.

By way of variety one arch may be entirely of ferns, dotted with tiny spangles. This simulates ferns sprinkled with dew, and is very pretty.

This style of decoration is especially available in the late autumn, for nearly all who have spent the summer at the mountains will return laden with woodland spoils.

Mottoes in colors are ornamental for all seasons. Such designs as the following, letters of which may be cut of colored flannels or paper, are in good taste. The initial letters

may be quite fanciful and the whole sentence tacked to the wall or fastened with mucilage. Such mottoes as express love are better cut from red flannel. Faith, confidence, and truth, are appropriate in blue. Pentitence, in lilac or purple. Yellow or gilt, for glory. Do not place the letters in a straight row, but around a curve, double curve or scroll.

The beauty of these illuminations will depend as much on

the neatness of their execution as their artistic design, in the first instance. We give a number of ornamental designs which

are very handsome when cut from dark green or crimson velvet paper.

If the ground against which they are placed is dark, the

lilies in the foregoing and following examples may be cut from white velvet or cotton flannel, with stems of gold paper;

the leaves may be gold or dark green, the cross and vase of gold.

Wreaths of ivy form the prettiest frames for your text or

ornamental designs; as we are chary of the natural vines at Christmas-time resort may be had to artificial ivy leaves, for the manufacture of which the *American Cultivator* gives the following directions:

"Artificial ivy leaves are made by taking green window Holland and using an English ivy leaf for a pattern. Cut out any number of leaves, making different sizes. Next lay them upon your paper and with a warm iron, upon which you first rub some beeswax, press each leaf. To shape and vein the leaves, fold the leaf from side to side, making a crease from stem to tip; then likewise through to each point, from stem. For stems take fine wire (not too fine to stand in shape) push the end through two small holds, previously made with a pin, far enough to turn back upon the under side, and twist carefully around to secure it in its place. The smallest leaves are placed upon the ends of the vine. Twine the wires with tissue paper, the color of leaves, and make long vines with branches here and there.

A wreath of natural thorn, will form an appropriate border to monogram I H S, instead of the stamped circlet given above.

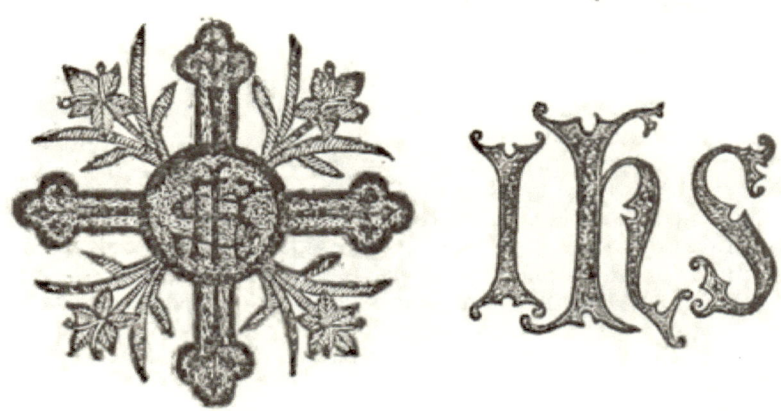

For Thanksgiving, the most appropriate decorations are the sickle and cornucopias filled with grain and grasses.

Cornucopia, flat for the wall.

The wedding bell, the flower canopy under which the bridal party stands to receive congratulations, although one of the costliest *chef d'œuvres* of the florist, may be improvised at home from a child's hoopskirt.

SCENERY, &c.

Mr. G. B. Bartlett, in his little book, Parlor Amusements, gives a list of the stage properties necessary for the presentation of tableaux, and instructions as to their manufacture. He gives an interesting account of an entertainment given in an old boat-house on an island near Plymouth Rock, where for a background to a vaudeville by amateur performances, when a garden scene was demanded, the rough beams were dressed with graceful vines, and arches made of clematis lighted up with gleaming sumac and coral-covered berries. Just as the play began the managers threw open the great doors at the end of the boat-house. The tide was high, and the sea came up close to the building, and the great, round, August moon began to rise slowly out of the water; and all agreed that no finer background could have been seen in any theatre.

The same writer gives the following directions for the construction of a boat to be used in such tableaux as "Cleopatra going to meet Mark Antony," "The Lily Maid of Astolat," "The Lady of Shalott," etc.

"Lay two boards, about fourteen feet in length and fourteen inches wide, side by side upon the floor so that they will fit together very closely at the edge. Screw three cleats firmly upon these flat boards, one near each edge, and one at the centre. Turn the whole over, and you have a flat surface fourteen feet in length and one and a half in width. Draw upon one end the profile of the bow of a boat, and upon the other the stern. Saw the ends carefully, following your drawing. Paint the whole a light shade of yellow. Shave the upper edge into a slight curve, beginning eight inches from the bow and descending to the middle, then ascending to within twenty-five inches of the stern. Then paint a black stripe three-fourths of an inch wide, six inches below the upper edge, following as nearly as possible the curve; and six inches apart two more stripes below it. Next shade the bow in black, also following the curve from the upper edge to a distance of two feet from the lower edge. Saw out a figurehead and rudder to fasten upon the ends by screws. Stretch a strip of blue cambric, eight inches wide, across the front of the stage having three wavy lines of white painted upon it for water. The boat is held up by the persons who sit behind it on boxes; the sail is made of a sheet tacked upon a mast, also held by one of the performers."

A boat scene of an entirely different character is described in the St. Nicholas for 1876, page 235, which describes the acting of Ballads and gives Lord Ullin's Daughter as an example. The ballad of The Mistletoe Bough prepared for acting, is given in St. Nicholas for January 1878, page 191.

For further practical and excellent hints on the arrangement of tableaux, and their accessories, we would refer to our chapter on Living Pictures or Picture-frame Tableaux. Another way of manufacturing angel's wings, and one which we prefer to marking the feathers with crayon on white muslin, is, after the cloth is stretched over wire frames four feet long, to coat it with varnish, and while still "sticky" sprinkle thickly with live-geese feathers.

The properties are, after all, the least important part, as any one who has thrilled under the reading of Charlotte Cushman, where no scenery whatever was attempted, can testify. The first requisite for a successful entertainment, is good acting, the first requisite of good acting is forgetfulness of self, and we beg our young readers to pay especial attention to Miss Hale's very sensible advice on this subject which precedes her little drama of Beauty and the Beast. If the acting is really fine it will be of little consequence whether a rosy sunrise or pallid moonlight floods the artistic scenery in prompt obedience to the manager's command, or whether instead some one follows the advice of Quince in Midsummer Nights Dream, and " come in with a bush of thorns and a hawthorn, and says he comes to disfigure, or to present the person of moonshine," while "some other presents *wall*, having some plaster or some loam or some rough cast about him to signify wall, holding his fingers thus, and through that cranny Pyramus and Thisby whisper."

THE END.

MISS JULIA A. EASTMAN is one of the most popular of our modern writers.

YOUNG RICK. By *Julia A. Eastman.* Large 16mo. Twelve illustrations by Sol Eytinge . $1 50

A bright, fascinating story of a little boy who was both a blessing and a bother. — *Boston Journal.*

The most delightful book on the list for the children of the family, being full of adventures and gay home scenes and merry play-times. "Paty" would have done credit to Dickens in his palmiest days. The strange glows and shadows of her character are put in lovingly and lingeringly, with the pencil of a master. Miss Margaret's character of light is admirably drawn, while Aunt Lesbia, Deacon Harkaway, Tom Dorrance, and the master and mistress of Graythorpe poor-house are genuine "charcoal sketches."

STRIKING FOR THE RIGHT. By *Julia A. Eastman.* Large 16mo. Illustrated . 1 75

While this story holds the reader breathless with expectancy and excitement, its civilizing influence in the family is hardly to be estimated. In all quarters it has met with the warmest praise.

THE ROMNEYS OF RIDGEMONT. By *Julia A. Eastman.* 16mo. Illustrated . 1 50

BEULAH ROMNEY. By *Julia A. Eastman.* 16 mo. Illustrated 1 50

Two stories wondrously alive, flashing with fun, sparkling with tears, throbbing with emotion. The next best thing to attending Mrs. Hale's big boarding-school is to read Beulah's experience there.

SHORT-COMINGS AND LONG-GOINGS. By *Julia A. Eastman.* 16 mo. Illustrated. 1 25

A remarkable book, crowded with remarkable characters. It is a picture gallery of human nature.

KITTY KENT'S TROUBLES. By *Julia A. Eastman.* 16 mo. Illustrated . . 1 50

"A delicious April-day style of book, sunshiny with smiles on one page while the next is misty with tender tears. Almost every type of American school-girl is here represented — the vain Helen Dart, the beauty, Amy Searle, the ambitious, high bred, conservative Anna Matson; but next to Kitty herself sunny little Pauline Sedgewick will prove the general favorite. It is a story fully calculated to win both girls and boys toward noble, royal ways of doing little as well as great things. All teachers should feel an interest in placing it in the hands of their pupils."

FOUR GIRLS AT CHAUTAUQUA. By
  Pansy. 12 mo. Illustrated . . . $1 50
    The most fascinating "watering-place" story ever published. Four friends, each a brilliant girl in her way, tired of Saratoga and Newport, try a fortnight at the new summer resort on Chautauqua Lake, choosing the time when the National Sunday-school Assembly is in camp. Rev. Drs. Vincent, Deems, Cuyler, Edward Eggleston, Mrs. Emily Huntington Miller, move prominently through the story.

HOUSEHOLD PUZZLES. By *Pansy.* 12mo.
  Illustrated 1 50
    How to make one dollar do the work of five. A family of beautiful girls seek to solve this "puzzle." Piquant, humorous, but written with an intense purpose.

THE RANDOLPHS. By *Pansy.* 12 mo. Illustrated 1 50
    A sequel to Household Puzzles, in which the Puzzles are agreeably disposed of.

GRANDPA'S DARLINGS. By *Pansy.* 16 mo.
  Illustrated 1 25
    A big book, full of "good times" for the little people of the family.

ESTER RIED	By *Pansy.*	1 50
JULIA RIED	,,	1 50
THREE PEOPLE	,,	1 50
THE KING'S DAUGHTER	,,	1 50
WISE AND OTHERWISE	,,	1 50
CUNNING WORKMEN	,,	1 25
JESSIE WELLS	,,	.75
DOCIA'S JOURNAL	,,	75
BERNIE'S WHITE CHICKEN	,,	75
HELEN LESTER	,,	75
A CHRISTMAS TIME	,,	15

"**MISS FARMAN** has the very desirable knack of imparting valuable ideas under the guise of a pleasing story."—*The New Century.*

MRS. HURD'S NIECE. By *Ella Farman.* Ill. $1 50

A thrilling story for the girls, especially for those who think they have a "mission," to whom we commend sturdy English Hannah, with her small means, and her grand success. Saidee Hurd is one of the sweetest girls ever embalmed in story, and Lois Gladstone one of the noblest.

THE COOKING CLUB OF TU-WHIT HOLLOW. By *Ella Farman.* 16 mo. Eight full-page illustrations 1 25

Worth reading by all who delight in domestic romance.—*Fall River Daily News.*

The practical instructions in housewifery, which are abundant, are set in the midst of a bright, wholesome story, and the little housewives who figure in it are good specimens of very human, but at the same time very lovable, little American girls. It ought to be the most successful little girls' book of the season.—*The Advance.*

A LITTLE WOMAN. By *Ella Farman.* 16m. 1 00

The daintiest of all juvenile books. From its merry pages, winsome Kinnie Crosby has stretched out her warm little hand to help thousands of young girls.

A WHITE HAND. By *Ella Farman.* 12m. Ill. 1 50

A genuine painting of American society. Millicent and Jack are drawn by a bold, firm hand. No one can lay this story down until the last leaf is turned.

WIDE AWAKE.

AN ILLUSTRATED MAGAZINE

For the Young Folks.

$2.00 PER ANNUM. POSTAGE PREPAID.

Edited by ELLA FARMAN.

Published by D. LOTHROP & CO., Boston, Mass.

It always contains a feast of fat things for the little folks, and folks who are no longer little find their lost childhood in its pages. We are not saying too much when we say that its versatile editor — Ella Farman, is more fully at home in the child's wonder-land than any other living American writer. She is thoroughly *en rapport* with her readers, gives them now a sugar plum of poesy, now a dainty jelly-cake of imagination, and cunningly intermixes all the solid bread of thought that the child's mind can digest and assimilate.—*York True Democrat.*

A Moment's Chat with our Friends.

WE take pleasure in offering our patrons a finer and more varied assortment of Juveniles and Holiday Books for 1876-77 than in any year heretofore. In presenting our catalogue, we would add that, in regard to Children's Books, there is one happy word to say: the easiest, surest way to prevent the formation of a desire for evil literature has been found to place in the little hands book upon book known to be pure and strong in influence, pure and vivid in impression, pure and fascinating in interest. Still, the parents who set out to do this are largely dependent upon what their Publishers and Booksellers set before them.——In our latest selection of books, we have borne the welfare of the young people constantly in mind, from the young men and women, down to the little folks in the Primary schools. There are, for these "dots," whose tastes the parents can reasonably hope to shape, some exquisite little "Libraries," in tasteful boxes. There is no way to render a little one so completely happy as to give it a box of books to be all its own. With these arranged upon a swing book-shelf — and no child's room should be considered furnished without a book-shelf — the child feels that it has a library; and by no other method is it possible to teach a child the use, the proper care, and the value, of books. —— In the matter of price these tiny "Libraries suit all purses. The LARGE PRINT LIBRARY, 6 vols., Illustrated, Cloth Bound, Chromo sides, $2.40. CHARMING STORY LIBRARY, exquisitely bound, 6 vols., $3.00. BOYS' HOLIDAY LIBRARY, GIRLS' HOLIDAY LIBRARY, each 6 vols., $3.00 each. THE TRUE STORIES LIBRARY, 12 vols., $2.40. This library comprises twelve tiny volumes, dainty in gray cloth, embossed with black, lighted up with gay chromos. The PANSY PICTURE LIBRARY, 4 vols., $3.00, is exquisite in paper, printing, illustrations and binding. For the very small folks in the nursery there are four merry books, with big print, full-page pictures, and gay, cloth-lined covers, MADAME MOBCAP, MERRY MICE, TONY and WINKET'S VALENTINE. —— With the same care the Holiday Gift-books have been selected. Gift-books hold a place for years upon the shelf and table; and the WIDE AWAKE

PLEASURE BOOK, PANSY'S PICTURE BOOK, PICTURES FOR OUR DARLINGS, TWO FORTUNE SEEKERS, WORD PICTURES, each deserve a permanent niche, being sweet and sound from the first page to the last. These are the work of our foremost authors, *Bayard Taylor, Miss Alcott, Mrs. Whitney, Rossiter Johnson, Ella Farman, Mrs. Louise Chandler Moulton, Elizabeth Stuart Phelps, Mrs. R. H. Stoddard, Sophie May*, etc.—— We also believe that we offer, in our List for Boys, volumes which may safely be read without first passing under parental scrutiny and excision, but which at the same time shall satisfy a boy's longing for adventure and his admiration for the stirring and the heroic, and shall leave him resolute instead of restless, ready for action and patient toil, instead of filling his brain with idle dreams.—— Our list for Girls is eqully wholesome and entertaining. We also offer for examination the WIDE AWAKE MAGAZINE, edited by *Ella Farman*, D. LOTHROP & Co., Boston, Publishers. This magazine is furnished at the low price of $2.00 per annum, post-paid. It is exquisitely illustrated by *Sol Eytinge, Waud, Merrill, Jessie Curtis, Miss Hallock, Miss Northam, Miss Humphrey, Mrs. Finley*. Miss Farman is supported by a brilliant array of contributors, *Mrs. R. H. Stoddard, Mrs. Celia Thaxter, Mrs. S. M. B. Piatt, Mrs. Moulton, Mrs. Emily Huntington Miller, Rossiter Johnson, Charles E. Hurd, Sophie May, Margaret Eytinge, Nora Perry*, etc. The attractions for 1877 include a serial by *Sophie May*, QUINNEBASSET GIRLS, GOOD-FOR-NOTHING POLLY, by *Ella Farman*, and CHILD MARIAN ABROAD, by *Wm. M. T. Rounds*, of the *N. Y. Independent*, the latter being records of a little girl's visits to the Pope, Empress Eugenie, Princess Marie Valerie, Madame McMahon, etc., illustrated with portraits. —— We shall show this magazine to our patrons with pride and satisfaction, and receive and forward subscriptions. We are also able to furnish a catalogue of Messrs. Lothrop & Co.'s choice publications, including 500 vols., upon application. We can cordially commend Messrs. Lothrop & Co.'s publications, for their wholesomeness of tone, their power of entertainment, and their superior graces of style.

BOOKS OF MERIT.

YOUNG FOLKS' HISTORY OF GERMANY. By Charlotte M. Yonge. Very fully illustrated. D. Lothrop & Co., Boston. Price $1.50.

We welcome the set of Histories of which this is the initial volume. Since Dickens' Child's History of England, nothing so tempting has been offered to our young folks, and we predict that these volumes will displace the stories of fictitious and improbable adventures now found on many a boy's bookshelf. Miss Yonge, while always boldly and continuously outlining the course of historical events, has the knack of seizing upon incidents which reveal the true character of historical personages; thus she makes her narrative very pleasing, especially to a young reader. Indeed her History of Germany ought to satisfy the most ardent lover of adventure, for its pages are crowded with soldiers, knights and heroes, baby kings, little girl queens, and boy emperors. German History, dating back before Christ, abounds with wonderful mythology, romantic exploits, and swift, bold deeds; and Miss Yonge begins with the giants of Valhalla and comes on down through the noisy days of Wallenstein into our own times to Bismark, who, perhaps, is quite as mighty a man as the boldest of the old Captains.

The book, besides assisting one to understand the whys and wherefores of the present geography of Europe, and giving an insight into modern European politics, has also an abundance of pictures which affords a good idea of German costumes and customs in the early ages.

ROYAL LOWRIE. A Boy's Book. By Charles R. Talbot. Large 16mo, with 12 pen-and-ink pictures by Hopkins. Boston: D. Lothrop & Co. Price, $1.25.

This capitally written story of school and vacation life is bound to become a standard in boys' libraries. It is full of fun, and yet not coarse fun. It tells the story of the troubles got into and blunders made by half a dozen people, young and old, the principal characters being two schoolfellows. Royal Lowrie and Archie Bishop. It is an essentially "live" book, and the boy who fails to read it loses just so much genuine enjoyment.

"THAT BOY OF NEWKIRK'S." By L. Bates. Boston: D. Lothrop & Co. Price, $1.25.

Another good book of the right type, with genuine boys, full of life, and, therefore, full of fun, eager for pleasure, and exposed to sharp perils. The moral is simple and tells itself, without any preaching by the author, that a Christian home, with an atmosphere of love, is a magnet to hold a boy to a pure life. Gordon Ferril, nurtured in such a home, grows naturally to a noble manhood, and becomes a helper to other boys less favored. The story brings out, also, with great beauty, the power of genuine sympathy in recovering the vicious, and the nature of true piety in begetting such loving sympathy. The story is well told, the characters clearly drawn, and the book will be sure to interest readers, and inspire them with higher aims in life.

CARRIE ELLSWORTH: OR SEED SOWING. By W. O. Johnson. Boston: D. Lothrop & Co. Price, $1.25.

Carrie Ellsworth is a pleasant book to read, and its influence hangs about one like the fragrance of luscious fruit. It is a quiet story, with no extraordinary incidents or characters, but teaching in a winning way how girls naturally impulsive and thoughtless may take on resolute purposes, and overcome the weaknesses that threaten to maim life. Good home and Sabbath school teaching inspire good aims; and every day endeavors, though often baffled, gradually bring strength and victory. It ought to be a favorite book, for it deals with people that everybody knows, and with incidents of daily occurrence.

BABYLAND. Boston: D. Lothrop & Co. Bound vol. 75c.

This is one of the charmingest of the many charming books for the little ones published by this house. Babies are critics in their way, and know right well whether what is written for and read and sung to them is genuine baby literature or make-believe. Every line in this volume was written by lovers of the little ones, who know just what they like and can appreciate. The stories are such as innumerable mammas will have to read and re-read and read again, while the verses will become as familiar in nurseries as the choicest rhymes of Mother Goose. Such are the verses about "Naughty Susie," "Baby's Complaint," "Washing Day," etc. The illuminated cover displays a choice selection of babies, doing all sorts of things.

The $1000 Prize Series.

Pronounced by the Examining Committee, Rev. Drs. Lincoln, Rankin and Day, superior to any similar series.

STRIKING FOR THE RIGHT,	$1.75
SILENT TOM,	1.75
EVENING REST,	1.50
THE OLD STONE HOUSE,	1.50
INTO THE LIGHT,	1.50
WALTER MCDONALD,	1.50
STORY OF THE BLOUNT FAMILY,	1.50
MARGARET WORTHINGTON,	1.50
THE WADSWORTH BOYS,	1.50
GRACE AVERY'S INFLUENCE,	1.50
GLIMPSES THROUGH,	1.50
RALPH'S POSSESSION,	1.50
LUCK OF ALDEN FARM,	1.50
CHRONICLES OF SUNSET MOUNTAIN,	1.50
THE MARBLE PREACHER,	1.50
GOLDEN LINES,	1.50

Sold by Booksellers generally, and sent by Mail, postpaid, on receipt of price.

BOSTON:
D. LOTHROP & CO., PUBLISHERS.

www.ingramcontent.com/pod-product-compliance
Lightning Source LLC
Chambersburg PA
CBHW021942240426
43668CB00037B/404